Rights of passage

Cambridge Studies in Work and Social Inequality

Series editors
R. M. Blackburn, Ken Prandy, Jenny Jarman

Rights of passage

Social change and the transition from youth to adulthood

Sarah Irwin
University of Leeds

UCL PRESS

© Sarah Irwin 1995

First published in 1995 by UCL Press

UCL Press Limited
University College London
Gower Street
London WC1E 6BT

and
1900 Frost Road, Suite 101
Bristol
Pennsylvania 19007-1598

The name of University College London (UCL) is a registered trade mark used
by UCL Press with the consent of the owner.

ISBNs:
1-85728-429-1 HB
1-85728-430-5 PB

British Library Cataloguing in Publication Data.
A catalogue record for this book is available from the British Library.

Library of Congress Cataloging-in-Publication Data are available.

Typeset in Palatino.
Printed and bound by
Page Bros (Norwich) Ltd, England.

To my parents, Ann and Hew

Contents

Acknowledgements

The idea for this book arose out of my PhD research, and my thanks are due to those whose enthusiasms, insights and encouragement were so important to me in the research and writing of the thesis and in its subsequent evolution. I am indebted to John Holmwood for contributing so much to the development of my ideas and for his incisive, and always constructive, criticism. Thanks also to Sandy Stewart for his important insights and comments. I am grateful to Colin Bell for reading and commenting on various drafts, and to Janet Siltanen for engaging with my research at a time when she had several pressing demands to contend with. The manuscript has benefited from the detailed reading and suggestions of Bob Blackburn and Ken Prandy. With warmest thanks also to my family and friends. I cannot name them all here but I am very grateful for the many ways in which they have given support. In particular, I wish to express my deep gratitude to Wendy Bottero, for sharing so much, and contributing so much in the development and sharpening of my ideas. Special thanks too, to Ian Jones, for his encouragement and support. I am grateful also to my survey respondents who gave their time so willingly in answering my questions.

Chapter 1

Locating transition

Introduction

The subject of this book is change in the transition from youth to adulthood. The approach endeavours to break with the boundaries that conventionally delimit discussion of this life course period, and offers an analysis that treats it as an integral aspect of more general social arrangements. Any separation of biography, or life course related processes, from such arrangements hinders analysis of social change. What is clear from the briefest survey of the experience of youth and young adults is the importance of a framework capable of furthering this sort of analysis. Recent decades have seen a pattern of deferral in the timing of transitions from the partial dependence of youth to the independence associated with adult status. Employment amongst teenagers has increasingly been displaced by youth training, unemployment and full-time education, the ages at which young people can expect to secure employment and a wage have risen, and amongst those young adults who are in employment, earnings have declined relative to average adult earnings. Young people tend to stay longer in their parental homes before establishing independent households, and a long run trend to younger ages at family formation was reversed in the 1970s since when a pattern of deferral by successive cohorts in the timing of marriage and parenthood has continued.

These changes indicate a set of developments in relation to both employment and family arrangements. The life course careers of young people through the labour market and the domestic sphere have been a central concern in recent analyses of youth and the transition to adult status. Much research in the area has been dominated by a concern with the family-related consequences of economic restructuring. Here, employment security is seen as important to the ability of young people to attain independence from the parental home, and establish new households and new families. Economic retrenchment, mass unemployment and the collapse of employment opportunities, and the increasingly limited scope for young people to secure the means to independence at a young age have made urgent the questions of their ability to attain adult lifestyles, and of their life chances. A number of writers have addressed a hypothesis of deferral amongst young people, in the attainment of adult status, and in the timing of independence, marriage and parenthood, as a consequence of changes in the structure of youth employment opportunities.

The research out of which this book has arisen started with a question shared by several other commentators: what are the consequences of economic change, in particular changing structures of employment and labour demand, for the transition from youth to adulthood? In the course of the research it became apparent that this question, and the ways in which it is variously formulated and addressed, is unhelpful. It suggests a causality from employment restructuring to life course relations that entails a division between "economic" and "social" processes. It is an argument of this book that an adequate account of change in the structure of the life course requires an understanding of "the economic" and "the social" as aspects of a unified, coherent social structure.

A defining characteristic of the transition from youth to adult status is the progression from partial dependence on parents to independence, and a reliance by individuals on themselves (and their partners) for resourcing their daily living arrangements. Now, this invites consideration of the social arrangements through which both dependence and independence are resourced. Financial dependence implies that the reproduction of people's day-to-day living arrangements is organized through claims on others, typically on those with "independent" access to earnings. The organization of social reproduction is itself reflected in a structure of earnings that rewards people not as equal before the labour market, but in relation to a general structure of claims and obligations. A hypothesis of deferral in the timing of the attainment of "independence" and "adult" obligations then, is necessarily also a hypothesis of change in the social

2

organization of dependence and obligation. However, as we will see, there has been a tendency to treat life course structure as influenced by, but nevertheless independent from, more general social and economic processes. It is for this reason that adequate explanations of change in the transition from youth to adulthood have proved elusive.

Recognition of the need for theoretical development is reflected in recent criticisms of youth research. These charge such research with a failure to locate youth and transitions to adulthood in their social context (Jones 1988; see also Chisholm 1990; Ashton & Lowe 1991; Jones & Wallace 1992). This state of affairs calls into question the efficacy of understandings that operate with an "unlocated" version of youth. The difficulties of "locating" youth do not arise from neglect; on the contrary, the problem has been important in shaping research agendas. "Youth" has been problematized in efforts to explain its social construction, and its relationship to "adult" forms of inequality, to citizenship and to economic change. Quickly, however, such reconstructions fall back onto a division between separate spheres: between family- and employment-related processes, and between "dependence" and "independence", and locating youth in relation to general processes becomes a *post hoc* affair. To define youth as a category and then to acknowledge a failure to locate it suggests that the category has attained precedence over the relations that give it social meaning. The difficulties of locating youth and transition in relation to general social arrangements have not been tackled head on. Indeed, recently, writers have placed a question mark over the validity of this endeavour. Evidence of change in the experience and organization of youth and transition have been described in terms of fragmentation, as youth are increasingly able to "construct their own biographies" in a more "open" (and uncertain) social world (Chisholm & du Bois-Reymond 1993; cf. Beck 1992). However, it appears premature to suggest that change amounts to "destandardization" or that youth is losing its coherence as a life course stage.

It will be argued that an elucidation of social change in the experience of youth, and in patterns of transition from youth to adulthood, requires a wider interpretation of youth as a life course stage than that offered by contemporary commentators. This is not proposed as an issue of simply broadening the scope of enquiry to incorporate more aspects of young adults' experience. The avenue of enquiry taken here traces the social and economic aspects of life course transitions, and the focus is on general processes of change. Youth and adulthood are used as terms for describing particular locations with respect to the organization of social reproduction. This refers both to the arrangements through which people resource their day-to-day livelihoods, relative to some customary standard of living, and the reproduction of households and of new generations of children. It is no more proposed that this is an exhaustive definition of adulthood, than that partial dependence offers an exhaustive definition of youth. However, that such definitions are not exhaustive should not detract from their general salience. The approach is one that locates youth and transition in relation to the processes that give rise to dependence and independence, and through which these statuses take on meaning. It addresses the ways in which changes in household and family structure, and changes in the division of labour between women and men, and across generations, are themselves bound up with changes in the structure of employment. The analysis of employment and family relations as aspects of a single process enables an improved explanation of social change in life course arrangements.

The changing experience of youth

Significant changes in the circumstances of youth have occurred over the past two decades. The period has been one of rapid change in the structure of demand and levels of reward to youth labour. The number of school leavers entering the labour force with no guarantee of a secure wage was a cause of increasing political and social concern in the 1980s. The percentage of 16 to 18 year-olds in Britain who were unemployed or on training schemes grew from 10.1% in 1979 to 27.0% in 1984 (Department of Education and Science (DES) figures, quoted in Raffe 1987). The percentages of 16 year-olds in paid employment fell from 60% in 1975 to 16% by 1986 (rising slightly to 20% by 1988). In 1988, 25% of the age group were on the Youth Training Scheme (YTS), a slight decline from the peak participation rate of 27% between 1985 and 1987; 47% were in full-time education and 8% were registered as unemployed. Of 17 year-olds in 1988, 33% were in full-time education compared to 25% in 1975. In 1986 YTS was extended to a two-year scheme, and the proportion of 17 year-olds on the scheme increased from 10% in 1987 to 21% in 1988. Those in employment fell from 45% to 36% between 1987 and 1988. In 1975, 84% of 18 year-olds were in paid employment, a percentage that fell to 62% by 1983 and recovered slightly to 68% by 1988 (Department of Employment, Labour Market Quarterly Report 1989). By 1988 the most common route into employment amongst 16 year-olds was via YTS, accounting for 36% of labour force entrants, compared to 30% who went directly into employment, and 30% who entered employment after full-time education beyond the minimum school-leaving age (Department of Employment, Labour Market Quarterly Report 1990).

Social security legislation was altered throughout the 1980s, effectively increasing the age at which independence, as recognized by social security arrangements, is deemed to start. In 1988 the Social Security Act replaced the Supplementary Benefit System with Income Support, since when it is only in exceptional circumstances that payments are made to 16 and 17 year-olds. Guarantees of a place on YTS, with its weekly allowance, replaced the automatic claim to benefit amongst the age group. While the YTS allowance was higher than rates of Income Support it was well below wage rates for most young people. It has been argued (Harris 1988) that the consequence of such policies has been to extend the dependence of young people on their parents, a situation that has grown through the twentieth century because of the extension of compulsory education and, more crucially, according to Harris, because of the growth of youth unemployment through the 1970s and 1980s.

The level of earnings of young, relative to older, workers has shown a significant downward trend since the mid 1970s, reversing improvements through the 1950s and 1960s. New Earnings Survey (NES) data demonstrate a decline, from 1976 to 1988, in the hourly earnings of young males aged 18 to 20 from 62% to 52% of the earnings of the highest earning age group, and a similarly sharp decline in the relative earnings of men in their twenties. Amongst the lower quartiles of the earnings distribution, successive cohorts of young adults have experienced a decline in real wages. These changes are indicative of important changes in the economic relations of youth and early adulthood. Since the unemployed and those on training allowances are not included in the earnings data, the evidence suggests more broadly based changes in the period of youth and early adulthood than is suggested by the emphasis of youth researchers on YTS and unemployment. While the decline in teenage wage rates has been broadly acknowledged, the decline in earnings of men in their twenties, relative to those of middle-aged men, has passed largely unremarked. What has also been neglected is the increase in the earnings of young women relative to young men. It will be argued that these developments are related, and integral to patterns of change in the resourcing of households.

Recent changes in the experience of young people have been followed by an attempt to locate them in relation to the economic and political events of the 1980s. Two general problems follow from this. The first is to do with the supposed causal relation between the employment structure and life course structure, where developments in the former are understood to be prior, to have consequences for the life course of individuals and families, but to be independent of this "social" sphere. The focus on the 1980s exacerbates the difficulties that have emerged in "locating" youth and the transition to adult status as life course periods. This is well illustrated by the hypothesis of deferral in the timing of departure from the parental home, marriage and birth of the first child amongst recent cohorts, posited as a consequence of the collapse in employment chances for young people that occurred through the early 1980s. The comparison of recent patterns of family-related transitions with those that obtained in earlier decades has been limited, and is usually set against a generalized description of "standard" transitions, made at younger ages than now, and underwritten by employment security. Yet a general trend, which is well known, if not well understood, has been largely neglected by youth researchers. National level demographic evidence demonstrates a reversal, since the early 1970s, of a long-term trend to younger ages at marriage and parenthood. *In other words, the sorts of changes envisaged as a consequence of the employment crisis of the early 1980s, principally amongst the most disadvantaged, were already in train across the general population.* It appears that the events of the 1980s did not precipitate a pattern of delay, but rather the claims of youth to independence at an early age were already being undermined by general processes.

Running in parallel with the neglect of demographic explanation is the limited engagement with historical change in the organization of the family and, in particular, the family life course. This is the second problem that ensues from the attempt to explain change in the organization of transition solely in relation to the economic restructuring and political climate of the 1980s. There has been little consideration of the processes underlying changes in family structure or in the organization of family resourcing amongst its members. Much of the youth debate concerns the undermining of claims by young people to adult lifestyles, and the increasing emphasis of government policy on parental responsibility for young adults without independent means. Change in the organization of the family has been described in terms of a "privatization" of unemployment and insecurity amongst young people where parents are increasingly expected to meet the costs of extended periods of dependence amongst their young adult children. This is an important element of changes in social security legislation but it is only a partial picture, reflecting a particular aspect of change in the organization of dependence and obligation at the level of the household. More general processes of change in the organization of the household as an economic unit have been sidelined in these accounts. The emphasis on employment and a wage as the key to independence and adulthood has led to a partial view of family-related life course transitions, where these are explained in relation to the "sphere" of paid employment but not in relation to the organization of households. Historical developments in the structure of households indicate quite significant changes in the relations of different family members to family income maintenance and related changes in the position of youth within the family. For example, recent generations of youth and young adults have grown up in a period of increasingly parent-centred obligations to household resourcing. This historically recent dispensation of the young from the sharing of economic obligations for maintaining their parental household is part of the background to contemporary studies of the transition to adult status, yet such studies barely address the processes by which changing household structures have enabled youth to experience a period of semi-autonomous independence, partly underwritten by the income of parents. These sorts of changes need to be incorporated into accounts of change in patterns of transition from youth to adulthood.

Any hypothesis of deferral in the timing of transition necessarily suggests structural change in the organization of social reproduction: in the ways in which dependence and independence are resourced. The concern with life course trajectories focuses attention on biographical journeys from dependence to independence, but in the absence of a theory of the mutual significance of these statuses, explanations of change in life course processes must be called into question. Claims by dependents for resources, for reproducing their day-to-day living, are met indirectly through the state or, more generally, through immediate kin with "independent" access to a wage. In the case of young children and to some extent amongst dependent young adults these claims are standardly met by parents. The ways in which claims to resources by children and women are met cannot be separated from the historical "success" of claims to a family wage by adult men. Where the transition to adulthood is defined in material terms in the youth literature, the definition is vague and entails a uniform notion of adult status being gradually achieved through the receipt of a secure wage. However, the longitudinal definition of transitions to adult status as a combination of life course events entails more than simply a transition from dependence to independence. For example, the "independence" enabled by a youth wage is partial, and contemporary household structures standardly enable dependent young adults to be net consumers where the costs of their day-to-day living are subsidized by their parents. The "independence" signalled by parenthood implies the need for access to resources sufficient to care for dependents. In short, transitions through these domestic life course events do not simply label a "more complete" independence, but entail changing circumstances with respect to the organization of social claims and obligations. A hypothesis of deferral speaks of change in the resourcing of youth, as a period of partial dependence, and is suggestive of change in the arrangements through which individuals and couples establish new households and families. *Changes in the structure of life course transitions from dependence to independence must simultaneously entail a restructuring of the relations between dependents and those on whom they make claims for resources.* The historical structuring and reproduction of these relationships has been of quite limited interest to recent youth research, and marginal to its methodology, yet an adequate understanding of processes of change in the structuring of life course transitions requires that it be placed centrally.

The organization of dependence and obligation

Locating the transition from youth to adult status in relation to the social organization of dependence and obligation enables a consideration of change in both family structure and employment structure. There has been a model in youth research (shared by life course studies more generally) of "parallel trajectories", or of life course careers both through family-related transitions and the labour market. While such "careers" are seen to interact, they are nevertheless understood to be based in independent, social and economic spheres. As we will see, existing studies of family-related life course transitions and studies of the youth labour market both embody, and reflect, this conceptual division between "social" and "economic" processes. The division, however, does not reflect real processes. To elaborate on this, it is useful to draw a parallel with theories of gender and inequality. Labour market theories and descriptions of inequality often bracket together women and young adults as disadvantaged in employment by virtue of either their low productivity relative to adult men, or their exclusion from forms of employment advantage by direct or indirect discrimination. Critiques of these descriptions of inequality, in which individuals are seen to be rewarded according to their productivity, have stressed the importance of the family, and the domestic division of labour, to patterns of inequality in employment. Drawing on Marx, but extending his argument to analyses of gender inequalities, labour is understood to be valued not according to its product but in relation to the costs of its reproduction (the day-to-day reproduction of people's livelihoods, relative to some customary standard of living). Thus, women in paid work are rewarded not at their true costs of reproduction but as partly dependent on others for the resourcing of their day-to-day livelihoods. Gender inequalities in rewards to employment are organized in relation to the domestic division of labour, and adult male earnings reflect men's particular relations to household income maintenance (Beechey 1978; Humphries & Rubery 1984; Brenner & Ramas 1984). The availability of labour at different costs affects the organization of labour demand, so people's differing relations to household income maintenance are themselves significant to the organization and reproduction of employment inequalities (Garnsey 1982; Stanworth 1984). In these arguments, the processes underlying inequalities in the "social" sphere of the family and in the "economic" sphere of employment are inseparable.

Conventional theories of stratification have been criticized for treating the occupational structure as a given, a system of rewards whose level is determined by "economic" processes, across which different labour force groups are allocated. Such theories fail to explain how the labour supply structure, and the varying success of claims to resources by different labour force groups, are implicated fundamentally in the patterning of access to, and rewards from, employment (cf. Garnsey 1982; Humphries & Rubery 1984; Stewart et al. 1985; Rainwater et al. 1986; Holmwood 1991). More specifically, labour is reproduced through the family, or through the domestic division of labour. Individual workers are not rewarded as if they have equivalent, or even potentially equivalent, value. Rather, the organization of rewards to employment is structured in relation to the costs of reproducing labour, and differing relations to household income maintenance are important to the structure of employment inequalities. The "labour market" is a process of distribution that embodies the relations of different groups to the resourcing of social reproduction. While the value of such an approach has been demonstrated in analyses of gender-related inequalities (e.g. Garnsey 1982; Stewart et al. 1985; Siltanen 1986) there are similarly good, and related, reasons why it is salient to an analysis of life course related inequalities.[1]

As we will see, developing an explanation of life course transitions in terms of social claims and obligations allows us to explore male and female transitions to adulthood as aspects of an integrated dynamic. In youth research, women are represented as being excluded from male forms of advantage because of their particular position in the family and their relation to childbearing and childcare. However, this approach neglects the ways in which aspects of male advantage are predicated precisely on their own, particular, relationship to domestic obligations. Defining both youth and adult statuses in terms of social and economic claims and obligations is theoretically coherent, enabling an exploration of salient aspects of both statuses within the same conceptual framework. *The need to "locate" youth in its social context is simultaneously a need to transform the ways in which youth as a life course stage is conceptualized.* Change in the structure and experience of youth and the transition to adult status can be adequately analyzed only as an aspect of the social relations through which these life course stages take on substance and meaning.

The research reported in the book draws on primary data collected in a survey of young people and their parents, locating these data in relation to existing evidence. A principal objective of the survey was to gather evidence on the processes underlying transitions from youth to adult status, and to contribute to a more general analysis of change in the structure and organization of early life course

10

transitions. The survey design and sample are described in Chapter 3. Here I confine discussion to some general methodological issues.

To understand the processes underlying change in life course event timing it is necessary to locate the data gathered in a small-scale, cross-sectional, survey in relation to more general evidence. Such a strategy will help to avoid the pitfalls of being too quick to generalize from a relatively small number of cases. While the problem of locating survey evidence is brought into sharper focus when the survey sample is small, a larger sample would not itself provide a simple solution. To locate the data next to other evidence helps in assessing the validity of the former and helps to "contextualize" such data. However, such a strategy is only a partial one. As well as evidence from other studies of youth in transition there is, of course, a wealth of data available on patterns of demographic change, on, for example, ages at marriage and parenthood. As we will see, this has not received the attention it deserves. Since such data reveal historical changes in life course event timing, that is, in precisely those family-related transitions generally considered as indices of the transition to adult status, they demand our consideration. While this macro-level evidence has not been totally ignored by youth researchers, it is generally invoked as a device for contextualizing analyses of contemporary patterns of transition. The aggregate level changes that it reveals tend to be vaguely specified and there has been little engagement by youth researchers with explanations of these changes. Why should this be? In part it appears to reflect a division between disciplines, with aggregate level, historical changes in patterns of marriage and fertility more the concern of demographers, economists and social historians than of sociologists. It may be too, that it reflects the methodological difficulties of relating macro- and micro-level evidence. However, these are difficulties that must be resolved in order to furnish a more adequate understanding of change in the organization and experience of transitions to adult status.

To address the problem of the division between macro- and micro-level evidence it is essential not only to locate the latter with respect to the former, but also to recognize a need to go beyond "contextualizing" our interpretation of the experience of survey respondents. Such an approach suggests that understandings of aggregate level changes are themselves unproblematic, and as we will see, this is not the case. Simply stated, the relationship between experience at an individual level and general changes in the organization of life course transitions is a conceptual as much as an empirical issue. The call to locate youth and transition within their social context seems to entail a dualism between youth and transition on the one hand and social structure on the other hand. Locating data on patterns of transition requires more than simply contextualizing empirical evidence, socially, historically or whatever: the "context", after all, is also the substance of the research problem. The format of the argument is not one of simply reporting evidence from my survey, suitably located. Rather, I analyze data from the survey, and from other sources, as part of an attempt to reconstruct a more general understanding of the transition from youth to adult status.

About the book

The book is organized as follows. Chapter 2 presents a review of research into youth and the transition to adulthood, describing developments in research as they relate to contemporary concerns about the consequences of economic change and employment restructuring for the experience of youth and young adults. The two main areas of research in the 1980s and since have addressed the impact of such changes on family and life course related transitions on the one hand, and on the structure of inequality, careers and life chances of young people in the labour market, on the other. These two research agendas, which have dominated recent discussion, are considered in turn. Both offer valuable insights into aspects of change in the experience of young people, yet both share a general theoretical framework that has hindered the development of a fuller description, and a more coherent explanation, of change in the organization of youth and transition as life course stages. This shortcoming arises out of a conceptual division between "social" life course processes and "economic" labour market processes, a division that is entailed within, and reflected by, their distinct research agendas.

The transition literature has addressed the consequences of employment restructuring for the ability of young people to resource independence and adult lifestyles. Changes in employment demand are taken as independent variables, and there is limited consideration of the ways in which life course arrangements are themselves structured into employment relations. These issues are discussed along with issues of gender, which need to be placed centrally in analyses of the changing structure of transition. Within the labour market approach, divisions of labour within the family are seen as important to understanding the structure of inequality, but this is immediately translated into a description of young people, women and men as comprising distinct labour supply groups. It is these categories that are then adopted as a description of inequality, and the more precise notion of household circumstances and relations is lost. Any changes in the structure of households, or in domestic divisions of labour, are elided. The following chapters develop an analysis that attempts to move beyond the dualism between life course and employment processes, in order to locate recent changes in the transition to adulthood as part of an historical process, and one that reflects the integrated development of social reproduction and employment structure.

Chapter 3 describes the research design and the location of survey respondents with respect to general arrangements. Aggregate level patterns of change in the organization and timing of life course events, in particular marriage and birth of the first child, over the twentieth century are then discussed. This evidence gives historical perspective to hypotheses of delay in the transition to adult status. Demographic evidence demonstrates that the long-term trend through this century, to younger ages at marriage and parenthood, was reversed in the early 1970s. Writers on youth in transition have compared the experience of the 1980s with "normal transitions" seen to have obtained during full employment in the 1950s and 1960s. However, a longer-term perspective illustrates clearly the historically specific nature of both periods. While this is an obvious point it is stressed because of the importance of locating contemporary patterns of transition as part of a wider historical process. The chapter considers patterns of event timing amongst the survey sample in relation to aggregate level evidence. Within the survey, information on parents' perceptions of changes between the experience of young people now and their own experience of transition was gathered. Their responses are described and examined in relation to other evidence on changes in factors that are salient to the timing of family formation. The most important changes are seen to lie in job security, housing availability and home ownership, female careers and expectations concerning living standards amongst contemporary cohorts of young adults. Female employment and careers are an aspect of change that was most frequently cited by respondents. This response touches on a set of issues that has been barely addressed by the youth literature, and is taken up in the next chapter.

Chapter 4 considers evidence that suggests that changes in gender relations, in employment and with respect to household resourcing, are of great importance in historically recent changes in the timing of family formation. To elucidate the processes that are operating here requires an understanding of the mutuality of productive and repro- ductive processes. Changes in the organization of the family and rela- tions to its resourcing by family members are inseparable from changes in the organization of labour demand and the patterning of rewards to employment. Changes in gender relations to employment and to the family are central to this dynamic. Economic theories of demographic change explain declines in fertility and delay in the tim- ing of marriage and parenthood in terms of historical changes in fe- male, relative to male, earnings. Economic models rely on macro-level data and have been criticized for their assumptions about individual behaviour. Their conclusions are contradicted by studies which, using data on household level earnings, identify stability in the relative con- tributions of female and male partners. However, this argument of continuity is misleading, and derives from still too general an inter- pretation of the data. An analysis of national level earnings data, disaggregated by age groups, reveals significant changes in gendered earnings ratios amongst recent cohorts of young adults. There has been an improvement in young women's earnings relative to those of young men. This is associated with a decline in the earnings of young men relative to peak adult earnings, i.e. earnings of men in the highest earning age group. Improving female to male earnings ratios are a consequence of differing, gendered, rates of decline relative to those of older workers. These developments in gender- and age-related pat- terns of earnings correspond with patterns of delay in the timing of family formation relative to previous cohorts. These processes are in- tegral to one another. An understanding of the coherence of relations in the domestic and economic "spheres" is essential to an explanation of change in the organization of the transition from youth to adult status.

In Chapter 4, peak adult earnings, against which changes in the earnings of young women and men are measured, are used as an index of general consumption standards. Chapter 5 disaggregates this general measure and considers the class-related patterning of life course event timing against a measure of consumption standards, derived from the survey data, which is sensitive to the differing socio-economic circumstances of the survey respondents. Recent research has failed to reconcile its hypothesis of delay in the attainment of independence, as a consequence of "new" forms of employment disadvantage amongst youth, with the traditional expectation that socio-economic disadvantage is associated with the attainment of independence at young ages. Associated with this problem is the limited analysis of class variation in life course event timing. Models of class differences propose that lifetime employment and earnings profiles are significant in shaping orientations that in turn are necessary to explaining class differences in the timing of marriage and parenthood. Middle-class life chances reward long-term planning and later ages at parenthood are seen to be a rational strategy in relation to an earnings profile that rises progressively over the working life. In contrast, early ages at family formation amongst the working class are seen as rational in relation to "careers" where earnings levels do not increase much beyond early adulthood and where insecurity is common. However, while a theory of orientations to the future is necessary to explain class-related differences, such orientations are typically deduced from a measure of class location. Consequently, such a theory adds little to the analysis of class differences.

Accepting a cross-sectional measure of class location as an adequate description of social difference is questionable because it neglects the way standard class-related employment trajectories may entail mobility across jobs. The analysis of Chapter 5 attempts to build in respondents' expectations for the future, in part through exploring their perceptions of the circumstances of salient reference groups. Gendered relations to employment careers and family formation are described, and illustrated through respondents' attitudes towards the timing of marriage and parenthood. The association between current employment position, orientations and patterns of life course event timing is explored. The discussion questions the marginality of life course processes to definitions of class-related inequality.

Chapter 6 considers recent critiques of sociological theories of inequality, critiques that are informed by a concern with demographic change and a growing dependent population. The literature on ageing, and inter-generational conflict, shares similarities with research into youth and transition. Both proceed as if economic processes and social relations over the life course have their own dynamic, yet it is precisely this dichotomy that compromises explanations of social change. The ageing population structure and claims on resources by non-working groups are seen by many to be contributing to a growing welfare crisis. In particular, the interests of the working, "productive" population and the interests of the non-working, "dependent" population are understood to be at odds with one another. Further, historical changes in the relative welfare of different non-working groups, in particular between the young and the elderly, are expected to engender perceptions of injustice. In these arguments, relations between age groups and generations will become increasingly fraught, as "unacceptable" levels of taxation are expected to blight the experience of a contracting workforce, required to resource a growing welfare population. Social conflict will ensue and undermine the welfare project. The chapter questions the division between "the political" and "the economic" on which these arguments rely. The division is part of a conceptual framework where the claims of particular (welfare) groups appear as problematic while other aspects of resource distribution (claims to employment) are not questioned. As it is, more seems to be known about researchers' views on distributive justice than is known about the perceptions of their subject populations. It has not been demonstrated that members of age groups share interests that are consonant with their cohort experience, or perceive their interests to be in conflict with those of members of other age groups or generations. Further, the literature offers little evidence on social actors' perceptions of inequality over the life course. Empirical evidence drawn from the survey suggests that standard processes do not place age groups or generations in an antagonistic relationship. The changing structure of the life course amongst women and men, and the diversity of experience of those not in paid employment, present a challenge to theories of inequality that prioritize people's location within the "productive" (employment) sphere over other areas of social experience. Understanding the relations between age groups and generations is essential to explaining change in patterns of inequality, but the interdependence of these relations is not necessarily a precursor to crisis but is part of a coherent social structure. The final chapter summarizes the main arguments and describes further their implications for understanding life course processes, inequality and social change.

Chapter 2

Economic change and the transition from youth to adulthood

Introduction

Youth research has reflected shifting sociological paradigms in recent decades, from neo-Marxist analyses of youth culture, and representations of the transition from school to work as a critical moment in the reproduction of the labour force (e.g. Willis 1977; Centre for Contemporary Cultural Studies 1981; Frith 1984; Rees & Atkinson 1982), to recent concerns about citizenship, gender inequality and socio-economic polarization in the transition from youth to adult status (e.g. Ashton et al. 1990; Jones & Wallace 1990; Ashton & Lowe 1991; Chisholm et al. 1991). The changing circumstance of youth, and the perceived inadequacy of previous theories for explaining contemporary developments have led to theoretical reformulations. These are aimed at exploring the consequences of economic restructuring for the experience of youth and the patterning of transitions from youth to adult lifestyles.

In the 1960s and 1970s, years of relatively full employment, processes of class continuity in the transition from school to work were a principal concern of youth research. Forms of socialization, through the family, school and work relations, were seen to underlie "smooth" transitions between these life course stages (Roberts 1968; Ashton and Field 1976; also cf. Willis 1977). This research was, in part, a critique of human capital theories of occupational selection. It emphasized the significance not only of structural constraint but attempted also to describe its "acceptability" through the structuring of young people's conceptions of their interests and capabilities. The social construction

17

of lifestyle orientations and orientations to the future was therefore a central theme. Class-related orientations, formed through the family and through school were seen to be "confirmed", and reified on entry into different career routes (Ashton & Field 1976). For Willis, the structuring of orientations was a dimension through which working-class schoolboys "seal their own fate" (Willis 1977). The issue of life course transitions amongst youth was directed at processes under-lying class continuity, as individuals traversed the distinct institutions of school and work.

Youth research in the 1980s was shaped by the experience of recession and mass unemployment at the beginning of the decade. Some writers suggested that the collapse in job opportunities amongst young people undermined traditional routes to independence and adult status (e.g. Willis 1984, 1985; Williamson 1985). This hypothesis was taken up and explored by those interested in the domestic, or family-related, consequences of economic insecurity amongst young people. Previous research on the transition from school to work was overtaken by an interest in life course trajectories, and in the con-sequences of economic change for the organization and timing of family-related life course events. In such accounts, employment is seen to underwrite the ability to secure the achievement of independ-ence and adult lifestyles through a series of status transitions, specifi-cally leaving the parental home, cohabitation, marriage and parent-hood. Most recent research in the area has focused on the experience of the 1980s, comparing the timing of life course transitions amongst unemployed and employed young people, and comparing their experience with that of cohorts seen to experience "normal transi-tions" during the 1950s and 1960s, decades of full employment. Dif-ferent conclusions have emerged as to the consequences of economic change for the transition to adulthood. Some writers argue that employment restructuring has, at least for some groups, underlain a prolonging of dependency at the parental home (e.g. Wallace 1987a; Harris 1988), and others maintain that economic change is not really significant to the attainment of adult status (e.g. Hutson & Jenkins 1989).

Other researchers have focused on youth in the labour market, employment restructuring and the extent and nature of change in the demand for, and opportunities available to, young workers. Central to recent research into the youth labour market is the concern with economic and institutional changes and their consequences for youth employment. Part of what was at stake in debates about the impact of recession, the growth of the YTS and industrial and occupational restructuring, was how best to characterize the nature of change in youth employment opportunities, and the consequences of such changes for the structure of social inequality and for the life chances of those generations of youth entering the labour force in the 1980s.

These two areas of research into youth and early adulthood, which will be referred to as the transition and labour market literature respectively, are reviewed in this chapter. Below, I describe the background to these debates, both the circumstances that they address, and earlier research and writing on youth. From there I focus on youth research through the 1980s, dominated by the debates outlined above, and highlight some of the reasons why the particular focus on the events of this decade has hindered explanations of change in youth and early adulthood as life course stages. In so doing I hope to set the stage for an account that is capable of elucidating change in these life course stages as integral to change in general social arrangements.

Transitions in the youth debate

Early accounts of the unemployment crisis amongst youth in the early 1980s presented vehement critiques of government policy during these early years of the Thatcher administration. Writers addressed the perceived discrepancies between youth labour supply and demand as they were manifest in training policies, and many argued that government intervention amounted to an ideological assault on working-class youth. Policies were argued to be restructuring the substance of youth as a life course stage, by forcing down youth wages and shaping the ambitions and expectations of the young in order to meet the demands of industry. The increased powers of the Manpower Services Commission (MSC) and, in particular, the development of the YTS were characterized as a form of ideological management by the state (e.g. Markall & Gregory 1982; Finn 1982, 1987; Benn & Fairley 1986). The "skill deficit" model implicit in YTS was a theme connecting the writing of several authors. Training policy, in particular the emphasis on training for "social and life skills", was argued to reify the popular myth that unemployment is a

19

consequence of a mismatch between young people's abilities and those required by employers (e.g. Bates et al. 1984; Rees & Atkinson 1982). State training policy was seen as an attempt to ingrain the work ethic in the young, and "to break people, especially working class young people, into a life of low wages and long periods of unemployment" (Benn & Fairley 1986: 3). The critiques were accompanied by rather vague policy recommendations, features of what now seems a dated political manifesto, with arguments for a participatory debate on the kind of work society needs (Benn & Fairley 1986) to teaching "subversive skills" (Atkinson et al. 1982).

A number of writers claimed that the sorts of changes occurring would effectively prolong the period of youth. The collapse in employment was simultaneously a collapse in the means by which young people could secure independence and adult lifestyles. Young "adults", in their early twenties and unemployed, or in work but without security or decent prospects, were said to be "trapped as teenagers" (Williamson 1985; see also Caffrey et al. 1986) or to experience an extended youth as a period of suspended animation, and be caught in a "frozen transition" (Willis 1985).

The argument that routes to adult status and independence were being undermined remained a euphemism for the problematic employment status of young people. However, it presented a hypothesis that wage security was necessary to "normal" transitions, through leaving the parental home, getting married and becoming parents in an independent household. A number of research projects were set up to explore the relationship between youth and young adults' experience in the labour force and the organization of family-related life course transitions (eg. Jones 1986, 1987; Wallace 1987a,b,c; Hutson & Jenkins 1987a,b, 1989; Furlong & Cooney 1990; Murphy & Sullivan 1986). Consequently the earlier emphasis on the transition from school to work shifted to a more general concern with labour force and life course trajectories. The ages at leaving parents, setting up a household, cohabiting, marrying and becoming a parent are standardly used as indicators of the attainment of adult status. Their incidence is not necessary, nor equivalent, to adulthood, their order not rigid nor uniform, but their timing serves as a useful and parsimonious framework for exploring class differences across the population and patterns of change across cohorts or generations. As life course events, of individuals and households, they provide indices to map out patterns of progression from childhood dependency through the partial independence of youth to the attainment of forms of "adult" independence and responsibilities.

Research into youth in transition has been dominated by qualitative evidence, with relatively small-scale studies often using in-depth interviews, and focusing on the experience of contemporary cohorts of youth and young adults (e.g. Sawdon et al. 1981; Griffin 1985; Coffield et al. 1986; Stafford 1981; Cockburn 1987; Wallace 1987a; Hutson & Jenkins 1989). The success in achieving detailed descriptions of the experience, social relationships and attitudes of young adults has not been matched by a similarly detailed account of the nature of change in the structuring of transitions to adult status. Evidence of historical change is used anecdotally, or general references are made to aggregate level patterns of change in the timing of early life course events but the processes underlying such changes are not explored and are not methodologically integrated in studies of the contemporary experience of young adults (Chisholm (1990) and Bynner (1991) make similar criticisms). So, for example, there has been no detailed analysis of the relation between ethnographic evidence on life course event timing and macro-level demographic changes. Further, while the class-related patterning of transitions to adulthood is well established (e.g. Dunnell 1979; Kiernan & Diamond 1983; Jones 1987), its relation to "new" forms of disadvantage (e.g. mass unemployment) is less clear.

The following discussion considers two recent research projects in some detail, those of Wallace, and of Hutson & Jenkins, since they are important in their attempts to move the youth debate forward by reframing its remit, and both help to illustrate problems that are general to conceptualizations of the transition to adult status. Parallel issues that confront theories of gender in the transition to adulthood are discussed in the next section. These problems are in need of resolution, and addressing them may enable us to move on from the current vogue of mutual chastisement, amongst youth researchers, for allowing the critical questions of the late twentieth century to pass us by (Bynner 1991; Chisholm 1990; Ashton & Lowe 1991).

Wallace argues that the "normal" paths to adulthood, established in the 1950s and 1960s during full employment, are no longer possible, and a substantial proportion of under-25s have joined a marginal, sub-employed, population (Wallace 1987a). A central theme of her research is the impact of new patterns of work and unemployment on patterns of transition on cohabitation, marriage and parenthood. The empirical basis of her work is a sample of young people living on the Isle of Sheppey, whom she interviewed three times between 1979 and 1984, from the age of 16 to 21. She examines their domestic and labour force careers, their experience of, and attitudes towards, family-related life course transitions. In the context of previous theories based on a narrow concept of "transition", and the tendency to equate youth with an age period, this longitudinal emphasis is welcome, although the structure of her sample still poses a methodological difficulty given that most people marry and have their first child at ages over 21. Wallace could therefore examine the *attitudes* of her interviewees to marriage, cohabitation and parenthood but could relate these to the *practice* of only a minority of her sample. Most of her respondents were opposed to the idea of marrying and having children while unemployed, but in practice a number did:

> Hence, unemployment would appear to inhibit "normal" family transitions in principle. However, in practice . . . those with irregular employment careers were just as likely to have had children by the time they were 21, particularly amongst the girls. This would confirm the idea that the unemployed tend to "drift" into parenthood for lack of any positive alternatives (Wallace 1987b: 126).

Wallace suggests that marriage was postponed as a consequence of unemployment. Unemployed people were more likely to be cohabiting with their partners, either independently or with their parents, than they were to have left home, married and established a household in a "conventional" way. She notes the growing significance of owner occupation to patterns of household formation amongst young couples and argues that female, as well as male partners' earnings were crucial to house purchase. This is an important point. It hints at a changing relationship between the earnings of young men and women, in relation to the timing of household formation, an issue to which I shall later return.

The tension in Wallace's argument between the attitudes of her sample as a whole and the practice of a few in terms of family formation is not resolved. The cut-off age of 21 amongst her sample presents a fundamental problem: only 13 of the 84 young adults interviewed at the age of 21 were parents. The point made by Wallace that those with irregular employment careers were as likely to have children as those with secure employment careers is based, amongst men, on a sample size of four. It is the attitudes of the sample as a whole and the level of unemployment amongst them that leads Wallace to her speculative conclusion that family formation amongst the unemployed is likely to be postponed "at least in principle" (Wallace 1987b: 133). Yet simultaneously "unplanned family formation . . . may increase as prospects look increasingly hopeless for young couples" (Wallace 1987b: 135). The need to make a distinction between principle and practice here highlights two related issues. First, it is not likely that there is any general single trend in the timing of life course events as a consequence of unemployment. Secondly, there has been a general pattern of delay in the timing of those life course events addressed by Wallace, a development in need of explanation, yet these aggregate level changes have received relatively little attention from youth researchers. Wallace, for example, points to the tendency towards younger ages at marriage and first pregnancy throughout the twentieth century, and only footnotes evidence, from the United States, of a pattern of delay in the timing of parenthood. Wallace, like many other youth researchers, does not locate the evidence of small-scale studies in relation to general patterns of change in life course event timing. The socially significant trend towards later ages at family formation over the past two decades suggests that this is a serious omission.

The tendency towards younger marriage and first pregnancy is true only as the most general characterization of change through the twentieth century. The long-term trend to lower ages at family formation, quite marked in the 1950s and 1960s, was reversed in the 1970s, with the trend to later ages becoming more pronounced through the 1980s (OPCS, Marriage and Birth Statistics). Since the mid 1960s there has been a significant decline in marriage and birth rates, most dramatically amongst younger age groups. The number of births per thousand women aged under 20 fell by 40% between 1971 and 1986, and by a similar rate amongst those aged 20–24 (Social Trends 1988, figures for England and Wales). These figures on birth *rates*, of course, do not clarify patterns of the timing of childbirth. However, other evidence suggests that cohorts of women born from the mid 1950s onward showed a significant change in the timing of their first births, relative to older cohorts. While up to age 18 the cohort born in 1955 had a fertility rate higher than that of previous generations, as the cohort aged it manifested a pattern of delayed starts in childbearing (Thompson 1980). Later cohorts have continued this trend.

These patterns of aggregate level demographic change are addressed in detail in Chapter 3, but have been sketched here in order to highlight the significance of their neglect, both theoretical and methodological, in the youth literature. The changes have been the subject of a largely separate research literature, the remit more of demographers and economists than sociologists. The explanatory problems raised by aggregate level theories have not been addressed in youth research. Busfield & Paddon attempted such a project in the 1970s (Busfield & Paddon 1977), but the implications of the framework they adopted, and the inferred necessity of cross-disciplinary engagement, has been passed over by recent youth research. The authors note that despite the widely acknowledged importance of economic factors to patterns of nuptuality and fertility, the relation of the latter to material standards, or orientations to living standards, has received little detailed study (Busfield & Paddon 1977). The writers address this omission and explain changes through the twentieth century, up until the 1960s, in terms of increasing affluence, and changes in the perceived value of accumulating material assets prior to marriage. They suggest that economic recession, and increased difficulties in attaining a mortgage at a time when there were newly-inflated expectations of home ownership, underlay the decline in marriage rates at young ages through the 1970s. While they are interested principally in questions concerning decisions to parent, and in family size and the spacing of children, they offer some evidence on the timing of first births, suggesting that economic considerations, particularly accumulating assets prior to family formation, are of particular significance in decisions about when to start a family (Busfield & Paddon 1977). As we will see, such considerations were important also to many of the young adult respondents in my own survey. The ambivalence amongst recent writers over the relationship between material circumstances and patterns of life course event timing is partly a consequence of the lack of interest in linking detailed evidence from ethnographic studies on attitudes and perceptions with aggregate level changes in life course event timing.

Wallace, however, does provide some evidence in support of the hypothesis that employment restructuring has been important to life course processes, arguing that unemployment may give rise to a postponement of family formation amongst those affected (Wallace

1987a,b). In contrast, Hutson & Jenkins vigorously oppose the suggestions that unemployment amongst young people undermines the process of "becoming adult". The significance of other aspects of adult status makes absurd, in their view, the idea that its attainment is somehow undermined by changing economic conditions. The authors take issue with the failure to theorize adult status within youth research and place this problem centrally in their research on youth transitions (Hutson & Jenkins 1987a,b; 1989). Their study is based on in-depth interviews of unemployed young adults and their parents, conducted in the mid 1980s in Swansea and Port Talbot. Most of their young respondents had been unemployed for six months or more, and were aged 18 to 25 at the time of interview. Broadly, Hutson & Jenkins approach the definition of adulthood, and the structuring of transitions, from two directions, first stressing the social psychological aspects of attaining adult status and secondly, developing an understanding of transitions in relation to a general concept of citizenship. In the first, the authors point out that most of their respondents considered themselves, or their sons and daughters, to be adult, and they ask why this should be so. Reasons given by respondents lay partly in terms simply of their age, but more typically in terms of achieving maturity and an "independence of mind and action, and responsibilities in their attitudes and behaviour" (Hutson & Jenkins 1987a: 94). So, the authors argue:

> The language which is used implies that the transition from childhood to adulthood is in large part a moral transition – a change in the individual's ability to make certain kinds of decisions – and that a bargain, and an agreed definition of adulthood, is struck between parents and children (Hutson & Jenkins 1987a: 94).

Ultimately, it may indeed be appropriate to characterize the transition to adulthood, and change in its social organization, as having a moral character, but in a broader sense than that implied by Hutson & Jenkins. For them the significance of inter-family relationships for young people's attainment of adult status lies in the "symbolic economy" of the family. Transitions to psychological independence are managed through financial and other exchanges, where young adult children negotiate greater responsibilities and independence with their parents. For example, the authors argue that the payment of board money by young people is of limited significance to household resourcing but that it is important symbolically, a precursor to managing one's own, adult, affairs.

Like Wallace, the authors appear to agree that economic change may have particular consequences for the attainment of adulthood. However, in their work they take issue with Paul Willis's argument that economic change undermined the transition to adulthood for disadvantaged youth, and they argue that the attainment of adult status is not as compromised as suggested by Willis because it is rooted in a much wider notion of citizenship than implied by the stress on economic relationships. In particular, jural and political adulthood is not dependent on employment status. Core components of adult status are independent of material resources. In criticism of Willis, they argue that:

> It is the failure to distinguish the legally constituted rights and duties defining adult status – which, taken together, may be conceptualised as a portfolio of enablement and obligation – from the capacity, whether economically based or whatever, to actualise the potential bound up in that status, which allows Willis to diagnose the suspension of adulthood for the young unemployed (Hutson & Jenkins 1989: 107).

Thus, the authors argue, independent living or marriage and sexual partnership are only facets of a much wider set of relationships that constitute adult status: "It is the *right* to each, not their presence at any particular instance, which is most important" (1989: 109; original emphasis). The substance of adult status, but not its attainment, is what is compromised by unemployment. Written in their slightly earlier publication, but consistent with their subsequent arguments, the authors maintain that:

> Young people continue – despite all the odds that are stacked against them – to achieve adult status. Although it would be stretching credulity too far to argue that they can achieve *full* adult status or *full* social membership as long as they are unemployed, neither is it the case that they are left in limbo, abandoned to a purgatorial appendix of the life cycle. Despite youth (and adult) unemployment life – of a sort – goes on (Hutson & Jenkins 1987a: 106; original emphasis).

Thus the authors highlight some of the problems inherent in arguments of a delay in the attainment of adult status, arguments they presumably see as potentially labelling disadvantaged young men and women as childlike dependents. Clearly adulthood is a vague concept and, as the authors maintain, not very developed in the youth literature; for example, the authors argue, pertinently, that many aspects of adult status are not dependent on material resources. They stress the importance of psychological and emotional independence, and of citizenship rights for a rounded definition of adult status. However, in their drive to an eclectic definition, adulthood is conceived in such general terms that their framework risks losing its purchase on those aspects of transition that are changing in structured ways. For example, in stressing the importance of citizenship rights over economic circumstances, they appear to understate the ways in which the latter may themselves be considered as an aspect of social citizenship issues, in terms both of people's living standards relative to customary norms, and in terms of class-varying ability to mobilize jural and political rights. The stress on rights over their realization diminishes the significance of social change.

The writers' emphasis on the symbolic, over the material, household economy serves to illustrate the relative freedom from domestic financial obligations of post-war cohorts of youth, compared to those of earlier generations. However, it is important to acknowledge how, historically, the "symbolic" exchanges within households could appear to take precedence over material exchanges. General evidence suggests that this shift must have come about as a consequence of parents being better able to resource their dependent young adult children than was standardly the case in the earlier part of this century, and before.

The patterning of income over the family life course demonstrates an historical continuity with relative poverty occurring around the family-building period and in old age, and relative affluence occurring during middle age. In their study of inter-generational income mobility, based on a 1970s follow-up survey of families interviewed by Rowntree in York in 1950, Atkinson and his colleagues present data that manifest a life course related profile of relative wealth and poverty, similar to that identified by Rowntree in his 1899 study of poverty (Atkinson et al. 1983). The reasons underlying the general pattern, however, have changed. At the turn of the century relative affluence occurred in the middle years because children had begun earning and contributing substantially to household income maintenance. In the latter part of the twentieth century the financial contributions of children are less important. The most important factor influencing relative affluence in the middle years is identified by the authors as mothers' employment (Atkinson et al. 1983).

The most significant aggregate change in women's employment patterns this century has been the increased participation rate. This is accounted for largely by the amount of time spent in employment over the life course, a period that has increased dramatically in association with the reduction in the time spent childbearing. Thus, there are many more women in the labour force at any one point in time. Fertility declined significantly in the inter-war period, in part because of the imbalanced sex ratio following the First World War, but also because improvements in infant survival rates and extended periods of familial dependence by young people meant that children had become an economic burden rather than an asset to their parents (Gittins 1982. Also cf. Banks (1954) on declines in fertility amongst the Victorian middle classes as this related to rising aspirations; and Lewis (1980) on declining fertility amongst the working class through the early decades of the twentieth century). Low fertility rates in the inter-war years meant smaller cohorts of new entrants to the labour force in the 1940s and 1950s. Economic growth and an increasing demand for labour faced labour supply-side shortages. High marriage rates and a trend to younger ages at marriage and childbirth after the Second World War further reduced the population of single women from which employers could recruit. Employers turned increasingly to the recruitment of married women (Tilly & Scott 1978). Compression in the ages of childbearing also have been identified as an important supply-side factor in the rise of female participation rates since the 1950s. While the overall female participation rate doubled between 1921 and 1981, the married women's participation rate increased from 12% in 1931 to 57% in 1981 (Joshi 1990).

These processes are essential to understanding the structure of contemporary households, and they demonstrate the interaction of economic and demographic processes. The domestic "sphere" interacts with economic processes not just in relation to daily resourcing but also in relation to fertility patterns, and to the restructuring of households and the composition of the family. Perhaps at first sight the changes described merely underline the current position of youth as a period of semi-dependence, partly enabled by an historically small typical family size and by the high labour force participation rate of middle-aged mothers. However, it will be argued that changes in gendered patterns of employment and rewards over the life course are bound up with recent patterns of delay in household and family formation. The relationship between economic and demographic changes is not merely "historical background" but part of the substance of a restructuring of transitions from youth to adulthood. The long-term changes in household structure and claims and obligations amongst household members have enabled a prolonging of the period of dependence at the parental home amongst young adults. Clearly this development raises questions about how youth as a period of partial dependence and transitions to independence is resourced, and about the ways in which this has changed. One development of central importance to understanding these developments is the issue of gender, and the changing relations of women and men to paid employment and to household income maintenance. It is to issues of gender and their representation in the literature that I now turn.

Gendered processes and the transition to adulthood

As we have seen, an earlier emphasis by youth research on the transition from school to work has been overtaken by more recent concerns with the impact of economic restructuring for early labour force careers. For many authors the emphasis on employment relationships was inadequate to the task of understanding female transitions to adulthood. For women, adult status appeared more appropriately thought of in terms of family formation, or motherhood in particular (e.g. Bazalgette 1978; West & Newton 1983; Busfield 1987). Surveys that asked young people about their expectations for the future found "gender typical" expectations that were argued to:

> reflect a prevailing view in society . . . that adulthood for the male is generally marked by his entry into the world of work whereas adulthood for the female appears to be contingent upon her marriage (West & Newton 1983: 162).

More recently, writers have begun to consider the relationship between work and parenthood for both men and women. However, there remains a tendency to emphasize the distinctness of work and family careers, although increasingly they are seen as relevant both to men and to women. The transition from youth to adulthood still appears to crystallize the divergence of female and male life course trajectories. Female life course trajectories are still seen to be shaped principally in relation to the domestic sphere. There is some recognition of the importance to employers' recruitment strategies of male domestic status. For some employers family men with financial obligations to dependents will be more reliable employees than those without similar obligations (e.g. Wallace 1987a; Hutson & Jenkins 1989; also cf. Blackburn & Mann 1979). In parallel, it is women's domestic responsibilities that are seen to exclude them from "male" career routes and the associated rewards. An extreme version of this argument is presented by Bynner, in his synopsis of a UK/USA comparison of transition made by Kerchkoff, where:

> The conflicting demands on girls, stemming from their desire to pursue a "domestic career", is seen to stunt their progress towards qualifications and consequently to depress their opportunities in the labour market (Bynner 1991: 649).

While many would be sceptical of locating gender inequalities in female "choices", there is nevertheless a general characterization of forms of gender inequality as residing in processes of discrimination, whether it is through labour market segmentation in the economic sphere (e.g. Ashton et al. 1990) or through patriarchal processes in general. Gender inequality, as a feature of social arrangements, is not so much addressed as taken for granted, even where the processes giving rise to it are seen to be of decreasing salience for the study of gender relations in youth. Such an approach again underlies a curiously isolated theory of youth. Hutson & Jenkins, for example, identify relative equality amongst young adults living with their parents, underwritten, they suggest, by mothers' domestic work. They therefore argue that:

> The apparent gender equality of young women within the family can . . . only be understood in the context of a wider, generational pattern of gender inequalities (Hutson & Jenkins 1989: 155).

In such a view, youth and adulthood appear as distinct spheres with respect to the general structure of inequality. The biographical, or life course transition between these "spheres" is abrupt:

> The young women's relative freedom within the [parental] household is likely to be shortlived, vanishing with marriage and the move into an independent household (Hutson & Jenkins 1989: 155).

There is no consideration here that "adult" forms of gender inequality might be anything other than static. The argument suggests that there is increasing equality in the treatment of young women and men while they are still dependent, but the domestic division of labour that follows parenthood reflects more general continuities in "wider gender inequalities". Such an understanding, as will be argued in detail later on, is problematic.

Cockburn, too, argues that continuity prevails, although aspects of change are apparent. Here differences lie not across life course stages but between social norms and social action. Her study of YTS schemes in London in the mid 1980s addressed the reproduction of gender inequalities amongst youth, via YTS, to gender inequality in adulthood. Critical of models of gender discrimination and stereotyping, models that cannot explain the dynamics of change, Cockburn maintains that her respondents were more liberal in their attitudes to "gender-appropriate" jobs than such models suggest. However, in the context of economic recession, and the associated risk of making gender-contrary choices "this openness at the level of ideas coexists with an actual behaviour that is almost always conformist" (Cockburn 1987: 198).

The characterization of gender inequality as general, uniform and unchanging is a common feature of research. In consequence there has been a neglect of processes of change in the structuring of forms of "adult" inequality. Change, it appears, requires a particularly dramatic quality to arrest attention. Recently, Chisholm has argued that gender has been marginalized due to the relative weighting of the sphere of production over the sphere of reproduction. She maintains that the latter effectively *"becomes that which cannot be allocated to the production sphere"* (Chisholm 1990: 38; original emphasis). As a result, she notes, reproduction is treated analytically as if it were secondary to, and dependent on, production. She argues that we should regard the two spheres as interdependent so that issues of gender are integrated rather than "tagged on". However, despite this promising statement of intent, she goes on to argue that:

> The changes in patterns of marriage, childbearing and house-hold size and structure over the course of this century are both fascinating and are becoming increasingly complex, but the central point remains that kinship and marriage expressed through the life cycle of the nuclear family still structures most people's domestic arrangements for most of their lives . . . all studies of the domestic division of labour show that neither ideologies nor (still less) practices have changed with respect to gender roles . . . Young people's experience of family life are unlikely to change dramatically in the near future, then (Chisholm 1990: 53).

Other authors, similarly, have argued in favour of a balance between research into the reproductive and productive spheres, between domestic and employment experience. Jones & Wallace suggest that "attempts to produce gender-symmetrical studies of men and women in terms of both their labour market behaviour and their domestic responsibilities are lacking" (Jones & Wallace 1990: 138). However, calls for a "gender-symmetrical" methodology seem bound to fail as a critique of the theoretical division between male and female experience because a dualism is already built into the call for symmetry. Such an approach would presumably endeavour to produce a theoretical balance between the significance of work to women and of domestic responsibilities to men. However, this sort of methodological "symmetry" would not redress the fragmented nature of explanations of male and female transitions, or of employment and household processes. Patterns of difference, whether in gender inequality or between the claims of youth and adults, are aspects of a coherent social structure. A symmetry would follow not from balancing the fragments, but from locating differences in relation to the processes that generate them. A number of problems ensue from the treatment of gendered relationships and inequalities in the transition to adult status, although these issues are salient also to the broader debate on gender, work and inequality. The problems relate to the use of the category "gender" as an adequate description of forms of gender-related inequality, to the tendency to treat male and female biographies through employment and the family as having distinct bases, and to the limited engagement with the dramatic changes in female labour force participation in the post-war period.

Conventional understandings suggest that the gender division is itself a sufficient statement of the causes and dimensions of gender-related inequality. In consequence, diversity and change in the organization of gendered relations becomes difficult to explain. As Siltanen has argued, the category "gender" provides an inadequate statement of the processes giving rise to related forms of inequality in employment (Siltanen 1986). She develops this argument through an analysis of forms of segregation amongst Post Office employees. Analyses of occupational segregation by sex tend to see gender as the defining characteristic and principal of such segregation. Such studies, however, fail to account for empirical "exceptions", and the presence of a minority of women or men in jobs atypical for their sex are glossed over. In her case study, Siltanen differentiates job types on the basis of their rewards, as these relate to domestic obligations. She defines as a full-wage job one that enables its incumbent to take sole responsibility for maintaining an independent household, which may entail contributing to the maintenance of dependents. In contrast, a component-wage job allows its incumbent to contribute to household financing, but not to resource the household single-handedly. Siltanen illustrates the way in which financial need and relations to household income maintenance structure the distribution of people to full- and component-wage jobs. Her evidence suggests that inequalities in employment, and patterns of segregation, correspond much more closely with relations to household income maintenance by job incumbents than with gender *per se*. "Exceptions" to conventional explanations of gender inequality, where people are employed in "gender-atypical" jobs, are accounted for within a more coherent explanation of employment inequalities. Material and social obligations to dependents are essential to understanding patterns of inequality in employment, and provide a more inclusive explanation of such inequality than do undifferentiated understandings of "gender" (Siltanen 1986). Later I will examine evidence that suggests that a full-wage job may be more appropriately defined as a principal wage job, and that two wages are increasingly necessary to family formation and household income maintenance. Siltanen's analysis suggests the value of considering the relations of young women and men to household resourcing, in their parental households and also in household and family formation, rather than adopting a "symmetrical" approach where women and men are given equal space but treated separately. Historical change in the relative contributions of women and men to household income maintenance suggests the value of such an approach.

Within the youth literature, "parallel" models of work and family-related trajectories maintain the significance of each to the other, but they fall short of locating the experience of men and women in relation to this interaction. In part, the methodological frameworks, which generally focus on young and single adults, detract from developing this argument. Young single adults have received more attention than young couples, and questions about change in the joint organization of family formation amongst couples are rarely addressed. Further, there has been little engagement with the causes and consequences of the post-war changes in female labour force participation rates. As we will see, there are strong grounds for being suspicious of arguments that the consequences of increasing levels of female employment mean simply "more of the same" in terms of inequality in earnings and in patterns of household income maintenance. These changes are important to understanding the underwriting of youth as a period of semi-dependence within the parental household, as well as to understanding change in patterns of household and family formation amongst recent cohorts of young adults.

Recent developments in the transition literature, then, have been of value in stressing the complexity and diversity of life course trajectories, in exploring the relation between labour force and domestic careers, and in highlighting the potential consequences of economic change for a generation of youth who, by virtue of their particular life course stage are particularly vulnerable to unemployment, and whose entire life chances may thereby be affected. However, the approaches have been less successful in offering a full account of developments in the organization of youth and early adulthood as life course stages. Approaches have treated life course stages as given categories, at least in research methodology, even though this has been questioned in general discussions. However, the social relations that give rise to the historically specific configuration and meaning of such life course stages must be central to any analysis of change in the experience that such categories endeavour to capture.

Labour market theories and the experience of youth

Labour market segmentation theory has been developed by a number of authors in their descriptions of change in youth employment opportunities (Ashton et al. 1990; Lee et al. 1987). Part of the reason for this appears to lie with a theoretical inclination towards structural, employment-demand led, explanations of inequality. In a segmentationist framework, gender and age are recognized as important dimensions of inequality. Their significance is seen to stem from the organization of household circumstances and constraints. As explanations of employment inequality, however, they are invoked at the point at which people "enter the labour market". Position within the family is seen as a constraint on access to certain types of employment. Ironically, through a framework that appears at first sight to challenge individualist explanations of inequality, household circumstance becomes simply another attribute that individuals bring to the labour market. Further, segmentationist approaches to youth employment opportunities operate with a taken-for-granted definition of youth as a life course stage. This is highlighted by the essentially static character of a division between youth and adult labour markets that is a feature of youth labour market research. The interest in labour force trajectories is sustained only up to this division, beyond which youth graduates to "adult" forms of employment. However, if young people are still partially dependent on others for their livelihoods or without extensive financial commitments of their own and can thereby afford to take low paying jobs, a trajectory approach that stops when "youth" become "adult" neglects a particularly interesting dimension of change in the experience of youth and transitions to adult status.

The youth labour market literature has drawn on developments in labour market segmentation theory directed at explaining patterns of gender inequality in employment. Below, I describe these developments and consider some difficulties presented by recent empirical analyses in the area. Similar difficulties are reflected in youth labour market theories and are taken up in the subsequent discussion.

Dissatisfaction with orthodox economic models of socio-economic inequality has led several authors to develop arguments that the labour market is segmented or organized around barriers to labour mobility. Important to both approaches is the relationship between labour demand and supply. In orthodox, neoclassical analyses of the labour market, all commodities, including labour, are seen as homogeneous economic units whose prices are a function of their scarcity and their marginal productivity (Del Mercato 1981). With respect to labour, differences in price, or wage inequalities, are seen to stem from the characteristics of individual workers, who compete freely in the labour market. In this approach, earnings differences are seen to measure inequalities in the quality of labour, whose productivity is largely dependent on its acquisition of human capital (Rubery 1988). Most criticisms of orthodox theory focus on its assumptions of open competition between workers. Segmentation theory formalizes the importance of institutional barriers to labour mobility, that is of barriers to a market equilibrium where rewards to employment would be in line with a worker's market value.

Early, dualistic versions of segmentation theory focused on the demand side of the labour market distinguishing between primary and secondary labour markets (e.g. Doeringer & Piore 1971; Piore 1975). White, male, middle-class workers are associated with the internal labour markets and career ladders that characterize primary sector employment, and women, young people and older workers, ethnic minorities and the disadvantaged working class are associated with secondary sector jobs characterized by low pay, poor conditions and high turnover. This characterization of the employment circumstances of young workers implies that all primary sector workers have spent some time in the secondary sector, a life course aspect to employment careers that is rarely addressed by segmentation theorists. Dual labour market theory has been criticized for its crude characterization of labour market structure, its stress on labour demand over labour supply-side factors, and the interpretation of divisions between labour market segments in terms of a capitalist conspiracy to divide and rule the labour force (Rubery et al. 1984). The emphasis on demand-side processes has been criticized for understating the importance of reproductive processes, or the way in which the resourcing of daily life is organized (Del Mercato 1981; Humphries & Rubery 1984). Processes of reproduction, in particular the organization of the family, and of waged and unwaged labour, underlie a heterogeneous wage labour force. In this argument, the broad divisions of labour that characterized family organization since industrialization, and most markedly so during the inter-war period of the twentieth century, have been embodied in a system where employment rewards are patterned in relation to claims by men for a family wage (Pahl 1984; Land 1980; Barrett 1980; Brenner & Ramas 1984; Humphries & Rubery 1984). Much of the literature here focuses on the dualisms that are part of the Marxist-feminist debates on the relation between gendered forms of inequality and the dynamics of capital accumulation. Women's lower earnings are explained in relation to expectations of their, at least partial, dependency on male earnings. Thus, jobs may be low-paid, or classified as low-skilled, on the basis not of technical content or the product market characteristics of firms, but because they are performed by female labour or by unqualified labour (Rubery 1988). In other words the market model, barriers or not, is an inadequate statement of how women standardly come to have lower remuneration from employment than do most men. The model operates with a division between labour supply and labour demand, and segmentation theory considers that certain groups are allocated to particular labour market segments on the basis of their perceived attributes. However, if labour demand and rewards to employment are patterned in relation to the costs of labour then the treatment of supply and demand as autonomous structures must be called into question. Humphries & Rubery criticize divisions made by segmentation theorists between pre- and in-market segmentation, where social, pre-market inequalities and divisions are invoked but not adequately explained. They argue that:

if [labour supply] differences are in fact endogenously determined by, for example, different current opportunities for market work and differences in family organisation resulting from historical differences in income earnings opportunities, then labour supply cannot be taken as independent of demand side variables and an historical interactive analysis of the relationship between production and reproduction must be undertaken (Humphries & Rubery 1984: 334).

However, in an attempt to operationalize the argument in an empirical study of employers' policies and recruitment decisions, rather than, as might be expected, locating these strategies in relation to more general social processes, Rubery (1988: 274) allows that some continuity exists between employers' recruitment decisions and labour supply inequalities, yet maintains that women "have already been categorised in the social and economic sphere as relatively disadvantaged workers'. The division between pre-market segments and labour market processes is thereby reproduced in her analysis, where employer recruitment decisions are no longer located with respect to the interaction of social and economic processes but take on an explanatory force of their own. In consequence, it is difficult to sustain the argument that labour supply and demand structures are integral to one another, and the claim that labour supply inequalities and demand processes interact in a dynamic relationship becomes suspended in her analysis of current processes:

> . . . the structuring or segmentation of the labour supply has been recognised to be itself in part the outcome of policies of recruitment, pay and promotion adopted by firms; women are available at low wages and relatively high efficiency because of the exclusion of women from large areas of the employment system. Thus the breaking of the direct link between current labour market demand and current labour market supply still allows for recognition of interdependency in an historical or long period sense (Burchell & Rubery 1989: 4).

The central argument in the revised segmentation model, of the inseparability of productive and reproductive processes, becomes merely the historical context of empirical analysis. This need to "bracket off" the explanatory claims of the earlier theoretical statement stems from a model of employers as gatekeepers where recruitment decisions are seen as constitutive of employment inequalities. Originally, for Humphries & Rubery, an explanation of such inequalities required an analysis of coherent social relations, and of the organization of the reproduction of labour. By treating ensuing inequalities as already determined they become static, their continuity explained only in relation to employers' recruitment strategies. Here, and, as we will see, in youth labour market theory, the salience of reproductive processes, and the associated endeavour towards a unified understanding of employment inequalities, are pushed into the wings as writers focus on the particular features of labour market segments.

Like women, youths are often seen to hold a distinct set of labour market characteristics that give them restricted access to adult male employment opportunities. In the case of women, it is their particular relation to childbearing and childrearing that is seen as a constraint to equality of opportunity in employment. However, changes in these relations, for example the reorganization of female labour force participation over the life course, are neglected because gender itself becomes treated as a principle of employment inequality. Similarly, as we will see, youth is not considered in terms of the social relations that constitute its particular character. Rather, youth as an age group appears as the principal dimension around which labour demand is organized. Paradoxically, approaches that operate with a division between youth and adult, in order to explore change in the former, become caught in a static analytical framework. To move beyond this requires a reappraisal of the social organization of dependence and obligation, structures that are reflected in patterns of transition from youth to adult lifestyles.

Structural and cyclical change and the youth labour market

The reorganization of youth employment opportunities through the 1980s has been heavily contested (Raffe 1986, 1987; Ashton & Maguire 1986; Ashton et al. 1987, 1990). A central issue in the debate is whether demand for youth labour is contingent on general labour demand, or whether school-leavers enter a youth labour market distinct from the adult market. In the former case, labour demand processes are seen to increase the vulnerability to unemployment of young people relative to adults. Unemployment has a cyclical nature, and during economic recession the slowing of new recruitment and the operation of last-in first-out policies has a disproportionate effect on levels of youth unemployment. During economic upturn, in this argument, youths are recruited more rapidly than other groups. These processes are represented by a job queue model, where young people are understood to be subject to the same processes as adults, but differently located in their attractiveness to employers depending on macro-economic circumstances (Raffe 1987). The empirical evidence for this argument is derived mostly from analyses of the relative concentration of youth in declining industries, which suggest that those sectors that declined the most rapidly during the recession of the early 1980s did not hold a disproportionate share of young employees. Raffe illustrates his argument through an analysis of change in employment rates across industries. Using data from the Scottish School Leavers' Survey for 1979 and 1983, he argues that the decline in school-leaver employment was a consequence of a heavy reduction in the recruitment of school-leavers within industries, rather than a consequence of a disproportionate concentration of youth in contracting industries (Raffe 1984; see also Main & Raffe 1983). Raffe is critical, then, of arguments that insist that structural change in youth employment has occurred, resulting in a permanent decline in youth employment opportunities (Raffe 1986, 1987).

Ashton and his colleagues are critical of Raffe's analysis, and of his argument that economic upturn would see a rapid rise in the recruitment of school-leavers, mirroring the decline in youth employment during recession. The authors argue that recession contributed to structural changes in the youth labour market, having long run consequences for the nature of youth employment opportunities. Using a measurement of the relative concentration of 16 to 19 year-olds across industrial orders and occupational sectors the authors criticize job queue theories. Their analysis of Labour Force Survey data suggests that there was a continued decline in the relative proportion of youth employed in most industrial sectors through the recession and early economic recovery between 1979 and 1984. Across occupations the measure suggests a decline in youth employment in the higher level occupations and an increase in the lower level ones, particularly in clerical employment for young men, and in selling and catering and cleaning both for young men and young women. They suggest that the extensive use of youth training measures in these sectors was partly responsible for job growth there. Changes in the organization of production, in particular technological change and the rationalization of labour, were responsible for a loss of many skilled and semi-skilled manual jobs in the manufacturing sectors (Ashton et al. 1990).

The authors, then, are critical of models of cyclical change in employment demand and argue that youth employment opportunities changed irrevocably over the decade to the mid-1980s. Economic recession contributed to change and may have quickened its pace, but its consequences were not separable from those of a more general economic restructuring. In particular there has been a decline in "traditional" routes of entry into employment, not least through the collapse of manufacturing industry, with a severe decline of employment opportunities for minimum age school-leavers. Further, there have been shifts in the composition of labour market segments as employers have switched between different types of labour. In the service sector the growth of part-time jobs and preferences for older, married, female workers has in many cases meant the further displacement of youth jobs. The growth of youth unemployment and of YTS have meant a diverse set of responses by employers to these changed circumstances (Ashton et al. 1990).

It is not the intention here to try and resolve the disagreements over the causes of youth unemployment. It seems that the authors may not be so irreconcilably at odds with each other as they maintain. Raffe concedes that during the early 1980s the demand for young workers may have changed in non-cyclical ways as youth unemployment has increased in its duration, and may permanently affect the life chances of disadvantaged groups in the relevant cohorts; that macro-economic processes may have changed, and that government training and employment policies may have encouraged employers to structure recruitment more along age lines than hitherto (Raffe 1987). Further, both Raffe and Ashton and his colleagues, examine the period 1979 to 1984, which appears to be a rather narrow timespan for analytical confirmation or rejection of Raffe's argument that economic recovery will underwrite the reabsorption of youth into employment. Lastly, the argument by Raffe that recession underlay the massive rise in youth unemployment in the early 1980s is not necessarily incompatible with the argument by Ashton and his colleagues that recession was accompanied by industrial reorganization that altered the structure of demand for young workers.

Segmentation and transition

The argument of significant and permanent changes in youth employment opportunities raises questions concerning the relation between youth and adult employment and concerning the nature of employment trajectories. It is here, however, that a segmentationist perspective and the focus on a distinct youth labour market provides only a partial description. Ashton and his colleagues provide an interesting and detailed account of change in patterns of employment amongst young adults. This is set out in relation to particular occupational groups, or labour market segments, defined by the authors as covering professional, administrative and managerial occupations, clerical occupations, skilled manual occupations and semi- and un-skilled occupations. Each of these segments, the authors maintain, manifests a dual, gendered, opportunity structure. The labour market consequently comprises eight segments (Ashton et al. 1990).

Age is understood to be another central dimension along which the labour market is organized. The authors argue that the significance of age discrimination in shaping the labour market has been largely neglected. Much here turns on employers' recruitment policies. Employers are seen to differentiate types of labour, principally on the basis of qualifications, gender and age, and through their recruitment decisions, to allocate labour force groups into different market segments with very different prospects for career advancement. These segments are represented as clusters of occupations into which young people tend to get "locked" after entry, with mechanisms operating to restrict movement across segments. Segments are created in part by employers' recruitment strategies, by legal requirements (e.g. under-18s cannot work shift systems, under-17s cannot do driving jobs), and by union pressures, for example restrictions on age of entry into apprenticeships. The general structure of the youth labour market, then, is one in which more jobs become available as young people grow older, although sectors into which young adults (defined by the authors as between 18 and 24) can enter from outside are limited. By the age of 18, those who have not obtained a formal training are excluded from large parts of the labour market (Ashton & Maguire 1986; Ashton et al. 1990).

How, then, are particular labour force groups typed and defined as appropriate labour by employers? The authors are critical of neo-classical treatments of labour as an undifferentiated commodity and stress the significance of sex and age discrimination in structuring the labour force. One of the most important sources of such discrimination is the way in which employers perceive worker characteristics as these relate to the position a person occupies in the domestic division of labour and in the life course:

It is the ability of employers to enforce their definitions of worker characteristics that provides one of the most important mechanisms linking the position a person occupies in the family to their position in the labour market (Ashton et al. 1990: 76).

The authors acknowledge the influence on their own work of members of the Cambridge Labour Market Studies Group (Rubery et al. 1984; Wilkinson 1981; Rubery 1978). However these writers' critique of the theoretical division between pre-market "social" inequalities and in-market "economic" inequalities (e.g. Humphries

42

& Rubery 1984) is not developed.[2] Ashton and his colleagues stress change in the access of young people to different job opportunities but do not consider together the organization of rewards to youth and change in the meaning of youth as a life course stage. The influence by the Labour Market Studies Group, as acknowledged by Ashton and his colleagues, appears to relate to their shared emphasis on macro-economic change and the position of Britain in the global economy, and the significance of technological change for patterns of employment at a national level, but not to issues concerning the interdependence of labour supply and labour demand structures. Household and family circumstances are seen by Ashton and his colleagues as constraints to equal participation in the labour market. Position within the family, through institutional constraints and discriminatory recruitment practices, appears as another attribute that *individuals* bring to the labour market. The family as a social institution is treated ahistorically. Thus, the authors address changes in the relative demand by capital for different types of labour but they do not discuss the social construction of such labour force groups nor, importantly, changes in the relations between them.

However, changes in household structure and the division of labour amongst its members appear to be important to changing patterns of, and rewards to, employment. For example, the growth in part-time work amongst older women, which Ashton and his colleagues see as displacing youth jobs in the service sector, cannot be separated from the increasing availability and preference for paid employment by women through the post-war period. By treating gender unproblematically, as a description of employment inequality, any changes in gendered relations in employment are elided. Similarly, youth is treated as a "type" of labour, but its meaning as a life course stage is treated obliquely. The majority of those aged 18–24 have no dependents of their own and many are partly dependent on others for the day-to-day reproduction of their lifestyles. The age group itself covers a diverse set of social relations with respect to household circumstances. While relations of dependence and independence are implicit in the definition of youth, it is youth as an age group that counts in the segmentation theorists' definition of a distinct youth labour market.

Ashton and his colleagues define as "adult jobs" those from which young people (16–18) are excluded on the grounds of age, and youth jobs as those that have sheltered access for young people (e.g.

apprenticeships) or those where young and older workers compete. On this definition, their data reveal that of 18 year-olds, 94% held youth jobs and 6% held adult jobs; and of 24 year-olds, 53% held adult jobs. This distribution would appear to reflect the salience of life course trajectories to employment processes, and it would be interesting, here, to know in more detail the circumstances of those in "youth" and "adult" jobs, and the pattern of movement between such jobs as it relates to domestic circumstances. The authors do point to household relations as having some significance for occupational mobility. For example, they see family formation as having important implications for the behaviour of young adults, and note that across their sample of young adults, 24 year-olds were almost twice as likely as 18 year-olds to mention "more money" as their reason for making a job move. This example suggests that a pattern of job movement may be related to domestic circumstances, but this relationship, pointed to by the authors, is not taken up in their analysis. Rather, patterns of job movement are seen as more firmly dictated by the labour market and processes of age discrimination. While the authors point to forms of occupational segregation that distinguish youth and adult labour markets, they do not analyze the differing rewards that accrue to jobs across the "markets". However, a patterning of rewards in relation to life course stages suggests that the potential value of an analysis of the relation between labour force trajectories on the one hand and domestic life course trajectories and the organization of dependence and obligation on the other.

For Ashton and his colleagues, the distinctness of youth and adult labour markets is attested to by age-related segregation across employment sectors. They note the skewed nature of the industrial composition of youth employment. The authors treat age-related differences across employment sectors as evidence of a segmented labour market. However, an examination of the earnings associated with the industrial sectors suggests a pattern that is consonant with patterns of movement over the life course into higher paying jobs, with youth and young adults concentrated into a relatively narrow band of lower paying occupational sectors. While the association between earnings and age is commensurate with different explanations, its very existence calls into question the treatment of youth and adult labour markets as structurally distinct entities. The significance of changes in the economic position of young people described by Ashton and his colleagues, suggests a reorganization of the labour force trajectories on which young people embark. They argue that household circumstances relate to position within the labour market through employers' appraisals of potential workers on the basis of their perceived attributes. This "gatekeeping" function shapes access to different occupations and different career routes. However, the interest in the salience of domestic circumstances to employment inequality might go beyond questions of access, which leave intact a notion of the reward structure dictated by economic and technological exigencies, to a consideration of the relation between the domestic division of labour and the patterning of rewards to employment (cf. Garnsey 1982). Rewards for employment are not independent of the social relations of labour. If young people standardly earn less than adult labour, yet are simultaneously partly dependent on the latter, as parents, for resourcing their lifestyles, then changes in patterns of demand for, and rewards to, youth labour raise questions about change in its relationship to adult labour. One might expect, too, that any changes in this relationship would necessarily be reflected in the organization of trajectories from youth to adulthood.

The difficulties that arise from treating "youth" and "adult" as subject to distinct labour market forces is repeated in descriptions of YTS as a distinct or "surrogate" labour market (Lee et al. 1987). The ways in which YTS was absorbed into employment processes, yet replaced a wage with a low, fixed, allowance, suggests that it has been important to changes in the relative position of young and older workers. The characterization of YTS as a distinct labour market appears to be bound up with the particular institutional features of YTS, yet the approach neglects the ways in which YTS became a part of more general processes that undermined the expectation of secure employment and a wage amongst early school-leavers. The significance of such developments to youth as a life course stage is marginal to such descriptions which, like analyses of youth labour markets discussed above, accept "youth" as a prior category. Paradoxically, perhaps, such approaches may understate the significance of the changes in the experience of youth that have occurred over recent decades.

Lee and his colleagues suggest that YTS and other government measures, through lowering the wages of young people, further lower their expectations as to what they can earn (Lee et al. 1987; see also Ashton et al. 1990). However, in this it would be useful to look at the long-term relationship between the earnings of youth and of older workers. Such an analysis is undertaken in Chapter 4. To anticipate the argument that will be elaborated there, national level earnings data demonstrate a decline in the earnings of young men relative to peak adult male earnings since the early 1970s. The rate of decline was faster for men in their twenties than for male teenagers, although post-war improvements in teenage earnings up until the early 1970s had levelled out well before the introduction of YTS and the recession of the early 1980s. It could therefore be argued that the context in which the government insisted that young people were "pricing themselves out of the market" was one in which claims by youth to adult wages were already being undermined by general processes. Whilst clearly YTS had far-reaching implications the evidence suggests that it was absorbed into general employment processes and became integral to a general restructuring of age-related claims to employment and earnings commensurate with independent living.

In Appendix 1 describe the relation of YTS and employment structures in the three occupational sectors in which the empirical work for this study was based. The evidence there suggests that the take-up of YTS by employers was contingent on existing recruitment strategies and employment structures. To treat YTS as a surrogate labour market seems warranted only to the extent that it was not directly attached to employment. However, the hierarchy of schemes of which Lee and his colleagues speak suggests that YTS, through "reflecting" general processes, contributed to a general restructuring of the demand for, and rewards to, youth labour. Theories of the youth labour market have not addressed problems intrinsic to more general statements on segmented labour forces, and have reproduced these problems in a new guise. The tendency of the general segmentation literature to treat disadvantage as a homogeneous attribute of women is not paralleled in the youth debate, where youth is understood as a temporary status covering a spectrum of inequality. However, "youth" is separated from the adult or "real" labour market as it is described by Lee and his colleagues (Lee et al. 1987). In consequence we appear to need different frameworks for analyzing the experience of youth and adulthood. Youth is equated with an age group yet, paradoxically, the life course circumstances that make such a description meaningful are marginalized.

Earlier I argued that problems that characterize general labour market segmentation theories have been reproduced in descriptions of a youth labour market. One of the central problems identified by Humphries & Rubery was the way in which "cruder" versions of segmentation theory take "pre-market" labour supply-side divisions as given, rather than as integral aspects of employment processes (Humphries & Rubery 1984). However, the revised versions end by reproducing the same divisions, accepting as given prior "social", inequalities. Thus Burchell & Rubery (1989) accept that, on entering the labour market, women are already categorized as disadvantaged, that is, secondary, workers. Similarly, Ashton and his colleagues accept age as a pre-given dimension of labour market inequality. The latter authors use a segmentationist framework as a way of exploring the differential consequences of economic change across age groups. However, the framework of distinct youth and adult labour markets leads to a position where changes in the former are assessed in isolation from the latter. In part this is a consequence of the stress in the associated literature on the causes of youth unemployment. The significance of change in the relative circumstances of, and opportunities for, youth, indicated by the writers, would seem to suggest the possibility of change in the structure of relative poverty and wealth, across the life course, and between age cohorts. In order to develop a general statement of change in youth and transition as life course stages it is necessary to further consider the organization of relations between life course stages.

Summary: transition and social reproduction

Youth research, focusing on the consequences of economic change for the labour force and domestic careers of young adults, has been shaped by a concern with individual, cohort and class trajectories. The integrated nature of the statuses of dependence and independence that youth is supposed to bridge is largely neglected, or ruled out by notions of transition between life course stages where different structural principles appear to operate. The dichotomy between youth and adult labour markets based in segmentation theory (e.g. Ashton et al. 1987) or between relative gender equality in youth that contrasts with its "wider context" of gender inequality in adulthood (Hutson & Jenkins 1989) are two examples of a more general paradigm that seeks to elucidate processes structuring life course continuity as individuals "traverse" different social statuses. It is the conceptual separation of individual trajectories from these statuses that is, in part, responsible for the difficulties that arise in locating youth and the transition to adult status in relation to general social arrangements.

This chapter has traced debates that are central to descriptions of youth and the transition to adult status and that follow two themes. The first addressed the issue of the social, domestic life course consequences of economic change, the second the consequences of economic restructuring, and the introduction of YTS, for youth employment opportunities. These research agendas share problematic assumptions over the nature of youth and the transition to adulthood as life course stages. Both have questioned "common-sense" definitions of youth as an age category, and emphasized the life course processes through which chronological age acquires social significance. In the transition literature adult status is defined in relation to the securing of economic independence and associated status transitions from dependence at the parental home to the "independence" of household headship, marriage, parenthood and so on. However, in tracing transitions in terms of life course trajectories, the literature has under-theorized the relation between dependence and independence, and has therefore faced difficulties in elucidating structural change in this life course period. There has been a tendency to leave intact a concept of "normal" transitions and not to question the social organization of occupations and rewards other than where there is a breakdown in standard expectations, that is, where there is unemployment. Economic change is treated as prior, and as neutral with respect to the life course, and family-related, processes. The historical evidence suggests that developments in household structure, and household divisions of labour are important to, and not separate from, changes in patterns of access to, and rewards from, employment, and change in the employment structure itself.

Within the labour market approach, segmentation theory has been quite widely adopted in studies of the consequences of economic restructuring for the life chances of recent cohorts of young people. Here age is seen as important in segmenting the labour market, and has been incorporated into analyses of the impact of economic restructuring on inter- as well as intra-cohort inequality. Within labour market theory, social divisions that separate out different labour supply groups are seen to affect the operation of the labour market. So, for example, women and young people are distinguishable from adult male workers, because social, in particular family-related, processes mean that such workers are located differently with respect to labour demand. Thus "pre-market" divisions in the population are "confirmed" by labour market processes. However, while the division of labour within the family is seen as important to understanding supply-side divisions, this is immediately transformed into a statement of generalized advantage and disadvantage of different labour supply categories, in particular women, men and young people. It is these categories that are then adopted as a description of inequality, and the more open, but potentially much more precise, notion of household circumstances and relations is lost. In consequence, the importance of changes in the structure of households, or in domestic divisions of labour, for understanding patterns of employment inequalities is elided.

In the following chapters an approach that moves beyond the division between "economic" employment processes and "social" domestic or life course related processes is developed. An historically rooted understanding of change in the transition to adult status would reflect the integrated processes through which the domestic division of labour, or family organization, and rewards to employment are linked. Change in the relative rewards to young adults cannot be separated from the social relations by which youth, and transitions to adult status, are resourced. Researchers have neglected to locate youth adequately in terms of these processes, beyond the question of "independent" access to employment. However, changes in family structure and in the family life course are of central importance in shaping contemporary patterns of departure from the parental home and of family formation. These changes are examined in the next chapter.

Chapter 3

Demographic change and rites of passage: locating "new" life course transitions

Introduction

Recent commentators have stressed the significance of the early 1980s to patterns of change in life course transitions, yet they have been vague in their descriptions of the historical specificity of this period. The emphasis on economic and government policy changes of the time has been accompanied by comparisons of recent transitions to adulthood with "normal transitions" seen to have characterized rites of passage to adulthood during the 1950s and 1960s, and seen to be a consequence of full employment (Wallace 1987a; Willis 1985). However, aggregate level changes in demographic event timing, in particular ages at household and family formation, show delays relative to previous cohorts beginning not in the 1980s but in the early to mid 1970s. The continuity into the 1990s of trends established two decades previously calls into question the value of seeing the recession, employment crisis and government policies of the early 1980s as a turning point in the patterning of life course transitions amongst young adults. Rather, the demographic evidence points to the problems that ensue from failing to properly differentiate hypotheses of delay in the attainment of adult lifestyles as a consequence of the changed circumstance of the early 1980s from the practice of delayed family formation that commenced a decade before. Further, the appeal to "normal transitions" of the 1950s and 1960s as an appropriate basis for comparison neglects the particular relation between full employment and life course processes during this post-war period.

Evidence surrounding the general patterns of delay in the timing of family formation since the early 1970s suggests that it is necessary to move beyond approximations of national economic prosperity or decline in order to understand the complexity of processes underlying changes in the life course.

Below I describe the research design, the structure of the survey sample as it relates to general social arrangements, and aspects of the data gathered through the questionnaire survey. I go on to outline the historical antecedents to post-war patterns of demographic change and describe in some detail subsequent changes in life course event timing. Patterns of historical change in the timing of household and family formation, and explanations of such changes, have been neglected by recent sociological research into transition, despite the importance accorded to life course event timing as a measure of change in the attainment of adult status. However, such evidence would help not only in placing recent patterns, but also in locating youth and transition, as life course stages, in relation to historical change in the social organization of reproduction. After describing some of the historical evidence on change in life course structure and family organization, data gathered in the surveys are analyzed in relation to aggregate level changes. Aspects of change, in the housing market, in employment security and in the importance of female careers, are discussed. These have all to varying degrees been identified as salient to contemporary patterns of transition from youth to adult status. Another set of issues, concerning resource availability and lifestyle aspirations, is frequently invoked in explanations of historical changes in the timing of family formation, as well as family size, but is rarely developed in detail. There is strong evidence to suggest that the salience of the relationship between resource availability and lifestyle aspirations for transitions to independence and family formation is currently bound up with the significance of change in women's labour force participation over recent decades. This relationship has been largely neglected, yet it appears to hold a central importance to the shape of contemporary life course transitions. Deserving of an extended treatment, it is taken up in detail in the next chapter.

The research design and general social processes

This section outlines the design of the survey, of young people and their parents, on which the book reports. A two-stage questionnaire survey was carried out in the spring and summer of 1988. The first stage of the survey was employer-based and comprised a series of interviews with 92 young people in varying occupations and in a range of domestic life course stages. The second stage was a linked survey of parents to 36 of the young respondents. These surveys will be referred to throughout as the Main Survey and the Parents' Survey. The survey was conducted in Scotland, principally in Edinburgh. The reader is referred to Appendix 1 for a discussion of the regional basis of the survey.

The Main Survey was principally employer-based, i.e. all respondents were in employment or on a training programme at the time of interview. It was conducted in the insurance, retailing and construction industries. Small-scale studies have provided valuable detailed descriptions of the experience and perceptions of youth (e.g. Coffield et al. 1986; Cockburn 1987; Wallace 1987a,b,c; Hutson & Jenkins 1987a,b; 1989). However, the focus on particular, often problematic, circumstances has contributed to the difficulties in locating hypotheses of delay in the attainment of adult status, as a consequence of economic recession and unemployment of the 1980s, in relation to more general and longer term patterns of change in life course structure. The survey was employer-based in order to furnish data on, and contribute to an analysis of, standard processes shaping the organization and experience of the transition to adulthood. The timing and, as we shall see, the organization of household and family formation has changed over recent decades across the population. It is the processes shaping these general changes with which I will be principally concerned.

Early in the design of the research project I was interested in the operation and consequences of YTS. However, it became apparent that this was a rather narrow approach, particularly as I became more interested in the general features of the transition from youth to adult status. Further, the operation of YTS, where it is employer-based, cannot easily be separated from more general employment processes. It was the relation between these general processes and the reorganization of life course transitions that became the central concern of the research. However, my initial concern with YTS is reflected in the choice of employment sectors in which the main survey was based. The insurance, retailing and construction sectors were chosen for the variety of youth training strategies and the differing articulation of YTS with their recruitment policies and employment structures. The inclusion of YTS-related factors did not limit the sample choice, but rather was consonant with a strategy of defining a sample that would cover a wide range of employment circumstances. The choice of sectors enabled the sample to cover manual and non-manual employees, different gender patterns of employment, and a range of socio-economic class backgrounds and employment and income prospects amongst respondents. The relationship between the use of YTS and the organization of recruitment and employment within the three sectors is described in Appendix 1.

Another important feature of the sample is its age structure. Much of the research into youth and transitions to adulthood has defined its subject in terms of a specific age group (e.g. Wallace 1987a; Hutson & Jenkins 1989; Banks et al. 1992; Ashton et al. 1990). Several authors maintain the inappropriateness of an arbitrary age limit to "youth", arguing that the "upper end" of youth transitions would be better defined in relation to household and family formation. However, even amongst its proponents this view is rarely matched by the design of data collection involving people aged over 25. The problem here is clear, since in 1988 the mean age at first marriage amongst men was 26.7, and the median age 25.6. The mean age at first marriage amongst women was 24.6, and the median age 23.6 (Population Trends 1989). Amongst married and unmarried women in 1989 mean ages at first childbirth were 26.9 and 24.4 respectively (Jones 1991). Samples that do not include respondents aged over 25 fail to do justice to the diversity of experience that is associated with older, as well as younger, ages at these family transitions. Further, the social meanings of age should properly be part of the analysis. An age-based definition of youth is inappropriate for exploring hypotheses of a prolonging of this life course stage. For this reason a strategy of the Main Survey was to furnish information on the experience, perceptions and attitudes of people in a range of life course stages. Respondents to the Main Survey were between 16 and 35. The sample, however, was defined with principal reference to life course related criteria.

The respondents left school between 1970 and 1988. In a larger survey it might be tempting to consider separately the experience of those leaving school at different periods in this timescale, taking into account the raising of the school-leaving age in 1972, the recession of that period, equal pay legislation, the recession and employment crisis of the early 1980s and the growth of YTS as a standard route into employment for many, especially disadvantaged, school-leavers. However, the consequences of such changes are not sensibly explored through disaggregating an already small data set. In analyses of the survey data the young adults are treated as if they form a single cohort. There are reasons why such a treatment may in any case be more appropriate than a division between the experience of young people before and after the recession of the early 1980s. The latter division might appear more valuable than is in fact the case because of the stress by youth researchers through the 1980s on this particular period. Data on aggregate level changes in event timing suggest that the early to mid 1970s marked the most significant turning point in patterns of leaving home and family formation that has occurred in the latter half of the twentieth century.

Interviews were conducted during work hours on the companies' premises. The main survey comprised 28 interviews in the insurance sector, 27 in the retailing sector and 32 in the construction sector. The insurance and retailing sample comprised similar numbers of female and male respondents. All respondents in the construction sector were male. The employers, and a Construction Industry Training Board representative, knew of no female apprentices or crafts workers in Lothian or Strathclyde. Interviews with young adults in the insurance and retailing sectors were conducted in Edinburgh, the sample drawn from two large, Edinburgh-based, insurance companies and two retailing organizations, one a national DIY chain and the other a supermarket retailer. Construction workers and trainees were drawn from two large companies, a College of Further Education and a Scottish District Council Direct Labour Organization, where interviewees were on the Community Programme, a government training programme for people aged 18–25 who had been unemployed for a year, or on a YTS Special Measures Programme established for those in particularly disadvantaged circumstances. Most respondents in the construction industry were apprenticed or qualified joiners and brickworkers, although some were in white-collar occupations.

Not all respondents were in employment at the time of interview. Access to a small group of respondents who were on YTS in building industry schemes was gained through a college of further education.

Also, in the building sector, some respondents were on a Scottish District Council Special Measures Youth Training Scheme, providing training for disadvantaged school-leavers, and some on the Community Programme. Other than these, all respondents were working in the private sector. The sample includes some, mostly those on the Community Programme, with a background of unemployment. In general, however, the most disadvantaged and those with continuous records of unemployment are excluded by the sample design. Another consequence of basing the survey in employing organizations is the particular gender structure of the sample. Women with young children were interviewed but their inclusion in an employer-based sample suggests that they may be in particular circumstances that require or enable them to work full-time, and that may differentiate them from their non-working peers (all of the five mothers in the Main Survey had divorced or separated from the father of their children). While all respondents were in employment or on a training programme at the time of interview, their backgrounds are diverse, some arriving at their current position through continuous employment and promotion through an internal career ladder, some with a background of unemployment, temporary jobs and training scheme placements and some women with children entering or returning to work after full-time childcare obligations.

Interviews lasted between 50 and 90 minutes, the typical interview lasting one hour. Interviews collected information on socio-economic circumstances, labour force histories and employment expectations; domestic or "demographic" histories and expectations, focusing in particular on the timing of life course events; and on attitudes towards "appropriate" forms of household resourcing and employment participation. The questionnaire design will be described in more detail shortly. At the end of each interview, I explained my interest in changes in people's experiences of youth and early adulthood, and that I hoped to speak with respondents' parents about their own experiences of this period of their lives. Respondents were asked for their parents' names, addresses and telephone numbers and, if willing, to tell their parents about the survey. A total of 63 contact names were given (14 from retailing, 24 from insurance and 25 from construction workers).[3]

Contact with parents was made by telephone where possible and interviews, with one of the parents, were arranged and carried out in their homes. A total of 20 parents (i.e. parents to 20 of the original respondents) were interviewed in this way. The schedule again followed a structured format but a number of open-ended questions were followed through in some detail. These interviews lasted from one to over three hours but were typically one and a half to two hours' duration. A number of parents lived outside Lothian. To supplement the face-to-face interviews the questionnaire schedule was revised and posted to 24 households, that is to all the remaining households who had not refused to participate over the telephone. Eleven completed schedules were returned. Adding questionnaires from pilots for the face-to-face interviews and postal survey gave a total of 36 completed parental questionnaires. The final sample of parents was inevitably self selected, the most obvious feature of which was a gender bias in the sample structure towards respondents' mothers. Access to parents was filtered through the permission of their children before approaches were made to parents themselves, and the sub-sample of parent–child pairs is liable to be biased towards households with more sympathetic relations between generations.

As well as providing a basis for inter-generational comparisons, in designing the survey I was exercised also by the question of how to explore class variation in the transition to adult status. This was in preference to exploring the experience of a particular (say, unemployed) group, without the resources for locating it adequately in relation to standard labour force careers and life course transition behaviour. Clearly, however, characterizing the class location of young people has particular problems, given that youths tend to be concentrated in fewer occupations than the (male) adult population, and given the potentially diverse labour force trajectories on which they have embarked. Research into the timing of family formation based on analyses of large data sets clearly demonstrates class-related differences, where working-class youths tend to leave their parental homes, marry and have children at younger ages than their middle-class counterparts (e.g. Dunnell 1979; Kiernan & Diamond 1983; Joshi 1985; Jones 1987; Oppenheimer 1982). Much of the variation is accounted for by socio-economic indicators: parents' (typically fathers') social class, own occupation, educational qualifications and so on, but most studies stress also the significance of orientations and class-related norms and expectations. Patterns of early event timing by working-class young adults is rational in relation to their lifetime labour force circumstances, which typically manifest a shallow, and often insecure, earnings profile. In contrast, later event timing by middle-class young adults is rational in relation to their standard career routes, which entail security, promotion and a rising earnings profile, at least to middle age. This clearly reflects standard male, rather than female, experience, as women, typically, are involved in childbearing at precisely those ages at which promotion decisions are important to male careers. It is male earnings profiles that are central to these explanations of class-related differences in life course event timing. To explain differences in event timing in relation to such earnings trajectories clearly requires a theory of orientations to the future, and all the studies just cited invoke concepts of class culture, norms and expectations as part of their explanation of class differences in life course event timing. However, attitudes are rarely available for empirical investigation in analyses of large data sets. Exploring attitudes and perceptions is more important in ethnographic studies of transition, and often detailed in research with a more qualitative leaning. In designing the survey an objective was to gather sufficient data to furnish some form of quantitative analysis, albeit within the methodological provisos already indicated. Within this format I wished to address perceptions and attitudes in some detail, and to do so in a way that would be amenable to quantitative analysis.[4]

I outline some of the questions designed to gather attitudinal data here, since they comprised a substantial element of the questionnaire schedule, and are important in subsequent analyses of the survey data. The questionnaire collected data on labour force and life course event histories. Where respondents were not yet married or parents they were asked if and when they expected to marry and have their first child, and to describe what they saw as important in deciding when to marry and have children. Those who had already married or become parents were asked parallel, retrospective, questions. These open-ended questions were designed to gather data on attitudes towards the timing of particular life course events. Given the varied ages and circumstances of respondents, the questions about cohabitation, marriage and parenthood clearly have differing salience, a problem that is taken into account in subsequent analyses of expectations.

To supplement these open-ended questions a series of other, structured, attitudinal questions were asked of respondents. The questions cover information on attitudes relating to life course event timing, to independence, and to the appropriate domestic division of labour in particular circumstances, and on perceptions of the strength of claims to employment and earnings by different social groups. Respondents were asked to self-complete a list of Likert-style attitudinal statements. However, a number of other forms of questions were used. Their inclusion has the advantage of providing a diverse array of attitudinal data, and also "livened up" the interviews, engaging respondents with a variety of questions and tasks. For example, a series of vignettes were read to respondents, outlining imaginary scenarios in which social actors are faced with some dilemma that needs resolving. Respondents were invited to advise on the best course of action. The vignettes covered questions concerning decisions about whether to marry without access to independent housing, decisions about childcare, employment and the division of labour in a marriage, and decisions around female earnings, careers and parenting. The use of vignettes was inspired by Finch's description of their possibilities (Finch 1987). One of the problems in their use that she identifies is the inability to know precisely the interpretation of the scenarios made by respondents and hence whether comparisons of responses are comparing like with like. However, this is a charge that presumably could be levelled at all "closed" attitudinal questions. The advantage of such questions is that they enable more straightforward groupings and comparisons of responses than do open-ended questions.

The questionnaire also invited respondents to rank the claims to employment of a series of individuals, described in terms of their household circumstances. Respondents were also asked about the structure of their employing organization through a series of questions asking for the typical attributes (sex, age, marital status) of employees across a series of job grades. Respondents were asked to say what the typical earnings carried by these grades were, and to say whether or not they felt that the pattern of earnings across job grades was fair. As well as revealing the significance of life course stage and domestic obligations in respondents' perceptions of appropriate actions in given circumstances, and in their perceptions of fairness, some of the questions revealed a pattern of attitudes that varied with respondents' own life course circumstances. Further, questions assessing the claims of young people relative to other groups reveal a broad consensus suggesting that such claims, while seen to be important, have less sympathy than the claims of groups seen to hold obligations to dependents. Domestic circumstances are clearly salient in respondents' perceptions of who should get (and do) what. It will be argued that these perceptions reflect the social arrangements through which relations to household resourcing are important to the structuring of social inequality.

Issues of transition to adulthood, then, are central in the questionnaire but the form of questioning is often structured, and indirect in its approach to perceptions of adulthood or adult status. Such questions, I believe, hold advantages over direct forms of questioning on this issue. For example, to ask respondents whether they feel, or perceive themselves to be, adult (e.g. Hutson & Jenkins 1989) is interesting, but interpreting responses is fraught with problems given that we do not know the basis on which responses are given. It seems likely that an important basis on which responses to such a question are made will be a desire by respondents to demonstrate to the interviewer that they possess the social competencies implied by adult status. To address the psychological and emotional aspects of the transition to adult status clearly has intrinsic interest and reflects on broader societal expectations and forms of support. The transition to adulthood entails more than a progression through a series of employment and family-related circumstances. Maturity reflects experience, and it is often a perception of maturity that is reflected in everyday distinctions between youth and adult status. However, in a study of change in the organization of transition, I have kept to a minimum questions addressing young respondents' perceptions of their own adult status, or parents' perceptions of their sons' and daughters' status.

In summary, the survey was designed to gather data on labour force circumstances and histories, domestic life course event histories and expectations, and on attitudes towards appropriate divisions of labour and claims on resources in relation to life course and gender related processes. While the sample is relatively small, it is possible to locate the primary data gathered there in relation to aggregate level evidence on employment and demographic processes. As indicated in Chapter 1, it is necessary to break with the conventionally made distinction between micro- and macro-level processes. In the youth and transition literature this is reflected in the separate treatment of life course processes and social structural change. Several writers have focused on the timing of life course events: departure from the parental home, cohabitation, marriage, and birth of the first child, as indices of the attainment of adult status. It is, however, meaningful to consider these life course events as more than simply proxies, or indices, of adulthood. Because they label transitions through forms of family dependence to forms of independence and obligation in the resourcing of households and dependents, they also reflect the social arrangements through which individuals and families reproduce their living conditions. It is not simply that change in the organization of transition is reflected in changes in these social arrangements, particular aspects of which have been identified by youth researchers. We might also consider that changes in the social organization of obligation and dependence will be reflected in the timing of transitions between life course stages. Such an approach acknowledges that changes in the structure of the life course are integral to change in the social organization of obligation and dependence. It meets the call to locate youth and the transition to adult status within "the structures and values of society" (Ashton & Lowe 1991) because it acknowledges that these life course processes are an integral aspect of those structures and values.

Demographic change and rites of passage

The making of the "modern" life course

Anderson, in his description of historical change in the individual and family life course, suggests that the 1960s and 1970s might be characterized as embodying "the modern life cycle" (Anderson 1985). However, the reversal in the 1970s of the long-term trend to younger ages at family formation gives some aspects of this characterization an already dated prospect. Anderson proposes that the historical tendency towards a clustering of the ages at life course events across the population is the principal feature in the emergence of the modern life course. For example, in the 1970s most people married within an eight year span, between ages 17 and 25. This compares with a spread of 20 years in the mid-nineteenth century and of 17 years in 1917 (Anderson 1985). Further, there has been a marked reduction in the span over which certain life course transitions occur over the life course of individuals. Accompanying the sharp decline in fertility from the mid-nineteenth century to the 1920s there was a clustering of childbearing in the early years of marriage and a continued decline in ages at marriage and childbearing until the 1960s. As we shall see, the age span over which childbearing occurs across the population

Table 3.1   Estimates of the average ages at different life course events.

Life course event	Year of birth					
	1850	1870	1890	1910	1930	1950
First marriage						
Men	27	27	28	27	27	24
Women	26	26	26	25	24	22
Birth of first child						
Men	29	29	30	29	28	26
Women	28	28	28	27	26	24
Birth of last child						
Men	37	36	35	32	30	28
Women	36	35	33	30	28	26
Spouse's death						
Men	56	60	62	64	66	63
Women	55	58	61	63	65	67
Own death as widow/er						
Men	75	77	79	80	81	82
Women	75	79	81	81	82	83

Source: Halsey 1986.

has subsequently widened. Through the eighteenth century until the mid-nineteenth century the median age of women at the birth of their last child is estimated by Anderson to have been 39, by the 1930s to have been 32 and by the 1970s to have been 28 (Anderson 1985; see also Modell et al. 1976, for a similar analysis of changes in life course event timing in the United States). Some of the changes in average ages at different life course events are illustrated in Table 3.1.

The ages at parenthood shown in Table 3.1 hint at, but do not fully reflect the dramatic nature of changes in fertility rates from the end of the nineteenth century to the 1930s. A decline in family size occurred amongst the middle classes from the 1870s, a pattern explained in terms of parents' aspirations for their children, in particular for maintaining customary living standards and for enabling provision for their children's education (Banks 1954). Significant reductions in fertility rates became the general pattern through the first decades of the twentieth century as working-class families had fewer children. In 1860 approximately 20% of married couples had two children or fewer, compared to 67% by 1925 (Royal Commission on Population 1949, reported by Gittins 1982). Gittins, in her research into change in family size and structure between 1900 and 1939, explores declining fertility rates amongst the working classes and, in particular, the diversity of family size and birth control across couples in different regions and occupations. In general the improvement in infant mortality rates was significant in shaping decisions that reduced family size. The position of mothers and children was, Gittins argues, bound up with an increasingly elaborate "ideology of childhood" and with policies that reinforced the centrality of the male wage to household resourcing (Gittins 1982; cf. Lewis 1980; Davin 1978). It is difficult to assess the contributions of different family members to household resourcing across the population, but there is a substantial amount of oral history evidence that points to the importance of the contributions of teenage children to working-class families, a development that Gillis associates with the removal of younger children from wage labour and the reduced participation of women (Gillis 1981). The importance of the contributions of teenage children to household resourcing in working-class families continued beyond the time of Rowntree's survey at the turn of the century through the inter-war years (Jamieson 1987).[5]

At a rate of 10%, fewer married women were active in the labour force during the period 1900 to 1939 than had been in the latter half of the nineteenth century (Hewitt 1959, reported by Lewis 1980). Pahl describes the inter-war period as "the high water mark of the privatized little domestic unit", a situation explained in part by the greater involvement of central government in family-related matters, including the introduction of the marriage bar, preventing women in some occupations working after marriage (Pahl 1984). In the context of a growing concern about the health of children and fears about population decline and national security, the child and maternal welfare movement and state policies reinforced a model of the family where "good mothering" was a full-time home-centred affair (Lewis 1980). It is important to stress the diverse experience of the period, and that many married women did work, particularly amongst the poorest households (Gittins 1982; Roberts 1986). However, the rise of the family wage system in the latter part of the nineteenth century, while not fully realized in practice, labels a general set of developments in the structure of employment and of household resourcing from the turn of the twentieth century into its early decades. It is interesting to consider how new notions about motherhood seem to have corresponded with improvements in earnings and living standards (for those in employment) and the level of adequacy of a single wage for resourcing households. Evidence suggests that the family wage was an ideal that was shared by the middle class and the skilled working class, where it was women's ability to remain out of wage labour, rather than their entry into it, which was seen as a sign of progress (cf. Lewis 1986; Roberts 1986).

It is worthy of note that high levels of abortion, estimated as terminating 16% to 20% of conceptions, were prevalent during the period (Inter-Departmental Committee on Abortion 1939, reported by Gittins 1982). Some commentators have pointed to the widespread availability of the Pill from the 1960s as a cause of recent patterns of delay in family formation but the dramatic changes in fertility in other periods must call into doubt this sort of technology-led explanation.

The Second World War is often seen as a convenient marker of change in life course patterns, in part because of the subsequent development of the modern Welfare State but, perhaps just as significantly, because it separates the Great Depression years from post-war prosperity and growth. Linked with the latter was a set of changes in the structure of the household as an economic unit, yet these changes have been understated in accounts of contemporary patterns of transition from youth to adulthood. This neglect has contributed to the incompleteness of accounts of the relationship between resource availability and orientations in shaping patterns of transition to adulthood. Anderson has suggested that prior to the Second World War the contours of the life course were shaped in relation to demographic and economic uncertainty. From the war to the 1970s, he argues, improved health and longevity, full employment and the Welfare State were essential in shaping the modern life course (Anderson 1985).

The historical tendency to an increasingly "normal" pattern in the timing of life course events as well as in, for example, family size, identified by Anderson, has been equated with a rise in individualism and in the salience of social norms in determining patterns of leaving home, household and family formation by a number of, mostly American, commentators. Social and economic security, concomitants of post-war prosperity, full employment and a state welfare system are seen in these arguments to have enabled a greater degree of choice than previously possible in the timing of early life course transitions. In part, too, this choice is seen as a consequence of changes in family structure, freeing youth from obligations to their parental family. The context in Britain in the early decades of this century, was one where young adult children were likely to have many more obligations to their parental household, both financial and caring, than is typical of the post-war period. Many had several siblings, and still high levels of mortality amongst the working class often disrupted households, and entailed the loss of the main bread-winner's earnings (Jamieson 1986). Hareven, writing in an American context in the early 1980s, argues that contemporary life course transitions are more strictly age-related and more strictly governed by age norms than they were historically. In the late nineteenth century familial obligations and duties prevailed over age norms, and the most important aspects of the timing of transitions were not age, but how such transitions were related to the position of other family members (Hareven 1981). Hareven argues that age norms have become more important, particularly since the Welfare State took over the underwriting of various economic risks and obligations, whose previous domestic resolution was very influential in structuring the life course. In the nineteenth century event timing was critical to families' efforts to maintain control over their resources, and in balancing the contribution of different members of the family economy. Familial assistance was an exclusive source of security. The multiplicity of obligations over the life course, Hareven argues, was a more complex affair, to be worked out amongst family and kin, prior to the extension of state welfare provision. She maintains that the decline in such obligations has led to an increased individualism in early life course transitions, where the timing of departure from the parental home, and of family formation is structured now less in relation to the family course, and more in accordance with age norms. The suggestion of a significant, yet inadequately explored role granted to normative aspects of life course timing is taken up by other authors (e.g. Hogan 1981; Elder 1978; Modell et al. 1976). The latter authors argue that there has been a relaxation of constraints on the ability to marry, allowing its timing to be increasingly preferential. Paradoxically, a greater uniformity of action is identified and simultaneously explained in terms of an increased individualism. However, patterns of event timing beg the question as to how "choices" are structured in particular ways, and how supposedly increasingly evaluative decisions should be located.

British writers have been less inclined to stress choices although, as we have seen, some have been quick to define "new" forms of constraint in contrast to the "normal transitions" of the 1950s and 1960s.

The latter, then, appear to hold a sort of authenticity, to suggest a "natural" set of life course processes accompanying full employment. However, reasons underlying the changed patterns from the 1960s on have been described in rather ambiguous terms. Busfield & Paddon, in their study of post-war fertility patterns, concur with Anderson and the above authors that the economic security and relative affluence of the 1950s and 1960s meant that individuals were less worried about their future material circumstances than previous generations, and were therefore less likely to defer family formation. They argue that through the 1970s the housing market and general economic circumstances became less favourable to early family formation and contributed to the reversal of earlier trends (Busfield & Paddon 1977). Similarly, Leonard speculates that these changes were related to the recession of the 1970s, a period where real wages levels became static and were consequently out of line with expectations of rising living standards and increasing house prices (Leonard 1980). In contrast, and from the more recent vantage point of the mid 1980s, Kiernan suggests that the lower rates of marriage amongst younger age groups in the 1970s were a consequence of greater choice than experienced by previous cohorts as, for example, increasing proportions chose to stay at school beyond the minimum leaving age. It is the 1980s' pattern of continuing decline in marriage rates that Kiernan identifies as a consequence of economic constraint (Kiernan 1986). The relative and contingent nature of economic choice and constraint, and the difficulties of addressing their relation to changing life course transitions are well illustrated by the ways in which one or the other are invoked in explanations of the experience of the 1970s depending on whether it is being compared with the preceding or subsequent decade. This problem is taken up later. First, it is appropriate to look in some detail at patterns of change in domestic life course event timing over recent decades.

Patterns of family formation

The long-term trend to lower ages at family formation from the early part of the twentieth century, quite marked during the 1950s and 1960s, was reversed in the early 1970s with a significant decline in marriage and birth rates, especially amongst those under 25. These demographic patterns are aggregate level measures of change in domestic life course events, central to the recent youth research

Table 3.2 Percentages of males and females who had ever married by certain ages, by birth cohort, 1900–65.

| | Age | | | | | | | |
| | Males | | | | Females | | | |
Birth year	20	25	30	50	20	25	30	50
1900	2	40	73	93	7	49	72	85
1905	1	31	68	91	6	44	69	85
1910	2	32	70	91	7	47	74	88
1915	2	36	69	90	8	54	76	89
1920	2	42	76	92	13	62	83	92
1925	4	47	77	91	15	67	84	92
1930	3	51	81	92	19	74	89	95
1935	3	57	83	93	21	79	91	96
1940	6	60	83		27	81	91	
1945	7	63	84		29	81	92	
1950	9	60	81		29	78	88	
1955	10	52	73		32	75	87	
1960	6	41			22	61		
1965	3				12			

Source: after Haskey 1987.

agenda, yet they have received remarkably little attention amongst youth researchers. This section outlines the changes that have occurred over recent decades in ages at departure from the parental home, household and family formation.

Full details of age at marriage were not recorded before the beginning of the twentieth century. Estimates of the percentages of men and women married by certain ages are shown in Table 3.2. Deaths in the First World War resulted in an imbalanced sex ratio, reflected in the contrasting proportions of men and women, born in the early 1900s, who ever married. The twentieth-century low point in marriage rates occurred amongst the cohort born in 1905, and is explained by Haskey as a consequence of the Great Depression (Haskey 1987).

The average age at first marriage amongst men rose from 26 to 27 between the mid 1880s and the early 1900s. By the end of the First World War it rose by a further year to 28, fell to 27 by the Second World War, then to 25 by the mid 1960s and reached a minimum of 24.4 in 1970. Since then it rose to 26 by 1985. Ages of women at first marriage followed similar trends over the century with average ages two years below those cited for men (Haskey 1987). Increasing ages at marriage and falling marriage rates have continued throughout the 1980s. Of all women aged 15 to 44, 61% were married in 1980 compared with 54% in 1989. These changes were accompanied by a continued rise in average ages at first marriage that reached 24.8 years amongst women, a rise of 22 months over the period (Cooper 1991).[6] While first marriages have been postponed and the proportion of women who have never married has increased, so pre-marital cohabitation has risen substantially over the last 20 years. More than half of the women marrying in 1987 had lived with their husband before marrying, compared with 36% of those marrying in 1980 and 8% of those marrying in 1970 (Haskey & Kiernan 1989). However, declines in marriage rates amongst younger age groups are not a simple consequence of increasing rates of unmarried cohabitation but part of a more general pattern of delay in the attainment of independence and in the timing of family formation. The decade from 1971 to 1981 saw an increase in the proportion of time spent by young people aged 16 to 30 living with their parental family, or living alone, and a decline in the amount of time spent living as part of a couple or with a child of their own. Using data from the OPCS Longitudinal Survey, a 1% sample linking individuals enumerated in the 1971 and 1981 censuses, Penhale estimates that over the decade the average period spent living with one or both parents increased from 35% to 38.6% of time amongst women, and from 48.8% to 51.5% of time amongst men aged 16 to 30.[7] More strikingly, the average time spent by members of the age group in a household of their own making (as a couple, with or without children, or as a lone parent) decreased from 55.8% to 49.4% amongst women, and from 39.4% to 32.8% amongst men (Penhale 1990). During the period the median age at leaving the parental home increased by six months to 22.8 for men and 20.9 for women. (Penhale 1990; see also Wall & Penhale 1989).

As well as a pattern of delay in ages at marriage from the early 1970s onwards, there has been a decline in fertility rates amongst younger age groups and a rise in average ages at first childbirth. Table 3.3 shows the decline in fertility rates, from the late 1960s, amongst women over 20. The small decline in fertility rates between 1976 and 1981 shown in Table 3.3 reflects a recovery between 1977 and 1980 that has been followed by a steady fall in fertility rates amongst women in their early twenties and a growing divergence in age-specific rates with significant increases in births to women in their early thirties (Werner 1985; Jones 1992). Age-specific fertility

Table 3.3 Age-specific fertility rates.

| Age group | Birth year | | | | | |
	1961	1966	1971	1976	1981	1986
Under 20	37.3	47.7	50.6	32.2	28.1	30.1
20–24	172.6	176.0	152.9	109.3	105.3	92.7
25–29	176.9	174.0	153.2	118.7	129.1	78.1
30–34	103.1	97.3	77.1	57.2	68.6	78.1

Source: Population trends 1988, figures for England and Wales.

rates refer to aggregate fertility within age groups and reveal less about the specific timing of births or birth order. Evidence on the timing of first births shows significant changes in patterns of family formation with women born from the mid 1950s onwards delaying the timing of their first birth, at ages over 20, relative to previous cohorts (Thompson 1980).[8] Birth rates continued to decline through the 1980s with the steepest decline over the decade occurring amongst women aged 20 to 24 amongst whom rates fell by 19% (Jones 1992). The mean female age at first birth within marriage was 26.6 years in 1988, the highest figure recorded since 1946 (Dollamore 1989). Mean ages of women at first birth within marriage rose from 24.2 in 1965 to 25.5 in 1982, and from 1971 to 1981 the percentages living with a child at age 29 fell from 79% to 69% amongst women and from 63% to 52% amongst men (Penhale 1990).

The median interval between marriage and first birth increased from 19 months in 1970 to 31 months by 1978, and declined to 27 months by 1988. The increase through the 1970s occurred alongside an increase in average ages at marriage (Shaw 1989). While there have been dramatic increases in the percentage of births outside marriage over recent years, this rise does not appear to explain the older ages at parenthood within marriage. In 1964, 7.2% of all births occurred outside marriage, rising to 10.2% in 1978, 15.8% in 1983 and reaching over 25% by 1988 (Population Trends 1989). The increase to the late 1970s was therefore quite gradual compared to the rapid increases over the last decade and does not coincide with the patterns of deferral of parenthood within marriage. Further, the upward trend in mean ages at childbirth has occurred both within and outside marriage (Dollamore 1989).[9]

Over the period 1970 to 1983 birth rates to women aged under 25 fell across all social classes. First-birth rates to women with husbands in skilled non-manual occupations were higher than to women with husbands in other social classes. In 1970 the lowest first-birth rates occurred to women with husbands in Registrar General social classes I and II, but by 1983 women married to men in skilled manual occupations had the lowest birth rates. In part this was due to middle-class women being increasingly likely to start childbearing in their thirties. It is amongst this age group that the most significant differences in class-related fertility trends emerged over the period. Amongst women aged 30 and over in 1970 the distribution of fertility rates across Registrar General social classes was within 4% of the average rate for all classes, yet by 1983 women married to men in social classes I and II had a fertility rate 29% above the national average and women married to men in skilled manual occupations had a fertility rate 21% below the national average (Werner 1985; figures for England and Wales). Class-related changes in first-birth rates to all married women aged 15 to 44 are shown in Table 3.4.

Werner suggests the possibility that childless married couples with husbands in skilled manual occupations may be more strongly committed to uninterrupted labour force participation than middle-class women married to men whose rising earnings through their thirties make it easier to forego, at least temporarily, wives' earnings (Werner 1985). The restructuring, through the 1980s especially, of skilled manual work, with increasing casualization and less security for workers in some sectors, may have contributed to a greater reliance on female income amongst affected couples. Evidence from the National Child Development Survey (NCDS) suggests that, in the late

Table 3.4 Legitimate first-birth rates per 1000 married women by social class of father.

Year of birth	National average	Social class of father			
		I/II	IIIN	IIIM	IV/V
1970	44	38	50	43	47
1973	39	38	43	38	39
1977	34	35	36	31	36
1980	38	36	43	37	42
1983	35	34	40	33	37

Source: Werner 1985. The rates are based on estimated populations of married women aged 15 to 44 in each social class. Birth rates up to 1977 are based on the 1970 OPCS classification of occupations; subsequent rates are based on the 1980 classification of occupations.

1970s, the men most likely to become young fathers were in skilled manual occupations. Amongst men in such occupations at age 26, the probability that they had become fathers by 22 was 80% greater than amongst their contemporaries in non-manual occupations but also, surprisingly, 30% greater than amongst their contemporaries in semi- and un-skilled occupations (Kiernan & Diamond 1983). This is contradicted by other evidence that shows a straightforward correlation between social class and age at childbirth, with those in the most disadvantaged circumstances likely to have children at the youngest ages (Joshi 1985; Jones 1986; Werner 1985). The traditional expectation that the most disadvantaged will attain independence and families of their own at young ages has not been satisfactorily reconciled with hypotheses of delay in family formation as a consequence of "new" forms of disadvantage in the labour force. This issue is taken up in detail in Chapter 5. With respect to characterizations of general patterns of change in the latter part of the twentieth century, it is clear that, along with new class-related differences, there is a growing diversity in the timing of family formation across the population. The supposed tendency to an increasingly age-related, "normal" pattern of life course transitions appears to reflect a temporary pattern specific to the 1950s and 1960s. However, the suggestion that national economic retrenchment and unemployment caused the subsequent patterns of delay in household and family formation is too narrow a model, embodying a static and deterministic notion of the relationship between economic processes and life course structure.

Given the emphasis by youth researchers on the value of life course event timing as an index of change in transitions from youth to adult status, it might be supposed that aggregate level demographic changes, and change in the organization of family structure, would be central to analyses of the changing experience of young people, yet this is not the case. Part of the difficulty here stems from the lack of detailed work towards linking analyses of small-scale studies with analyses of macro-level trends in the timing of household and family formation. The particular findings of small-scale studies have not been located adequately with respect to general processes of change in life course event timing. My own survey is clearly modest in its ability to furnish a "quantitative" analysis, so it is essential to locate the information gathered in the survey in relation to more general evidence on patterns and processes of change in transitions to adult status.

Life course event timing and attitudes
across two generations

The main survey of young adults collected information on changes in domestic living arrangements and ages at which a series of life course events occurred. Expectations of marriage, parenthood and their timing were asked of those who were single and/or childless. Table 3.5 shows patterns of dependence at, and independence from, the parental home across different age groups over the sample. The majority of male respondents were living with their parents at ages up to 22. Half of those who were aged 22 and over had left home by age 25. Amongst women, half of those who were 19 and over were living independently of their parents, and around three quarters had left before their 25th birthday.[10] These broad patterns correspond with aggregate level data where median ages at leaving home are 23 for men and 21 for women (Penhale 1990). Data from the 1981 Labour Force Survey indicate that the main period of leaving home amongst young women is between the ages of 19 and 23 by when 80% of women have left home. Amongst men the main period of leaving is between the ages 20 and 25 although approximately 20% of young men aged 26 still live at their parental home (Kiernan 1986). Respondents to the NCDS were asked their reasons for leaving home. 39% of men and 52% of women left to marry or to live with a partner. The next most common reason for leaving was for an educational or training course, accounting for 21% of male and 18% of female departures, and the third most common reason was to take up, or look for, a job, accounting for 19% of men and 11% of women. Friction with parents was cited as a reason for leaving by 5% of men and by 6% of women (Kiernan 1986). There is some evidence that increasing numbers of young people are living independently of their parents prior to cohabiting, marrying or having children (Penhale 1990). However, the exact nature of these patterns is difficult to specify due to the lack of comprehensive evidence.

Table 3.6 shows the distribution of marital status, by age, across the sample. Amongst men it is at ages 25 and above that marriage or cohabitation is the majority experience, amongst women this is the case at ages over 22. Aggregate level data show significant changes in the timing of family formation occurring amongst cohorts born from the mid 1950s onwards. The decline in marriage rates at young ages through this period is shown in Table 3.2. There was a national

Table 3.5 Distribution of dependence at, and independence from, the parental home by age group and employment sector.*

	Age and household status									
	19 and under		19.1–22		22.1–25		25.1–28		over 28	
Sector	dep	ind	dep	ind	dep	ind	dep	ind	dep	ind
Men										
Construction	32	1	19	5	7	6	2	7	1	5
Insurance	14	0	8	5	5	2	1	3	0	1
Retailing	13	1	7	5	3	7	0	3	0	3
Total	59	2	34	15	15	15	3	13	1	9
Women										
Insurance	13	5	9	8	2	13	0	9	0	4
Retailing	11	2	6	7	4	6	2	1	1	1
Total	24	7	15	15	6	19	2	10	1	5

* *Source:* Main Survey; "dep" and "ind" refer to dependent and independent status amongst respondents.

Table 3.6 Distribution of single and cohabiting/married status, by age group and employment sector.*

	Age and marital status									
	19 and under		19.1–22		22.1–25		25.1–28		over 28	
Sector	s	c/m	s	c/m	s	c/m	s	c/m	s	c/m
Men										
Construction	31	2	20	4	8	5	3	6	1	5
Insurance	14	0	10	3	4	3	1	3	0	1
Retailing	14	0	10	2	5	5	0	3	0	3
Total	59	2	40	9	17	13	4	12	1	9
Women										
Insurance	15	3	12	5	3	12	1	8	0	4
Retailing	12	1	8	5	4	6	2	1	1	1
Total	27	4	20	10	7	18	3	9	1	5

* *Source:* Main Survey, "s" and "c/m" refer to single and cohabiting/married status amongst survey respondents.

decline from 52% to 41% of men getting married by age 25 over this period. At ages 22 to 25 43% (or 13/30) of men in my survey had married or were cohabiting. Amongst women there was a national decline from 75% to 61% in the numbers who had married by age 25, over this period. At ages 22 to 25, 72% (or 18/25) of women in my survey had married or were cohabiting.

The patterning of dependence and independence, and of single and married status, by age, are disaggregated by occupational sector in Tables 3.5 and 3.6. Amongst men employed in retailing there is a higher rate of leaving home at ages under 25 than in the other sectors, although age-specific marriage patterns do not show sectoral differences that are marked enough to warrant comment on rather small cell sizes. Amongst women, those in insurance are more likely to have attained independence by age 25, and to have married at ages between 22 and 25 than are women in the retailing sector. It is not immediately apparent why women in retailing should be slower to attain independence than women in insurance, nor why men in retailing should attain independence at younger ages than men in construction and insurance. Rather than speculating here over various interactions that may account for such patterns it is appropriate to suspend judgement over the extent to which respondents' employment sectors marks a homogeneity of experience in their labour force careers. The issue of how best to disaggregate the survey data with respect to labour force trajectories is addressed in Chapter 5.

The remainder of this chapter describes some of the responses made by members of both surveys to questions on the timing of marriage and parenthood, and considers their relation to changes over recent decades in those circumstances that respondents see as salient to decisions about the timing of family formation. The first set of responses illustrate some of the stated concerns of young women and men in their decisions about when they will marry and start families. Unmarried respondents were asked if, and when, they expected to marry, and childless respondents were asked if, and when, they expected to have their first child. The reader is referred to Appendix 2 for the context and detail of these questions within the questionnaire. The questions about the timing of family formation and reasons given were placed quite early in the questionnaire, so that open-ended responses would not be shaped in relation to prior questions, which might act as prompts to particular types of response. Asking respondents if they expect to marry and expect to have children may, of course, encourage a positive response even where individuals are ambivalent about whether or not they will marry or have children. Further, such questions will have a differing salience to respondents depending on their current circumstances and whether or not they anticipate a change in their household circumstances in the short- or the long-term future. These issues are addressed later in the book, when I will look in more detail at attitudes to family formation and their relation to social circumstances and orientations to the future.

Within the Parents' Survey, respondents were asked to think about the experience of their young adult children, in relation to leaving home, getting married and having children, and to compare it with their own experience. They were asked to consider a range of circumstances, relating to male and female job security and career prospects, independent accommodation, home ownership and savings, and to say if they felt that any of these had become more, or less, important since the time that they married, and since the time that they had children. They were invited to talk about their responses. Respondents in the Parents' Survey were then asked to continue thinking of their children, and their children's generation, and to say what they thought of as sensible ages for young men and women to leave home, marry and have their first child. I then asked them to say if they felt that things are different nowadays in deciding when to leave home, and in deciding when to marry and start a family, than they were when they themselves were young. The initial questions asked of the parents were structured, reflecting my own perceptions of the issues that would be seen as most salient. Part of the background to this was an optimism about the value of a quantitative form of analysis, an optimism that the final sample size did not warrant. The quotes from parents that are presented below are drawn from the responses to the open-ended questions. The sample, of course, is small and the responses can be no more than illustrative of the issues that are seen to be salient to decisions around family formation.

The responses given here, and later in the book, I have chosen to illustrate the sorts of circumstances and concerns that respondents held to be important for the timing of marriage and parenthood. I lay no claim to a systematic procedure for deciding which responses to include and which to exclude, but I have chosen responses in part to convey the variety in people's concerns. It is of course tempting to choose the more articulate, and lengthy, responses, a temptation that I have not wholly resisted at this juncture. However, a shrug and a "dunno", while a rare form of response, is significant since it may illustrate the irrelevance of the question to the respondent, a possibility that needs attention. Later, in considering the relation between decision-making issues and patterns of event timing I pay more detailed consideration to those who, because of the brevity of their response, are so easy to exclude from a report on attitudes. The following are examples of responses by young adults to the questions about the timing of marriage and family formation.[11] Issues of change

in the organization of transition are returned to through a consideration of the perceptions of parents, and continued in the next chapter.

One respondent, employed by the supermarket, was a 28 year-old
man, working as a baker. He had left school at just under 16 and
started a painting and decorating apprenticeship. He left after two
months and took up a bakery apprenticeship. He qualified as a time-
served baker at 20 and continued working in the bakery until he was
24. He then took a job as a baker at the supermarket where I interviewed him, because of better pay and prospects, and so that he
would not have to work the nightshifts which, he explained, his wife
did not like. When he left school he was living with his aunt and
uncle, since some years previously family problems had led to him
and his brothers being, as he put it, split between family. At 17 he
moved into private rented lodgings, because he did not get on with
his cousins. He stayed in similar accommodation until he bought a
flat with his fiancée at 23, and they married one month later. At the
time of interview she was employed as a clerk. When I asked him
why he married when he did, he replied:

> I thought it was the right time. I had enjoyed myself with my
> mates . . . time was getting on. We looked for a house January
> and February of the year we got married. We didn't plan the
> wedding until about the same time. I was not prepared to stay
> with family, as it's the worst way to start. So we got a house. We
> had decided it would be the summer [when we married] but
> we decided we would make it soon after we got the house.

They do not have any children, and the respondent explained that
he expected to start a family in about 18 months' time, when he
would be 30. When I asked "Why then?" he explained:

> We have discussed it quite a lot. We could have a family now
> but we want to buy a bigger house, rather than the flat, with a
> garden, so now we are looking for a new house. We hope to
> move by next January or February, and maybe be there a year
> before children. We try to plan ahead rather than throw our-
> selves in at the deep end.

Another respondent in the retailing sector, this time in the DIY
store, was a female, aged 27 and a supervisor in the home decorating

department. She was living with her parents, engaged and expecting to marry the next year. She had, she said, started work as a shop assistant after leaving school in 1976, when she was 15. She had worked as a checkout operator and general assistant since, until she was promoted to a supervisory position at age 22. She had been engaged from age 24. Her partner was a technician with an electronics company. She expected to marry at 29. When I asked her "Why then?" she replied:

> I would get married tomorrow but I don't have the money. We need to save. I want no hassles with bills. I want to do things now with money, I'm feeling that when we are married we will need to put money aside to pay for bills etc. I like life now how it is. I sometimes wish I had saved up, I'm starting to save up now. We want to buy a house.

She expected that she would have children, and to start when she was 30 or 31, after she and her husband had lived together, wanting "a couple of years to ourselves before children". When I asked her for more detail about the sorts of things she saw as important in deciding when to have children, she replied:

> I think I will be happier then to give up my time and devote it to kids. [My partner] is younger than myself, he's 24. About my own work, I hope [my partner] will have more money, we'll be thinking about whether we can afford to have children. When I have them I would like to bring them up myself, and maybe get a part-time job when they are school age. I wouldn't like to be not working at any time, I would hate to be out of a job when they are old enough.

The following respondent was on the Community Programme when I interviewed him. Aged 25, he had left school at 15 and subsequently worked in a number of labouring jobs, interspersed with spells of unemployment. He had been made redundant from his labouring job at a leatherworks at age 23, and after 18 months' unemployment joined the Community Programme. He left his parents' home at 23 and moved into a privately rented flat with his girlfriend. They moved into council rented accommodation when he was 25, and his girlfriend was pregnant with their first child at the time of interview. She was working as a laundry assistant at a hospital. He explained that he had moved in with his girlfriend in order to get away from his parents. He was, he said, about to get thrown out of his parents' house anyway. He said that he and his girlfriend had no plans to marry, feeling that there was no point. He explained that the current pregnancy was an accident. I asked him if he wanted more children in the future. He explained that he would, eventually, when he and his girlfriend were sorted out, that they wanted to leave the area in which they were living, and when he had a more secure future. When I asked later what he expected to be doing in five years' time he replied that he hadn't got a clue, and that he expected his girlfriend would not work again "until after the kids have grown".

The next two respondents both worked in the insurance sector. The first provides a good example of the complexity of many life course trajectories, and of the ways in which transitions are not necessarily "cumulative" but may entail moves back to prior living arrangements. This respondent was female, aged 29 and a junior supervisor in an insurance company. She left school at 17, planning to work before going to university. She started working as a senior clerk in the pensions department of a large insurance company. She left at 19, in order to travel, and spent time working as a waitress and chambermaid. At 20 she returned to Edinburgh, was unemployed for seven months, and then took a job as a bank teller for ten months. She then started work as a clerk at her present employer, where she achieved promotions to her present grade, by age 27. When she returned to Edinburgh she rented a flat, and then bought a flat at 22, where she lived with her boyfriend. They broke up 18 months later and she sold the flat and returned to stay with her mother (her father died when she was 20). She bought a flat again when she was 28 and a house at 29 where she lives with her current boyfriend and they own the property jointly. She expected to marry, but was not sure when. She anticipated it might be when she was around 35, when she thought they might start a family. She thought 35 would be a good age to have her first child because, she said, she did not want to be too old.

The final example here illustrates well the range of concerns that were raised by many respondents, in particular the combination of "personal" and material concerns standardly seen as relevant to decisions around household and family formation. The respondent was male, the supervisor of the new business policy section of an insurance company. He had left school at 17, and started working as a junior clerk with his current employer after being unemployed for two months. He had achieved promotion over the years and become a section supervisor at age 22. He bought a house at 21 and moved in with his girlfriend. She was a clerk, working in the same company. He was 22 at the time I interviewed him, and engaged to be married later that year, shortly after his 23rd birthday. When I asked him why he and his girlfriend moved in together when they did, he replied that: "We knew each other well enough, and qualified for a staff loan. I had been at home for long enough. Sharing with someone halves the cost." He explained that he planned to marry in the autumn. When I asked "Why then?" he said:

> We have been living together for two years. We decided we were compatible, and it's the normal thing to do, with living together. We got engaged in February, there's no need to save up as we have got a house sorted out. Normal folk have to save up and have a long engagement.

When I asked if he expected that they would have children at some stage, he replied:

> I was going to try and put my fiancée off the idea, me not liking children, [pause] not in the immediate future, I may have changed my attitude toward them. At the moment I see them as a tie. I would not want to be too old, at about 30 would be old enough.

When I asked him to say more about why he thought 30 would be the sort of age to start a family, he replied:

> There is certainly no way that we could afford it just now. So we would need a lot more than now. We would need to be earning in excess – our combined salary is £14,000 before tax – we would need to be earning in excess of that before even contemplating it. If we were comfortably off I might contemplate it. [My partner] would probably stay off work with kids. We would need to be financially secure before we even thought about it.

It may be that pressing the question of why people anticipate marrying or having children when they say they expect to do so, encourages responses that highlight material considerations, where these are not as central to patterns of family formation as theory would suggest. Wallace, for example, argues that while material considerations, particularly job security, are central to people's statements about the circumstances in which to marry and start a family, in practice people tend to "drift into" marriage and parenthood (Wallace 1987a). However, this still leaves the task of explaining patterns of change in the timing of family formation, a task that does not require people to state precisely their future actions or provide "the full story". Later I return to the question of change in the organization of transitions to adult status. As we have seen, recent research has focused on the experience of recent cohorts of youth and young adults who have "come of age" (or not) in the 1980s. Much emphasis has been placed on their particular experience but, without an adequate comparative or historical framework, it has proved difficult to locate understandings of the consequences of economic change for the organization and timing of transitions. While the perceptions and attitudes of contemporary cohorts of youth must be central to an understanding of their experience, the latter is not in itself sufficient as a framework for analyzing contemporary processes. A more adequate framework requires not only an historical "background" but also that contemporary experience itself be understood as part of an historical process. In the rest of this chapter I describe some of the perceptions, of parents, of continuity and change in the experience of youth and transition. The experience of recent cohorts of youth in transition are then considered in relation to more general evidence of change in the processes that are seen to be significant to the timing of household and family formation.

Parents to approximately one third of the young adults were surveyed, one parent in each household. They were born between 1920 and 1950, and apart from one who married in 1948, all married in the 1950s and 1960s. Aggregate level trends in ages at family formation broadly follow a U-shaped curve from the post-war period, with lowest ages occurring in the late 1960s. Since the parents' generation were young adults over a period of decreasing ages at family formation and the younger generation are growing up over a period of later ages at family formation we may be agnostic about what to expect of an inter-generational comparison of ages at marriage and parenthood across the sample. The clearest difference between generations lies in female ages at marriage. In the Parents' Survey, the 12 male respondents' ages at marriage ranged from 19–28, with a mean age of 24 and a median age of 26. Amongst the 24 female respondents, ages at marriage ranged from 17–26, with a mean age of 22 and a median age of 20.5. Amongst men, ages at first childbirth ranged from 19 to 32, with a median age of 26, and amongst women ages ranged between 18 and 31, with a median age of 23.5. Amongst men in the Main Survey approximately half who had married did so at a younger age than did their fathers, and half at older ages. Amongst the women there was a tendency to marry at ages older than their mothers. Of the 13 women who had married, three did so at younger ages, and ten did so at older ages than had their mothers.

The structure of the sample across youth and parent generations confounds a comprehensive analysis of generational differences in patterns of event timing within the survey data. However, a more informal but nonetheless interesting insight is possible through a consideration of parents' perceptions of change in the experience of youth over recent decades. The variation of event timing amongst respondents in the Main Survey is explored later. This and the subsequent chapter focus on general processes underlying change in patterns of transition to adult status over recent decades. Certain areas were identified by parents, as they have been by other commentators, in influencing the attainment of independence by young people. Housing costs and availability, job security, careers and, in particular, female careers and general lifestyle orientations were seen by parents as important to household and family formation. These latter areas have been poorly attended to in explanations of change in life course event timing, and will be taken up in further detail in the next chapters.

In drawing up the questionnaire an aim was to see if any patterning amongst perceptions and priorities would be apparent. There is a tendency for parents of children working in insurance to identify several aspects of change, in particular referring to heightened expectations amongst young people now, and a tendency for parents of children working in the retailing sector to be more ambivalent in identifying aspects of change, or suggest that things have not really changed. Divisions between groups of responses are not clear-cut however. The following quotes are drawn from the sample of 20 parents whom I interviewed in their own homes. The purpose is not to be representative of the sample, some respondents felt that little had changed in relation to these issues, but the responses cited are indicative of the most important aspects of change that were identified by parents.

One father was born in 1930, and had been a time-served sheet-metal worker and had held a variety of jobs as a labourer, bus conductor, and clerical worker prior to early retirement. His wife was unwell and had stopped working four years previously. He married at 21, and had no children by his first marriage. His first wife died aged 25, when he was 26, and he remarried when he was 29. He had four children with his second wife. The son whom I had interviewed was working on the Community Programme and living with his parents in a council house. Aged 19 he was engaged to be married to a secretary in the civil service. He expected to marry at 22 or 23. I asked his father if he thought that things are different for young people now in deciding when to leave home than they were when he was young. He replied:

> We never thought of leaving home. Life was so different, it is hard to put it into context. You were in a family unit, life was much slower . . . The way we were brought up, the first time I thought of leaving home was to get married.

I asked him then if he thought that things are different for young people nowadays in deciding when to get married and start a family than they were when he was young. He said:

> To get married nowadays you've got to give it an awful lot of thought. The attitudes of young people are entirely different. Women used to be trained for marriage, if you couldn't do certain things you weren't fit to be a wife. Now young men and women are much more similar. A girl in our time wasn't giving up very much. Now a girl's got to think . . . and neither are prepared to settle down. For ourselves, a marriage could survive through hard times. Now young people wouldn't accept it, there would be rows.

Another, female, respondent was interviewed while she was visiting her son. She lived abroad. She was born in 1941, left her parents to marry at 17 and moved into private rented accommodation with her husband. She had her first child a year later. At the time of interview she was a printer, her husband a chemist, and they had lived outside Britain since 1972. Her son was a trainee butcher, aged 23. He had lived overseas with his parents since he was seven, and he returned to Britain at age 21, staying with his godparents initially and then moving into private rented accommodation. At 22 he bought a flat with his partner whom he married when he was 23. He expects to become a father at age 26. I asked his mother to consider those circumstances, job security, housing, career prospects and so on which might be relevant to decisions about marriage and parenthood, (see question 65, Appendix 2b). I then asked if she thought that any of these have become any more important or less important since the time that she married. She replied: "Home ownership is more important now. Then you were just keen to rent a place, anything to have a roof over your head."

When I asked her in general terms: "Do you feel that things are different for young people nowadays in deciding when to get married and start a family than they were when you were young?" she replied:

> It's a lot better. They've got money to buy things now. I had secondhand stuff. The first washing machine I got was eight years ago. It's the same over the world. [Where I live] now kids have got to have things new . . . TVs, videos, fridges . . . its a good thing.

Another respondent was the mother of a 17 year-old boy whom I had interviewed. He was on a Special Measures YTS, painting and decorating. He was not currently engaged nor in a steady relationship. He lived alone with his mother in a council house. His father died seven years after marrying his mother and had been receiving hospital treatment out of the country, being away most of the time when his son was a baby. His mother went to work when he was one year old. She is currently an audio-typist in a solicitor's office. She was born in 1950, left home to marry age 20, and her son was born when she was 21. In response to the question on what issues had changed in their importance since the time that she married, she replied:

> The woman having good career prospects has become more important. I think a woman nowadays thinks about having a career . . . I think the other things are just as important as they were in our day.

I asked her then if she thought that any of the considerations had become more, or less, important since the time that she had children. She said: "The man having a secure job is important. There is no point in bringing kids into the world to suffer nowadays, though other people would think differently."

I then asked her: "Are there any other changes, do you think?" and she replied:

I don't know. I think they would think twice with the unemployment, I think so, I know I would think twice if I couldn't afford . . . if I was with someone who didn't have a secure job. I have done it myself with my husband's low income but I think it's unfair. I think maybe being able to own their own homes as well. I think it's more important for people to own their own house, maybe as it's an investment. Before it didn't matter so long as you had somewhere to live. Security over the years has become more important to people, they like to, or do, buy their own home. A lot of women have to work. I feel that's changed, they have to work and have a secure job for example if they are married, or if they are widowed. Money in the bank is more important now, we never used to think about it so much.

Another father whom I interviewed was semi-retired from a career in the police force, and was working half time as an office messenger. He had been born in 1930, had left home at 17 to complete his National Service, stayed in the Marines for seven years, married at 24, and was 26 at the birth of his first child. His wife was a seamstress in a dress shop at the time of interview. Their son was an actuarial clerk in an insurance company, aged 22 and living with his parents in their own home. He was engaged to another clerk, and expected to marry at 26 or 27. I asked his father to think about the relative importance of the issues listed, in decisions about marriage and parenthood. I asked him if he thought that any had become more or less important to decisions about marriage now, since the time when he got married. He answered:

Being able to afford home ownership is more important because of the present circumstances. Then there was no possibility of being able to buy a council house. Now tenants are able to purchase.

I asked him if any of the issues had become any more or less important to decisions about parenthood now, since the time that he had children. He said:

I don't see any as more or less important. I would say women having a secure job now has changed tremendously with the number of career women now. It's maybe that women want a bit more security behind themselves now because of, for example, the possibility of break up of marriage, there seem to be more break-ups now. There is more emphasis now on women having a secure job rather than an ordinary job . . . as so many women are into careers rather than marriages.

When I asked him in general terms whether he thought things are different for young people nowadays in deciding when to get married and start a family than when he was young, he replied:

Generally I would suppose they are just the same. On average people tend to marry about the same age as we did. It appears now that more are having to get married because of pre-marital pregnancy . . . In my younger days . . . employment, it's a big factor, it has to be taken into consideration now, security and prospects. Things are more expensive now, although salaries are comparable, though things seem to be very tight, as they were in my day. As you grow older you have more money to do things, but it must be the same nowadays. In later life, as you get on, the amount you need to be paying doesn't seem so difficult to be committed to than in the early days of marriage. As you get older you get more secure in life, with promotion etc. I remember my parents always struggled in one way or another, largely due to the size of the family. It was common then to have seven or more children, now there is a reduced family size. Things were difficult for parents then. It doesn't seem to be the case nowadays.

It is interesting to note the significance of relative wealth and poverty across the family life course emphasized by the above respondent, and his reference to the way in which this pattern has changed between his own household and that of his parents, an issue to which I shall return.

Another father I interviewed was born in 1941, was a labourer in a bakery at the time of interview, and married when he was 22. He and his wife stayed with his brother for two months, and then moved into private rented accommodation and into a council rented flat in 1968, where they currently live. He became a father at 24. His 16 year-old son was on a Special Measures training scheme. When I asked him what issues he felt had changed in their importance with regard to having children he replied:

> Then you never thought about it. Now I'd be inclined to think before . . . the young fellows at work want savings, a house of their own, a good job. They are all more important than when we were married . . . They expect more than we did. They expect they should be getting something better. In my day you had kids and got a rented flat. Nowadays they want to be established.

Across the parents' responses to the questions described the most commonly cited areas of change, all seen to have increased in their importance for transitions to independence and family formation, were female employment and female careers; housing costs, availability and expectations of home ownership; job security and unemployment, and higher expectations regarding living standards. Of the 20 parents interviewed face-to-face, 12 mentioned female careers, 9 mentioned unemployment and the increased significance of job security, 9 mentioned housing and 6 aspirations as significant to changes in the experience of youth. The stress by some respondents on changes in the costs of living and increased aspirations, sometimes identified together as sides of the same coin, were not prompted in the same way as those issues that had been identified by the preceding fixed-choice question.

Aspirations, or orientations to particular standards of living, are often drawn on in the literature in a general way in attempts to locate the inevitably relative quality of economic circumstance and resource availability as a cause of changes in the timing of household and family formation. Most work that draws on orientations in any formal way stresses their variability across social classes. There has been little analysis of lifestyle orientations and their relation to social practice. In part this is responsible for a paradox at the centre of the youth debate, where recent hypotheses of deferral in the attainment of adult lifestyles amongst young unemployed people have not been reconciled with understandings of patterns of early independence and parenthood as they are associated with disadvantage. The concentration of unemployment amongst groups who would generally attain independence and families of their own making at young ages complicates hypotheses of delay in ways that have not been adequately addressed. A recent study presents evidence that demonstrates that women who are unemployed at 17–19 are more likely, across all social classes, to become mothers at younger ages than their class peers (Penhale 1989). Evidence on the domestic careers of young men, and on the linked domestic careers of young couples is, as we have seen, not well established. There is, for example, contradictory evidence over whether or not young unemployed people are likely to remain dependent on their parents longer than their employed peers. Data from the 1981 Labour Force Survey indicate that unemployed men and women in their late teens and early twenties are more likely to be living with their parents than are their employed age peers (Kiernan 1986). Wallace presents evidence to suggest that young adults living at home are more likely to be unemployed than are those who have left (Wallace 1987a). In contrast, evidence from the Scottish Young People's Survey suggests that teenagers remaining at their parental home were more likely to be employed than teenagers who had left home (Furlong & Cooney 1990). Furlong suggests that this discrepancy with Wallace's data may be a consequence of the older sample interviewed by Wallace, where unemployed people who had attained independence from their parents had later returned, unable to support themselves on State Benefits (Furlong & Cooney 1990; see also Harris 1988).

Many of the interviewed parents as well as general commentators saw unemployment and the need for job security as holding a central significance in the experience of contemporary youth, although it is significant that, across respondents, the perceived significance of these issues, along with housing considerations, took second place to changes in women's labour force commitment. This may reflect the particular socio-economic composition of the sample, and the employed status of most young adult respondents. With regard to unemployment and insecurity, and their relationship to domestic life course transitions, it is important that theorists should address explicitly issues of citizenship and justice in the shaping of life chances. If a pattern of delayed transitions to independence is general over the population, as indicated by the demographic evidence, life course event timing is necessarily a poor indicator of changes in class-related disadvantage. Too great a stress on the timing of transitions to adult status as measured by particular life course events also risks neglecting the plight of young families bringing up children on State Benefits. It seems probable that unemployment has a variable relationship to the timing of family formation and parenthood, and that suggestions of uniform consequences with regard to the timing of life course transitions are misplaced. For example, prolonged dependency on parents amongst recent cohorts of youth may be as much an aspect of relative privilege as of disadvantage. There is no simple relationship between dependence and disadvantage or independence and advantage.

Housing availability, too, is central to the ability to attain independent lifestyles, and seen to be important to changes in patterns of transition. Busfield & Paddon, in their survey of two cohorts of couples who married in the 1950s and 1960s noted that, despite their younger ages at marriage, 29% of those marrying in the 1960s had a mortgage on their own home, compared to 10% of those marrying in the 1950s (Busfield & Paddon 1977). The authors suggest that difficulties in achieving home ownership in the 1970s, when fewer houses were being built and prices were rising, contributed to the trend to older ages at marriage during the period. From 1956 to 1984 the average house price to earnings ratio was 3.5. Over the period this peaked dramatically at 4.95 in 1973, declined to 3.34 in 1977 and rose to 3.82 before declining to the mid-1980s (Building Societies Association 1985a). By 1989 a disaggregation of rates of owner occupation by socio-economic group of the household head revealed that 89% of intermediate non-manual workers, 72% of skilled manual workers and 70% of junior non-manual workers were owner-occupiers, as were 53% of semi-skilled manual and personal service workers and 43% of unskilled manual workers (General Household Survey (GHS) 1989). While home ownership increased dramatically through the 1980s this was not the case for households with a head aged under 25, amongst whom 30% owned their own home throughout the decade. However, amongst 25 to 29 year-old household heads levels of ownership rose from 52% to 66%, slightly faster than overall rates which rose from 54% to 66% (GHS 1981, 1989).

In an international comparative study the Building Societies Association presents data that show British levels of owner occupation amongst young adults to be markedly different to those in other countries, with especially high levels of home ownership amongst householders aged under 30 (Building Societies Association 1985b). In this context it is interesting to note that the majority of respondents, over both generations interviewed, believed that young adults should delay getting married until they could live independently. The interview schedule presented respondents with a series of vignettes, which were described in the first chapter. One of the vignettes presented to respondents read: "Iain and Lynn intend to get married. They don't have a place of their own to move into yet though. What should they do?" The majority of respondents (67 out of the sample of 92 young respondents and 24 out of the sample of 36 parents) said the couple should delay getting married until they can get a place of their own. Thirteen young respondents and six parents said that the couple should marry and stay with parents until they can get their own place. While having a place of their own is not necessarily equivalent to owning it, the responses point to a general expectation of home ownership as the principal tenure of young couples. This pattern may be somewhat exaggerated amongst the sample, given the policy of insurance companies in which the survey was partly based to subsidize the mortgages of its employees. However, actual rates of home ownership amongst the sample are in line with evidence on general rates from the GHS. Table 3.7 shows first housing tenure at marriage and cohabitation amongst the respondents to the Main Survey and first housing tenure at marriage for respondents to the Parents' Survey. The prevalence of cohabitation prior to marriage amongst the parent sample was negligible. Amongst young adults the distribution of housing circumstances at cohabitation is similar to that recorded at marriage, with a slight increase in home ownership and a decline to a

Table 3.7 First housing tenure at marriage amongst respondents to the Parents' Survey and first housing tenure at cohabitation and marriage amongst respondents to the Main Survey.

Tenure	Parents	Young adults at cohabitation	marriage
Owner occupied	10	15	17
Council rented	1	4	4
Private rented	13	4	1
At parental home	4	5	2
With other relatives	4	0	0
Housing association	0	1	1
Other	3	0	0

very limited number living with parents or in private rented accommodation.

The table shows general rates across both samples, so only some of the parents are related to some of the young adults, and vice versa. Of the sub-sample of youth with parents who were interviewed and who were themselves married, four out of eight had owned their own home at marriage compared to the parents of only one out of eight of the young adults (not shown in the table). These changes are in general accord with aggregate level changes revealed in larger scale surveys that demonstrate the increased prevalence of home ownership amongst young couples. This change is reflected by several parents in their perceptions of the increased salience of home ownership for young people's decisions about family formation. Home ownership, and increased aspirations in general amongst contemporary cohorts of youth, were standard themes that were taken up by parents. While the sample of parents was to some extent self-selected and consequently may be biased to more advantaged households, the evidence suggests that the processes identified are general to a large proportion of the population.

The most common single aspect of change in transitions to independence identified by parents, more frequently than either the increased expectation of home ownership or the significance of unemployment and job security, was the greater salience of female labour force participation and female careers. Here the informants appear to part company with youth researchers. The latter, as we saw in Chapter 2, have stressed that continuities in patterns of gender inequality are more persistent than a first reading of recent "superficial" changes might suggest. In such arguments, any increases in gender equality amongst young single adults are understood to be subsequently lost at family formation, beyond which point the "traditional" division of labour is seen to persist. Interestingly, some of the parents who identified changes in female employment, and the importance of female job security and earnings, related these changes to rising expectations regarding living standards and home ownership amongst young adults and in the ability to afford children. General evidence demonstrates that changes in gendered patterns of employment and earnings are indeed bound up with change in household structure and life course processes. These processes should be placed centrally in understandings of change in patterns of transition from youth to adulthood.

Some of the processes operating here are caught well in the following quotes from two interview respondents, both middle-aged mothers of young adults, who were asked, in relation to leaving home, marriage and parenthood, how they felt things had changed since their own youth. One of the women was born in 1942, she was a clerk in a stockbrokers, and her son, a respondent in the Main Survey, was a sales assistant. She came from a family of two children, has three children herself, the youngest of whom was born when she was 25. She returned to work when the youngest child was three years old. She said:

> A woman needs to work a lot longer than we did to be able to afford a family. People don't have a family so quick as we did. We made do with a lot less. I think we were more content with less, they want a lot more now.

Another respondent, born in 1931, was head of a retail payroll department, and her interviewed daughter was a junior supervisor in an insurance company. The mother was an only child, and she herself had two children, the first at age 29. She returned to work when the youngest child was ten years old. She replied to the question on change in the circumstances of young people as follows:

> I really don't know, the cost of living now and the standards. I would think young people getting married today expect what to them are essentials, to us were luxuries. Quite a few start families later now, and then again they get so used to the good earnings the woman is making that they couldn't do without it. When we were married my earnings were extra as opposed to bread and butter.

The processes indicated are not uniform or universal ones, but nor are they particular to a narrow set of "career women". The responses identify changes in female contributions to household resourcing, changes that are seen to be inseparable from changes in orientations towards living standards or perceptions of living costs. What the respondents point to is a relationship that has not been satisfactorily addressed in research on life course transitions, specifically the relationship between resource availability and general consumption standards, and the significance of female labour force commitment. These relationships are explored in the next chapter.

Summary

This chapter has described aggregate level patterns of change in the organization of life course event timing over this century, and considered perceptions, of continuity and change in the experience of youth and transition, amongst respondents to my survey of parents of young adults. A detailed historical perspective is missing from recent literature on the transition from youth to adulthood. Despite its authors' central concern with life course event timing as an index of change in the organization of transition, the literature has focused almost exclusively on the experience of the 1980s. Some have compared this with "normal transitions" seen to obtain during full employment in the 1950s and 1960s. The evidence on historical change in life course event timing, however, demonstrates that these decades were characterized by patterns of transition that were no more "normal", and no less historically particular, than are recent developments. An understanding of such developments requires not simply an historical context to add sophistication to our interpretation of current experience, but the development of a framework capable of locating such experience as itself historically specific. This requires a more comprehensive understanding of the processes underlying change in the organization of transition. Youth theorists have defined economic change in rather particular terms, reflecting a concern with the consequences of unemployment for patterns of transition. The issue of an age-related deferral in the attainment of a "full" wage, capable of resourcing an independent household, has received less attention, paradoxically so, since it would seem essential to locating the life course related consequences of unemployment amongst youth. The theme of this chapter, of locating "new" life course transitions, is continued in Chapter 4, which explores historically recent patterns of deferral in marriage and parenthood as they relate to changes in age- and gender-related employment inequalities.

Chapter 4

Earnings, gender and reproduction

Introduction

Economic processes are central to most explanations of change in the timing and organization of marriage, and birth of the first child, and to change in fertility rates.[12] Youth research, however, has not adequately located its hypothesis of change in patterns of life course event timing in relation to economic change. To explain the significance of material resources to patterns of life course event timing necessarily requires an understanding of the ways in which life course stages are resourced, and an understanding of their relation to general orientations or aspirations to some standard of living. It is an argument of this chapter that an adequate account of change in the organization of the transition to adult status requires an understanding of change in the gender- and age-related patterning of rewards to employment. The neglect of such changes by youth theorists is surprising, given the significance accorded to material resources for underwriting "normal" transitions. However, this emphasis is typically reflected in a concern with labour force status and class-related inequalities. In their discussions of economic change, youth researchers have contrasted the life course consequences of unemployment and subemployment with transitions that are underwritten by "traditional" forms of employment security and continuity. The operation of the labour market is an object of analysis, then, only in relation to what is seen as the most problematic facet of market processes: that of exclusion. There has, in consequence, been little interest amongst youth theorists in the causes or consequences of age-related change in the structuring of rewards within employment. However, evidence of change here must speak of related changes in the relative position of youth as a life course stage.

Aggregate level earnings data demonstrate that the earnings of male youth increased relative to adult earnings through the post-war period up until the mid 1970s. Earnings appear to have increased quite rapidly in the early 1970s, following the lowering of the age of majority from 21 to 18 in 1969, and the subsequent reduction in ages at which adult rates were paid to young employees, and with the raising of the school-leaving age from 15 to 16 in September 1972. From the mid 1970s onwards there has been a pattern of decline in the earnings of young men relative to those of older men. This trend has been accompanied by an increase in the earnings of young women, relative to those of young men. These developments have not been addressed in youth research, yet they are potentially very significant, since they point to changes in the relative position of youth and early adulthood as life course stages. Indeed, the trends parallel changes in the timing of family formation, where there was a reversal of the post-war trend to lower ages at family formation from the early to mid 1970s onwards, as described in the last chapter. It has been argued that employment processes and life course relations are interrelated. This dynamic appears to be reflected in the historical coincidence of change in gender- and age-related earnings structures and patterns of deferral in the timing of family formation.

Evidence of change in the relative earnings of young women and men, relative to each other and relative to the earnings of older workers, are suggestive of changes in the organization of resources on which young people draw in attaining independence from their parental home, in setting up an independent household and in commencing a family. There has, however, been very limited research on the resources seen to be necessary to household and family formation or, importantly, on the organization of resource acquisition amongst young couples involved in household and family formation. The organization of parenthood, *as a joint enterprise*, has received limited attention amongst youth theorists. In part this is due to an age-related definition of survey samples, in studies of transition, which fall short of furnishing general evidence on patterns of family formation. In part, too, it would appear irrelevant if we were to accept conventional statements of continuity in the structure of gender inequalities. However, the separate treatment of female and male

transitions is theoretically problematic. Youth research has characterized the transition to adult status amongst women and men in terms
of a divergence in employment chances, a divergence organized in
relation to parenthood and differing, gendered, childcare obligations.
As we have seen, gender inequalities are described in terms of female
exclusion from male forms of advantage. However, if the latter are
predicated on men's particular relations to household income maintenance it would be more appropriate to consider the interrelatedness of female and male life course transitions. In this way we can see
them as different facets of a single process, rather than accept such
differences between male and female rites of passage to adulthood as
an adequate description of gendered patterns of transition.

Further, arguments of continuity in gender inequalities in employment and in household resourcing are at odds with empirical
evidence. It will be argued that the closing of gendered earnings
differentials amongst young adults is an integral aspect of changes in
earnings relations across age groups over recent decades. While there
is limited evidence available on changes in gendered contributions to
household income maintenance, there is some evidence that suggests
an increase in the importance of female contributions to the financing
of households. Such developments need to be understood in relation
to orientations towards living standards. As one of the parents
quoted towards the end of the last chapter said: "What to them are
essentials, to us were luxuries." In other words, achieving a level of
material sufficiency prior to family formation or parenthood may be
as much to do with meeting the costs of living as with furnishing a
particularly high living standard. Further, in these quotes, there was
a perception that the change in orientations towards living standards
amongst young couples cannot be separated from the increased
importance of the employment and earnings achievements of young
women. The aggregate earnings data explored in this chapter suggest
that these processes, largely neglected by youth researchers, have
a general significance to change in patterns of transition to adult
status.

Transition, gender and the labour force

In the last chapter, descriptions of historical changes in transition
couched in terms of greater choice and an increase in individualism

were questioned for their suggestion that values and attitudes have a greater salience now than in the past, and a different role to play in the explanation of life course event timing. This chapter continues to develop the argument begun in the last, that contemporary patterns of event timing are organized in relation to the social and economic resources that underwrite the attainment of independence and that structure its relationship to privilege and disadvantage. As Hareven argues, the development of the Welfare State and the post-war organization of resource transfers in the public domain have been very important to the structure of the individual and family life course (Hareven 1981; cf. Mayer & Schoepflin 1989). The structure of social security, housing costs and availability, inter-generational resource transfers, as well as labour force opportunities and rewards are all essential to an explanation of life course structure. However, welfare provision and changes in household demography have not increased choice in the sense argued by Hareven, but are rather part of a changing structure of which life course transitions are an inseparable part.

Arguments that posit an increase in choice amongst young adults in their decisions about family formation, on the grounds that they do not face the economic or familial constraints and obligations faced by earlier generations, impose an historically relative interpretation that may have little salience for current generations of youth. Young people do not measure their actions against those of their forebears, and few would appear to perceive a large degree of choice in the opportunities available to them. However, there are at least two ways in which the experience of prior generations has a direct bearing on the organization of transition amongst contemporary cohorts of young adults. First, family background may be significant to orientations towards living standards, although any such influence would need to be considered in conjunction with that of other, perhaps more salient, reference groups, such as age peers. Secondly, the experience of the parents of young adults is significant to their particular household circumstance, to the composition and resourcing of households. As indicated previously, the relative freedom amongst youth from financial obligations to their parental family cannot be separated from long-term changes in family structures nor from changes in the respective obligations of different household members to household resourcing.

It was noted earlier that the youth debate has not engaged with aggregate level patterns of demographic change nor with the literature that addresses these changes. Research from a different tradition, into aggregate level rates and timing of marriage and fertility, explains historically novel patterns in terms of gendered changes in employment relations, in particular stressing female employment and earnings opportunities. There, changing fertility patterns are seen to be a consequence of increases in female, relative to male, earnings. While theorists writing in the area take gendered earnings differences as a starting point rather than as an explanatory issue, it is notable that sexual inequality is central to explanations of change in the life course, in particular to changes to the incidence and timing of marriage and parenthood. While the approach, based in utility theory, has been subject to many pertinent criticisms, it is interesting since it locates centrally the interaction of demography and economy, and identifies gender relations as important to this process. Before examining the arguments of these approaches, I will consider some of the developments in gendered patterns of employment over the post-war period. These developments demonstrate the mutuality of reproductive and economic processes. The dynamic is important to contemporary household structures and to the resourcing of household social reproduction. The interaction of supply and demand is significant to youth, not solely in terms of late twentieth-century employment processes, but also through its being embedded in current household and family structures.

Patterns of demographic change and developments in family organization through the twentieth century were described earlier. Below I consider post-war developments in patterns of female labour force participation, and their relation to changes in household organization and resourcing. The increase in female employment participation since the war has occurred mostly amongst married women in their thirties and forties, and largely in part-time employment (Martin & Roberts 1984). The increased participation rate is accounted for by the greater spread of employment amongst married women, across the population and over the life course, as intervals out of work around childbearing have contracted (e.g. Main 1988). This latter trend has continued since the war, with it being rare now to quit the labour force prior to pregnancy, and with increasingly rapid returns to employment after childbearing. The proportion of women who did not work at all between their marriage and first birth fell from 37% of those with a first birth in the 1940s, to 12% of those with a first birth in the 1970s. A significant proportion of the latter were pregnant at the time of marriage (Martin & Roberts 1984). Declines in periods out of employment during the childbearing years are summarized by Martin & Roberts, who provide data on the cumulative percentages of women making an initial return to work after given periods. Of women having their first birth in 1950–54 the percentages returning to work within one, three and five years stood at 13%, 20% and 28% respectively. Of those having their first birth in 1975–9 the equivalent percentages stood at 25%, 37% and 58%. While 51% of women had returned to work within ten years of their first birth in 1950–54, by 1970–74 the proportion was 79% (Martin & Roberts 1984). A recent survey suggests that by 1988 28% of women were in work within nine months of giving birth and of those who had worked during their pregnancy, 45% were in work within nine months of giving birth. (McRae 1994).[13]

A United Nations survey shows an increase in employment participation rates, from 1971 to 1981, of 28% amongst women aged 25–9, and of 18% amongst women aged 30–34 (United Nations 1985). Although these rates seem high they are substantially lower than those of a number of other countries. The authors of the report explain the growth in terms of the increasing speed with which women return to work after childbearing. They argue that this did not change significantly in Britain over the period, where in 1979 67% of children aged three and four had mothers not engaged in paid employment, a decrease of 5% since 1973. This change is smaller than that identified in a number of countries that exhibit rapid growth in economic activity rates of mothers of very young children, specifically in Canada, United States, Sweden, Norway and Italy (United Nations 1985). Britain has increasing participation rates but they are relatively low where children are very young. It is likely that another important influence on change in younger women's participation rates is the decline in fertility and the postponement of childbearing. The drop in fertility, reductions in family size, and the increasingly compressed childbearing period must be extremely significant to high levels of participation amongst the age group.

A number of authors cite as highly significant the relationship between demographic and employment structures at an aggregate level. Economy influences the timing and level of fertility. This in turn influences potential labour supply structure. The population that is socially "available for work" is an important factor in recruitment strategies. For example, the availability of labour prepared to work part-time is important to the restructuring of particular sectors. Growth and change in employment opportunities in some service sectors have in large part been constructed around this option, retailing being the outstanding example, where part-time labour allows a flexibility and a cost-efficient employment strategy on the part of employers (e.g. National Institute of Economic and Social Research 1986; Hart 1988). Some employers have reassessed their reluctance to recruit youth labour on a part-time basis given the willingness of youth, in the context of high unemployment, to accept available employment on less than preferable terms (e.g. Ashton et al. 1990).

In the 1950s and 1960s, as ages at childbearing fell and periods between births decreased, and as returns to work by mothers were made increasingly quickly, so the standard middle family course phase was one where household resourcing became increasingly parent-centred. Economic growth meant that most youngsters could firmly expect to enter employment on leaving school. The growing affluence amongst youth underlay its new significance to commerce. The targeting of this section of the population as a significant consumer group reflected a circumstance where young people, with limited family obligations, could spend their income in the market rather than dedicate it to household finances. The general importance of parental earnings in supporting a reduced family size contributed to the enablement of youth as an extended period of semi-dependency. Change in household structures over the long term is important as an aspect of contemporary economic processes. Positioning with respect to household obligations is important to the structuring of relative rewards for different groups within the labour force, but also in terms of how, and under what circumstances, people organize the resources required for daily reproduction.

While over recent decades young people in general have fewer financial obligations to their parental families than did their parents and grandparents, these changes do not equate with an increase in individualism, or a greater salience of norms to the timing of life course transitions. The suggestion of greater choice, and of a change in the explanatory validity of norms, is problematic, and begs the question as to how such evaluative decisions should be located.[14] An argument that social norms are historically more important, like the emphasis by Hutson & Jenkins on payments of board money as an exercise in money management (Hutson & Jenkins 1989), suggests that family, or household, structure is less relevant now to an understanding of the life course than it once was. However, changes in household structures over the long term are an important aspect of contemporary economic processes and are inseparable from developments in labour demand, levels of female participation, changing expectations concerning women's employment and changes in the significance of female contributions to household income maintenance.

Pay structures and household reproduction

Economic models of fertility

Unlike the youth literature, economic models of fertility patterns take as axiomatic the interaction of economic structure and patterns of household and family formation. Two schools dominate explanations of change in fertility patterns: Easterlin's Relative Income Hypothesis and the New Home Economics (NHE) model of fertility. Both approaches identify significant changes in life course patterns and place economic relations centrally within their explanation of change. A problem for demographic forecasting has been measuring the extent to which dramatic falls in period fertility rates signal an overall drop in total fertility, or a deferral amongst younger age groups. The economic models are concerned primarily with aggregate patterns of fertility but also, as an aspect of this, with the timing of first and subsequent births. Within the models the significance of economic change to the timing of parenthood is formalized. They present an explanation of early life course transitions, formulated at an aggregate national level. Although they are concerned with similar issues these explanations have had a negligible impact within sociological discussions of transitions from youth to adulthood.

Easterlin explains change in fertility in terms of aspirations towards living standards, as these are determined by relative cohort size. The size of successive generations is seen to affect economic opportunities, with large cohorts depressing opportunities through increased competition for available work, and small cohorts, conversely, experiencing more favourable economic circumstances. Fertility is a function of relative economic status, or relative income: the ratio of young men's earnings relative to their aspirations. These aspirations are formed during adolescence in relation to fathers' income. Fertility is positively associated with economic status so the model predicts a cyclical variation in fertility rates. In the American example, the generation of childbearing age in the early post-war period were members of small cohorts born during the Depression years of the 1930s. Faced with limited competition as they entered work, they experienced high achievement and earnings relative to their older peers. Combined with relatively low aspirations formed during the Depression, economic achievement encouraged earlier marriage and high fertility. In contrast, cohorts born in the 1950s and 1960s grew up in a period of relative affluence and formed high aspirations, but met with relative economic disadvantage on entering the labour force. This cohort was therefore responsible for delays in marriage and a reduction in fertility rates (Easterlin 1968; also see Oppenheimer 1982).

In this model, incomes of young relative to older men is assumed to be a function of relative cohort size. This, of course, assumes a perfectly competitive labour market (or one where the aggregate consequences are the same), a finite level of employment and an aggregate structure of rewards that accords with aggregate fertility patterns. British evidence indicates a co-variation between relative cohort size and fertility rates, but not between relative income and fertility rates (Ermisch 1979). That is, the relationship between cohort size and relative income across generations does not accord with the Easterlin hypothesis. Easterlin has admitted that co-variation of fertility and age structure may be coincidental (Easterlin & Condran 1976, quoted in Ermisch 1979). This patterning is anyway country-specific, and the hypothesized relationship between cohort size and fertility fails to provide an adequate description of fertility patterns across several countries (Wright 1989).

Oppenheimer, in her analysis of patterns of marriage and fertility in the United States, is influenced by Easterlin, but develops a more detailed analysis of the importance of changes in female labour force participation (Oppenheimer 1982). One of her principle concerns is to explain class-related differences in the timing of marriage and parenthood, which she explores through an analysis of reference groups. Social classes with steep age earnings profiles form families at later ages in part because of an "economic squeeze", an imbalance between their lifestyle aspirations and their current resources. Oppenheimer analyzes data from the United States census for the period 1959–69, a period that saw a decline in the earnings of young, relative to older, men (in contrast to British developments). She suggests that, other things remaining equal, the period would have seen a postponement in the timing of marriage, but, critical of Easterlin, she argues that the increasing employment commitment of young women became a functional substitute for young men's earnings, and that female contributions to household resourcing became increasingly significant. She challenges Easterlin's model of a cyclical relation between economic circumstances and aspirations, arguing that the more extensive work commitment of women, and their financial contributions to the household economy, has been incorporated into family strategies in the timing of parenthood (Oppenheimer 1982).

The NHE school similarly stresses the importance of changes in female employment participation, and claims a more accurate description and explanation of changes in fertility patterns than that proposed by Easterlin (e.g. De Cooman et al. 1987; Ermisch 1988). Ermisch criticizes the significance granted by Easterlin to relative economic status, since empirical evidence suggests its failure to accord with recent declines in fertility (Ermisch 1983, 1988). The preferred model emphasizes changes in women's labour force participation rates, and in female relative to male earnings. Here the relationship between female and male positions and rewards in the labour market is the most important motor of change in fertility rates and timing. As with Easterlin, the relationship between economic and domestic spheres is central, but here it is articulated in terms of the gendered patterning of rewards. Based in utility theory, the NHE model assumes that the relative disparities between male and female earning opportunities underlie the household sexual division of labour. Marriage is seen as a partnership whose aim is to maximize the expected wellbeing of a couple, where the complementarity of their time is related to differential earnings opportunities. The gain from the domestic division of labour increases with the disparity in spouses' wages. Rises in women's wages relative to men's therefore reduce incentives to marry and similarly the desirability of children is inversely related to the ratio of female to male wages (Ermisch 1981). The probability that a woman of childbearing age will enter the labour force is a function of her husband's earnings and her own earnings capacity. For working wives, as their earnings increase, so do the opportunity costs of having children. The model predicts then, that for any level of male income, as relative female wages increase, women will have fewer children and space them more closely. The models also predict a delay in the timing of first births, with later marriage, and a longer childless period in the early years of marriage (Ermisch 1983, 1988). Increases in earnings capacities of women relative to men will increase female lifetime labour force attachment and this, along with high income ratios, will result in lower marriage and fertility rates, and a delay in marriage and parenthood relative to previous cohorts. The steep decline in fertility since the late 1960s, and older ages at parenthood are interpreted in Ermisch's argument as a consequence of increased female labour force commitment and increased female, relative to male, earnings.

Cast at an aggregate level, the NHE argument posits that increases in female employment opportunities and earnings levels are central to an explanation of declines in fertility rates and to deferral of marriage and parenthood. Other factors are acknowledged as important, for example, housing costs and housing availability, the subjective costs and ease of contraception, and lifestyle aspirations. The theory does not address women's career paths in any detail and nor does it attempt to explain why later family formation should be an optimum strategy in relation to employment sector specific career and earnings prospects. The argument does not predict a continuing decrease in fertility in the hypothetical event that aggregate earnings ratios were to continue their trend to increasing parity, but that fertility rates would follow an asymptotic approach to a minimum level (Ermisch 1979). There are a number of critiques of the characterization of individual level behaviour in these models (e.g. Blake 1968; Turchi 1975; Sanderson 1976; Wright 1989). Turchi criticizes the NHE models for their assumption of homogeneous tastes across the population, and asks whether reproduction is governed by differential social norms. It is not so much potential parents' objective situation with respect to income and expenditure but their subjective assessment of their current and future situation that is important to understanding reproductive behaviour. This issue is taken up in Chapter 5. Turchi also argues that the aggregate level data used for the models are often inappropriate for factors affecting individual or family decisions (Turchi 1975). The purpose here is not to dwell on all the standard objections but to consider the nature of causality as it is represented in the NHE explanation of change in fertility patterns.

Diversity and explanation

Models, of course, simplify complex processes, but their strength is dependent on the efficacy with which they correctly identify and reconstruct the most salient of these processes, and on their success in reproducing patterns to be explained. The latter of course is no guarantee of the former, in which case such models will mislead as to their explanatory and predictive potential. In simplifying change in gendered earnings patterns, the economic models use average earnings data. However, given the interrelatedness of life course stage and earnings this is problematic. For example as a youth cohort ages so its working female population will divide between those with continuous and those with discontinuous employment histories. Further, aggregate earnings data ignore those women who are temporarily out of the labour force. Gender earnings inequalities increase with age. This pattern reflects different earnings opportunities, and greater access to internal labour markets and career routes for young men. However it is also likely that the ratio of female to male earnings for those women with continuous employment histories falls at a slower rate than the aggregate average. As cohorts age this average will cover a great diversity of labour force experiences. With ample evidence that female returners experience downward mobility (e.g. Dex & Shaw 1986; Martin & Roberts 1984; Elias & Main 1982), their earnings average is expected to be lower than women of equivalent age with continuous work histories.

There has been limited research conducted into the patterning of earnings amongst continuous and discontinuous workers. Better earnings ratios amongst female continuous workers are a consequence not solely of their continuity but also of their positioning within employment. Discontinuity is more likely to be attached to employment disadvantage, and continuity to advantage. A study of earnings of continuous workers is likely to select out women involved in careers and with a better ratio to age-equivalent men. There is some empirical evidence in support of this argument. A comparative European study found that in most countries across Europe, and in most employment sectors, length of job tenure reduces the female to male earnings gap (United Nations 1985). The implications of this for aggregate earnings data are not entirely clear. On the one hand, earnings ratios decrease as age increases. This would suggest that the overall average might be reduced as more

Table 4.1 Female-to-male earnings ratios amongst partners, by sex of respondent to the Main Survey.

	20–23	N	Age 24–7	N	28+	N
Income (all)	£6700	10	£8200	9	£9000	7
*Men**						
Ratio (all)	0.99	5	0.79	6	0.71	4
Women						
Income (all)	£5000	8	£6400	9	£7800	6
Income (childless)	£5000	8	£6800	7	£8700	3
Ratio (all)	0.85	8	0.71	5	0.88	4

* Only male retail and insurance workers are included to enable sector-specific comparability with women.

women at older ages are included in a sample of the working population at any point in time. On the other hand, it seems possible that reduced fertility amongst younger age groups, and longer continuous periods in work prior to childbirth would inflate a cohort's female to male average earnings ratio, relative to that of earlier cohorts. The direction of causality implied by the NHE models is not as straightforward as it might at first appear. Inter-cohort improvements in earnings ratios between women and men may be a consequence as well as a cause of decreased fertility and later ages at parenthood.

Data from my own survey are limited with respect to these issues, but evidence is in accord with the argument that female continuous workers maintain a level of income more similar to their male peers than do discontinuous workers. Individual level data on female to male income ratios are obviously restricted to those members of the sample who had a partner. The survey did not collect detailed income history data of partners, so amongst the sample the following uses only the current ratio of partners' income. Dividing the sample into three age groups, each with a similar number of respondents, indicates a female to male ratio that declines over successive age groups; that is, women's earnings do not keep pace with male partner's earnings. This pattern in shown in Table 4.1.

The data amongst female respondents shows no patterning of earnings ratios over age groups. It may be that the high ratio of the oldest groups is related to long, unbroken careers. Seven out of the eight women aged 20 to 23, a group with very low earnings, are employed in the retailing sector. Their high income ratios suggest that, with their partners, they are in quite disadvantaged economic circumstances. A comparison between income for all women in this sample, and income for childless women, shows a higher level of earnings for the latter group. These women have an earnings average that is much closer to the male average amongst equivalent (insurance and retailing) sectors. While the numbers are very small the evidence corresponds with what we would expect: women with continuous employment experience have earnings profiles that are more similar to those of their male peers than do women with discontinuous employment profiles.

Ermisch rejects the validity of the Easterlin Hypothesis through an analysis of British data that indicates the earnings of young men, relative to older cohorts, continued to rise over a period of both increasing and decreasing fertility rates. Older cohorts' earnings are assumed to match fathers' earnings during sons' adolescence. "Sons'" real wages are shown to increase relative to "fathers'" throughout the period 1955–75, although they are quite constant between 1966 and 1973. The theoretical significance of "fathers'" income at a point fixed 15 years previously does not take into account current cost of living. It may be that it is considered to serve as a proxy for perceptions of age-related distributive justice, although this is not developed. Ermisch, in comparing fathers' and sons' earnings, constructs a series of cohort earnings relativities by taking average earnings for seven years before time t (to represent sons' earnings) and comparing this figure to the average over ten years before $t–5$. The resulting series shows increasing relative wages of young men from 1955 to 1975, a period of both increasing and decreasing fertility. Ermisch uses these results to reject the validity of a relative income hypothesis. However, these results reflect the earnings of youth relative to those of still quite young men. Ermisch graphs change in fertility rates amongst 20–24 year-old women, and these demonstrate the downturn in fertility in the mid 1960s. This he uses to argue a discrepancy between fertility and (male) relative earnings (Ermisch 1979). Yet other evidence on the *timing* of first births shows the most dramatic recent historical change to have occurred somewhat later, through the cohorts born in the mid 1950s on (Thompson 1980). This along with another measure of relative earnings suggests the value of reconsidering the relationship between youth and adult earnings in explaining patterns of parenthood.

It is suggested that the models of fertility described above are most interesting for their stress on the link between female and male earnings in relation to family formation, and their concern with gendered processes as important to the patterning of life course transitions. It is possible to develop this emphasis without adhering to the tenets of a model based in utility theory but to develop it in a way that addresses the nature of change in the domestic division of labour, rather than taking it as a given.

Diversity and change

Models from within the NHE school were criticized above for focusing on aggregate patterns of change without taking on their manifestation at the level of the household, and of earnings relationships between spouses. There is some research that has been conducted into this issue, and analyses made of the relationship between increases in female labour force participation and financial contributions within the household. Findings here indicate a high level of stability in female contributions to family finances. A more detailed disaggregation of available data suggests that arguments of stability flow from a still quite aggregate level of analysis, one that hides important processes underlying change.

Two recent research studies argue a relative stability in the level of wives' earnings contributions to their households. Rainwater and his colleagues (1986), in a comparative study of the United States, Britain and Sweden, argue there has been continuity of female contributions over their data period from the late 1950s to the late 1970s, with slight increases only in the Swedish case. Joshi, using British data, argues that there was an increase in wives' income contributions in the 1970s, and that its level stabilized thereafter. It is argued below that both studies reach their conclusions on the basis of too general an interpretation of their data, since a more detailed reading suggests that, contrary to their conclusions, significant changes are occurring both in gendered contributions to household resourcing, and in the age patterning of earnings.

Rainwater and his colleagues criticize the "two revolution" description of change in gender inequalities which posits that the revolution in female labour force participation is associated with an equity revolution where women, in consequence, become more equal partners with their husbands. They argue that the framework treats women as an homogeneous category, and fails to differentiate changes in participation rates amongst different categories of women. They prefer to distinguish aspects of female employment in terms of participation, attachment, continuity and contribution to family income. Their analyses are based on mothers' earnings, and they emphasize in particular the importance of separating labour force participation and contributions to family income (Rainwater et al. 1986). Thus, in the United States in 1959, 20% of mothers had earnings. This had increased to 42% by 1969, and to 64% by 1978. Over the same period, according to the authors, women's contribution remained quite constant at around 20% of the total household income package.

In the analysis by Rainwater and his colleagues there is no distinction between the different career stages of women. Given that the sample is based on mothers, it must cover a range of different ages of children, periods spent back in the labour force, presence in full- and part-time work, and of course, availability of employment and income opportunities. Because the analysis is conducted in cross-section it tells nothing about change in longitudinal earnings contributions to household resourcing. In a further analysis the authors examine mothers' earnings, differentiating by periods of unbroken labour force attachment (Rainwater et al. 1986). Here there is some association between level of continuity and contribution, but it is argued to be still quite limited. The authors note the furthest progression in patterns of continuity is in Sweden, where by 1978, 69% of women with pre-school children were labour force participants. Here they find that there has been a substantial rise in female contributions to family income. Yet, they argue, once continuity is controlled for, there is no trend towards a growing contribution in either the United States or Sweden. The process of change, it appears, is illusory. However, by standardizing for continuity the authors drop a fundamental aspect of gender inequality. What they suggest may be important to arguments that gendered earnings differences cannot be accounted for solely in terms of labour force discontinuity. However, it is surprising that this aspect of female experience and gender inequality should be "controlled" for so readily. Continuity is extremely important to income patterns, and to contribution profiles over the individual and family life course. Evidence of change in female employment continuity over the life course suggests that we might be especially interested in its relation to household resourcing.

Data on participation rates amongst American birth cohorts, presented by Rainwater and his colleagues (Rainwater et al. 1986) illustrate the dramatic changes over this century, with the cohort born in 1946–50 being the first to manifest a profile involving a higher cohort participation rate amongst the 25–9 year-olds than amongst 20–24 year-olds. This is almost certainly a consequence of declines in fertility and historically later ages at childbearing. However, the analysis of continuous participation extends only to 1979. If the most "revolutionary" change occurred in patterns of fertility amongst those born in the late 1940s and on, for these women to fall within the analysis of mothers' participation rates would require them to be young mothers. Included women would, therefore, be representative of a particular sub-sample, and not amongst the vanguard of "postponers". The authors' analyses of continuity, and its relationship to contribution, do not differentiate by cohorts, and do not contain data on those with the most historically novel fertility behaviour. Yet it is amongst such women that more significant changes in earnings contributions are likely to occur.

Joshi, using Department of Employment data, also notes evidence of continuities in levels of female contribution to household finances. While there was an increase in female-relative-to-male earnings ratios during the 1970s it was, Joshi maintains, a one-off occurrence. The ratio amongst manual sectors rose from 60% from the late 1960s to over 70% by 1977. This ratio has remained quite stable since that increase that Joshi associates with the Equal Pay Act (Joshi 1989). It is possible to reproduce this finding from an appraisal of New Earnings Survey (NES) data that demonstrate very similar aggregate patterns of stability from the late 1970s onwards, as shown in Table 4.2.

Disaggregating these earnings ratios by age suggests the above figures impose a uniformity that is at odds with the experience of different groups within the labour force.

Table 4.2 Gross hourly pay: female as a percentage of male earnings (medians).

Year	Occupation	
	Manual	Non-manual
1968	58	54
1976	72	63
1982	70	61
1988	70	62

Estimated from the NES.

Table 4.3 Gross hourly pay: female as a percentage of male earnings by age group (medians).

Year Age group	1968	1976	1982	1988
Under 18	100.0	100.8	97.4	105.2
18–20	81.3	90.5	90.4	92.9
21–24	72.8	84.6	85.4	89.0
25–29	70.2	81.8	84.7	89.3

Source: estimated from the NES.

The data shown in Table 4.3 illustrate the similarities in male and female earnings averages at the youngest ages, and their rising discrepancy over successive age groups as employment processes reward men more highly than women. Joshi's data indicate a stability in average earnings ratios from 1977 to 1988. However, the age-disaggregated data reveal that disparities between female and male earnings have continued to decline throughout the 1980s.

However, while female earnings appear to be improving relative to male ones, the data say nothing of the relative wealth or poverty of young people. They might hide a pattern where earnings relative to those of the general population have declined so that young people are worse off in relation to general consumption standards than they were say 20 years ago. This, indeed, appears to be the case. There are no consistent data series on age-related earnings patterns across all workers throughout the post-war period. It is, however, possible to reconstruct available data to show the trends in the earnings of youth relative to older workers. Wells undertook such a reconstruction in his analysis of data from the October Enquiry and the NES. The former is a survey into the earnings and hours of manual workers, carried out annually from 1948, and providing data on age related earnings until 1980, based on aggregate returns by employing establishments. The NES is based on a sample of employees, covers all occupations and industries, and provides a disaggregation of earnings by age group and gender.[15]

Wells analyzes the October Enquiry data (on manual workers) for the period between 1948 and 1979. The average earnings of males under 21 relative to those of adult men rose, gradually, from 41.6% in 1951 to 49.0% in 1972. The average earnings of females under 18 relative to those of adult men remained constant at 33–4% between 1952 and 1972, the earnings of both girls and boys, relative to adult male workers, having fallen slightly between 1948 and 1951. From 1972 the average earnings of young men and women relative to those of adult males rose rapidly until the mid 1970s. After this period they remained constant, at around 56.5% for young males under 21 and at around 40% for young females under 18 (Wells 1983). Wells explains the relatively sharp increase in the earnings of young men from the late 1960s to the mid 1970s, and the similarly sharp increase in the earnings of young women from 1972 to 1974 as attributable to a number of factors, specifically the lowering of the age of majority from 21 to 18 in 1969, the raising of the school-leaving age from 15 to 16 in September 1972, and as a consequence of income policies of the period. After the lowering of the age of majority, there was a rapid decrease in the ages at which adult rates were paid to employees. Department of Employment statistics cited by Wells show that in 1970, 72% of young workers did not receive adult rates until they were aged 21 or over, a figure that fell to 16% by 1975 (Wells 1983).

After the mid 1970s there was a decline in the earnings of young relative to older workers (Wells 1983; Black 1990). Both of these authors examine NES data up to 1982. In Table 4.4, I reproduce data from NES from the early 1970s up until 1990. Young adults' earnings are shown as a percentage of male peak earnings. The latter serves as an index of general consumption standards, or living costs, and is based on the median earnings of the highest earning age group across the population, that is of men aged 30–39 or 40–49, whichever is the higher. It might be considered as a measure of a "full adult wage", that is, a wage that can carry the major part of household resourcing (cf. Siltanen 1986). The table presents percentages derived from data on gross hourly earnings, but an analysis of gross weekly earnings shows a very similar trend, in the continued decline through the 1980s in the earnings of young men and young women, relative to male peak earnings. I have chosen to use the measure in preference to an aggregate average of those aged over 21. Indeed, the changes amongst age groups in their twenties is suggestive of a general "stretching" of age-related earnings, with an increasing differential between young male and older male workers, where the former includes those in their twenties. Amongst men in their twenties, the decline in earnings relative to the highest earning age group commenced prior to the decline amongst the youngest age groups. This trend is not apparent from Wells's comparison of youth and adult earnings, and suggests that the average of adult earnings over the period of his analysis disguises changes in the age distribution of male adult earnings.

The earnings of young women and men relative to the full adult wage index reveal a pattern of decline from the late 1970s onwards. As female-to-male earnings have narrowed so this has been accompanied by a decline in the earnings of young men, relative to full adult earnings, starting in the mid to late 1970s and becoming pronounced through the 1980s. It is apparent from Table 4.4 that the improving female-to-male earnings ratio cannot be separated from the decline in young men's earnings. The earnings of teenage women and men declined relative to adult peak earnings from 1976 to 1990. Over this period, there was a decline in the relative earnings of women aged 20–24, relative to peak adult earnings, but it was less marked than amongst age equivalent men. Amongst women aged 25–9 relative earnings held quite constant, even improving slightly between 1988 and 1990. The improving ratio of female-to-male earnings through the 1980s appears to be a consequence of differing, gendered, rates of decline. The change in gendered earnings patterns amongst young adults has as much to do with declines in young men's earnings relative to peak adult earnings as with improvements in the earnings of young women. Among the youngest age group the increase from 1970 to 1974 coincided with the raising of the school-leaving age, which is expected to raise average earnings amongst the sample.

From 1974 to 1982, men aged 30–39 were the highest earning age group. By 1988, gross hourly earnings, as well as gross weekly earnings, were achieved by the men aged between 40 and 49. Black notes the decline in the relative earnings of 20–24, and 25–9 year-old males from 1974 to 1975 onwards but, like Wells, in his discussion of changing age differentials he focuses on the experience of those aged 20 and under. He notes the widening of the (teenage) youth to adult pay differential since 1979 which, he suggests, may be due to increases in the relative pay of more highly-paid workers, who tend to be older, rather than due to a widening of age differentials *per se* (Black 1990). Given his acceptance that the age-earnings profile across the population is a reflection of increases in human capital attributes, in the form of skills and work experience, this argument seems disingenuous. That the highest paid workers "happen to be older" does not undermine the significance of age-related changes in the structure of earnings differentials.

112

Table 4.4 Young adults' earnings as a percentage of those of the highest earning age group (median, gross hourly, earnings).[16]

Age-group	Year										
	1968	1970	1974	1976	1978	1980	1982	1984	1986	1988	1990
Males											
Under 18	31	33	39	40	40	40	39	36	35	36	35
18–20	57	57	61	62	62	61	57	55	53	52	52
21–24	82	82	83	82	81	79	75	73	72	70	71
25–29	93	94	96	95	94	92	89	88	86	85	85
Females											
Under 18	31	32	37	41	40	40	38	35	38	38	39
18–20	46	47	51	55	55	54	52	50	49	48	50
21–24	60	61	63	69	68	66	64	63	62	63	64
25–29	65	66	69	77	77	77	76	76	76	76	78

Aggregate level evidence indicates that the earnings of male youth relative to those of adult men improved gradually through the post-war period up until 1972, and female youth earnings remained constant as a proportion of male youth earnings. From this year until 1975, there was a rapid rate of increase in the earnings of both male and female youth relative to those of adult male average earnings (Wells 1983). Full age-disaggregated data are not available for this period. From the mid 1970s onwards, and considering also young adults in their twenties, there was an improvement in the earnings of young women relative to young men, and a decline in the earnings of young men relative to the median earnings of the highest earning age group. The increasing discrepancy between young men's earnings and peak adult earnings from the mid 1970s on, and improvements in young women's earnings, coincide with patterns of deferral in family formation, relative to previous cohorts.

This pattern also corresponds with expectations concerning home ownership, and with escalating house prices through the 1980s, and corresponds with evidence of the current importance of joint contributions to house purchase, and with expectations concerning women's employment continuity prior to childbirth. The series of events that occurred in this period very probably coincided in their influence on patterns of birth timing, so their effects are difficult to isolate. The raising of the school-leaving age in 1972, the onset of world recession, equal opportunities and equal pay legislation are expected to have been important to the "deferral" of parenthood. The male and female earnings figures should not be seen in isolation from one another. Changes in female and male earnings relative to general consumption standards, and their association with changing patterns of family formation, suggest a growing salience of female earnings to patterns of family formation as well as to household income maintenance over the family life course. Improvements in the earnings position of young women relative to young men should not be seen straightforwardly as a positive reason for later ages at parenthood as suggested by the New Home Economists' assumptions of opportunity cost. Rather, patterns of deferral in family formation are inseparable from changes in the income of both young women and young men, relative to general consumptions standards.

Summary

Contrary to arguments of continuity in gendered earnings ratios since the mid 1970s, the empirical evidence shows that the gap between the earnings of young men and women has narrowed, and that this pattern has coincided with an increasing discrepancy between the earnings of young people, and those of older age groups. In turn, these developments are associated with patterns of deferral in the timing of family formation, relative to previous cohorts, from the mid 1970s onwards. It is argued that declines in the earnings of young men, relative to those of the highest earning age group, and improvements in the earnings of young women relative to those of young men, both embody and reflect changes in the ways young adults organize the resourcing of new households. The literature on transitions from youth to adult status has considered the impact of economic change *on* event timing or *on* the life course, but the way the research questions have been formulated has resulted in a static notion of the life course, as if it were an autonomous area of social experience. This chapter has attempted to demonstrate the value of exploring the dynamic relationship between life course processes and economic change.

It is suggested that improvements in young women's earnings are inseparable from the general decline in young men's earnings, relative to those of the highest earning age group. There is a restructuring of gendered earnings patterns amongst young adults, which appears to be linked to the increased discrepancy between rewards to youth and full adult earnings. The latter is considered as an index of general consumption standards. It is suggested that, in not keeping pace with improvements in the earnings of the highest earning age group, the earnings of young men have lagged behind increases in living costs. A corresponding trend is the improvement in young women's earnings. These aggregate level trends reflect on changes in the importance of young women's earnings in patterns of family formation. These joint processes, of changes in the relative earnings amongst young adults, and their relation to changes in the position of young adults relative to general consumption standards, are inseparable from patterns of deferral in the timing of family formation. In the aggregate level analysis, median earnings of the highest earning age group have been used as a proxy for general living costs, or life-style orientations, against which to appraise changes in the relative position of young adults. Such an analysis is theoretically coherent, reflecting as it does the inseparability of resource availability and orientations towards living standards in decisions around household and family formation. The next chapter develops this theme at a more disaggregated level of analysis, in order to examine social inequalities in the organization of transition.

Chapter 5

Lifestyles, orientations and occupational careers

Introduction

Youth research, in hypothesizing and exploring the possibility of an extended period of dependency, has inadvertently set something of a riddle: why should labour force disadvantage prolong youth dependency when traditionally it has been associated with early independence? Research that argued the collapse in employment opportunities, and social polarization between those with and those without secure employment, suggested that young people, displaced by economic change, faced novel social circumstances as a consequence of their labour force disadvantage. The hypothesized social disruption was set up in terms of researchers' expectations that employment, however limited in its rewards and opportunities, is a prerequisite to "normal" transitions from youth to adulthood. Deferral in the attainment of independence and adult lifestyles has been seen as a potential consequence of resource disadvantage, yet this argument has not been located in relation to the traditional expectation that economic disadvantage is associated with early adult status. In the last chapter, a method of relating the resource circumstances of youth to an index of general consumption standards proved valuable for elucidating patterns of change in the position of youth and young adults relative to the population as a whole. This chapter disaggregates the index of general consumption or living standards, and explores the relation between inequality and the organization of early transitions from dependence to independence.

A positive feature of the life course literature lies in its inter-

117

pretation of the interaction between transitions to adult status and longitudinal, or lifetime, career and income prospects. Through emphasizing the relationship between patterns of event timing and differing lifetime resource and income profiles, it forces attention to prospective, as well as current and "background" socio-economic circumstances. Class-related differences in the timing of domestic life course events are explained with reference to future, lifetime, economic prospects. Rising earnings over (male) middle-class careers suggest that later ages at parenthood can better accommodate the probable, if temporary, loss of mothers' earnings and the costs of children, relative to lifestyle aspirations. Job insecurity and a shallow earnings gradient over working-class employment trajectories, where young adults quite rapidly attain earnings levels that they will not progress far beyond, are seen to encourage younger ages at family formation since there is little to be gained by delay. A class-related patterning of early life course transition behaviour, whose explanation invokes future careers and life chances, requires a theory of the orientations through which such futures are rendered meaningful for individual action. However, the structuring of orientations is rarely addressed in detail. Models of class differences in life course event timing rely on rather crude distinctions between class categories, from which orientations are deduced, and equated with a set of attitudes and expectations. In these descriptions, class processes are seen to underlie differences in life course event timing because of differences in lifetime income profiles and life chances, where middle-class careers reward long-term planning and working-class circumstances render it irrelevant (e.g. Roberts 1968; Ashton & Field 1976; Wallace 1987a; Jones 1986; Dunnell 1979; Kiernan & Diamond 1983).

The problem, then, is one of translating the relationship between *lifetime* careers and earnings profiles on the one hand, and the patterning of life course transitions amongst young adults on the other. Prospective careers are standardly seen to be significant to current behaviour through social actors' orientations to their futures. Orientations are seen to be strongly class-related. However, in studies of life course event timing, particularly those using large data sets (e.g. Kiernan & Diamond 1983; Jones 1986; Oppenheimer 1982) orientations are rarely subject to empirical analysis. Rather, they are deduced from a cross-sectional definition of class, based on current employment position. However, given the problems that arise from assuming current employment position to be an adequate indicator

of a "class career" (Jones 1986; cf. Stewart et al. 1980), such a definition of orientations is reductionist, and fails to improve our understanding of actors' socio-economic location and subjectivities.
Assumptions of orientations based on current class location impose
their authors' understandings of rational action, in the absence of
data on lifetime labour force trajectories, or empirical investigation of
the perceptions of young adults themselves. An adequate theory of
orientations requires that we locate actors' perceptions of their
circumstances in relation not only to measures of their current social
location but also to the processes that shape labour force and
domestic careers over the life course. Indeed, standard patterns of
movement through employment over the life course suggest that an
adequate understanding of current class location necessarily requires
a sensitivity to potentially diverse career routes. Orientations, then,
should necessarily be integral to an understanding of class-related
variation in life course event timing. However, it is necessary to
explore the ways in which orientations are constituted in relation to
lifetime trajectories, rather than attempt to read them from cross-
sectional definitions of class.

This chapter considers variation in patterns of life course event
timing amongst survey respondents, in relation to a measure of
respondents' orientations to the future derived from respondents'
perceptions of the circumstances of others in their employing organization. Orientations are defined here as perceptions of current circumstance and wellbeing, relative to significant reference groups and
relative to associated expectations for the future. Through data gathered in the main survey the analysis explores the relationship
between employment circumstances and life course trajectories and
develops a theory of orientations that makes central the perceptions,
amongst respondents, of the relationship between their current and
future circumstances.

Class and careers

Goldthorpe and his colleagues provide a succinct statement of the
standard understanding of class-related orientations, an understanding that is conventionally reflected in descriptions of class differences
in the timing of marriage, parenthood and so on (Goldthorpe et al.
1969; Ashton & Field 1976; Oppenheimer 1982; Jones 1986; Wallace

1987a). The "traditional" working-class model is one where a structured lack of opportunity corresponds with orientations that are immediate in their outlook: "the major economic concern is with being able to *maintain* a certain standard and style of living, not with the continuous advancement of consumption norms and widening of cultural experience . . . This emphasis on the present and lack of concern for 'planning ahead' are . . . encouraged by the view that there is in fact little to be done about the future, that it is not to any major extent under the individual's control. Fatalism, acceptance and an orientation to the present thus hold together as a mutually reinforcing set of attitudes" (Goldthorpe et al. 1969: 118–19). In contrast and "consistently with the notion of a social ladder that all have the opportunity to climb, wants and expectations are, from a middle-class standpoint, capable of continuous enlargement" (Goldthorpe et al. 1969: 120). The typical objective amongst the middle classes then, is to make a progressive improvement in consumption standards, social prestige and lifestyles over their careers. Goldthorpe and his colleagues maintain that, from the point of view of the individual or family, it is a key expectation that these lifetime advances will occur, through promotion, a progressively rising income and so on.

Orientations, then, are seen to be organized on a class basis. Indeed, general statements frequently invoke such orientations as part of class culture which, in descriptions of transitions to adulthood, is important to understandings of class differences in the timing of independence, parenthood and so on (Dunnell 1979, Kiernan & Diamond 1983; Wallace 1987a). Goldthorpe places some importance on employment trajectories, over the life course, as part of the substance of class inequality. This appears to be at odds with his later statements of the lack of consequence of life course related processes for understandings of class (Goldthorpe 1984; Erikson & Goldthorpe 1992). This latter position is made explicit by Goldthorpe in his "defence of the conventional view" of descriptions of women's location in stratification theory (Goldthorpe 1983, 1984). In maintaining that the secondary earners' jobs do not make a difference to household class position, Goldthorpe argues that such differences as do occur:

> we should regard . . . as being among those resulting from changes in household composition – in turn often associated with life cycle stages – and, hence, as ones that are *independent*

of class position and that can, and typically do, occur while class position remains stable (Goldthorpe 1984: 498; original emphasis).

However, if life course changes occur while class position remains stable might we not just as easily see such changes as contributing to the definition of stability? Goldthorpe refers to Rowntree's cycle of poverty model to illustrate the logic of his argument. Exposure to threat of poverty was an abiding feature of the class position of labourers' families. Whether or not such a family was below the poverty line at any time was largely influenced by its composition, particularly its balance of dependents and of secondary workers (most importantly the presence of older children). Goldthorpe acknowledges the significance of family composition but, he argues: "it would have been rather obviously unhelpful to see it as testifying to high rates of mobility in and out of the class of labourers" (Goldthorpe 1984: 498). Indeed it would seem rather unhelpful. If the threat of poverty is seen as an abiding feature of a particular class position why should its realization undermine that position? Goldthorpe appears to maintain a division between these two aspects of social experience, but the argument of an independent life course dynamic is at odds with his earlier statement of its class-related reproduction.

To separate, as Goldthorpe does, the work of secondary earners, associated with changes in household composition, or the consequences of life course changes, from household class position, defined by the head's occupation, is a curious position if we acknowledge that family structure and the family life course are themselves organized in relation to class processes (cf. Irwin & Morris 1993). They are not, however, reducible to class. Changes in the life course of individuals and families have significant consequences for the organization of employment demand and rewards and, by extension, might be seen to have their own consequences for class-related processes. Goldthorpe argues that married women standardly can be allocated to their husbands' class position on the grounds that they are secondary wage earners (Goldthorpe 1984; Erikson & Goldthorpe 1992). However, this neglects the significance of changes in female, relative to male, earnings. These changes, described in the last chapter, are bound up with life course changes, such as changes in patterns of childbearing and in returns to work, changes in the organization of households: their formation, structure and resourcing, and changes in the relation of members to household income maintenance. To accept the employment position of the household head as an index of inter-household inequalities would, quite inappropriately, place such changes outside the concerns of theories of class and stratification.

The division between life course processes and definitions of class is echoed by Jones in her study of class reproduction and transitions from youth to adulthood (Jones 1986, 1987). She argues that conventional models of stratification are inadequate for describing the experience of youth and early adulthood, a period characterized by high levels of occupational mobility. Transitions to adulthood are stratified by class, but current socio-economic position is a poor indicator of future class location. Jones proposes that the class position of young people is best defined by the class of their families of origin. One's relation to fathers' social class is considered a better indicator of class position than current occupation, since the latter is only "a stepping stone in a class career" (Jones 1986: 78). Over time, as young adults attain a more stable occupational identity, class is better defined by their own occupational position. An understanding of class arrangements amongst youth, then, needs to take account of current class position but also, importantly, the life course trajectory on which it is situated (Jones 1986, 1987). However, while such an approach suggests the value of treating life course processes as integral to class careers, Jones accepts the validity of prior class categories, without discussion of their relation to longitudinal, life course, processes.

In her analysis of patterns of transition based on GHS and NCDS data, Jones develops a typology of youth classes, based on a comparison of occupations across generations.[17] This typology forms the basis for comparison of life course event timing amongst young adults. The stable middle class and stable working class are those who "reproduce", on entry into the labour force, their fathers' current position in non-manual and manual work. Between these two extremes lie youth who are described as upwardly mobile from a manual background into non-manual jobs and those who are downwardly mobile from a non-manual background into manual jobs. Of the latter, those who "regain" a middle-class, non-manual position are described as counter-mobile. Jones argues that:

> inter-generational stability is not a matter of simple and direct class reproduction, but may be achieved through mobility on

an intra-generational basis. Intra-generational mobility is therefore important not only as a means of achieving upward mobility for those from working class backgrounds, but also a means of achieving class stability, through counter-mobility of the middle class. A surprisingly high proportion of the early school leavers among sons and daughters of middle class fathers are downwardly mobile on entry into the labour market (Jones 1986: 505).

Jones's youth classes are defined in terms of occupational mobility *vis-à-vis* fathers' social class. This shades the complexity of inequality within the youth classes. For example, if working-class respondents are not upwardly mobile to non-manual employment they remain classified as a single group, and variation in the experience of those in skilled, semi- and un-skilled work is occluded.[18] Despite her acknowledgement of the problems of accepting current employment position as an adequate description of class position amongst youth, Jones accepts as an appropriate index for defining youth classes a cross-sectional measurement of class background: fathers' current employment positions. There is no description of fathers' own employment careers. Evidence from my survey, however, suggests that where the young adults' social class are compared to their fathers' social class position where the latter were themselves young adults, there is a much greater level of inter-generational stability than suggested by Jones. This suggests that those occupational trajectories that she describes as counter-mobile, where a "lost" position is regained, might be better described as reflecting inter-generational class stability, where occupational mobility is a standard career over the life course.[19]

Jones is right to pause over the appropriateness of assigning a class position to youth on the basis of current occupation, but the problem of cross-sectional definitions of class inequalities is not confined to the particular occupational circumstances of youth. Jones's study falls short of defining life course processes as part of the substance of class-related inequality. This problem echoes that of studies, important to the debate on stratification, of the class position of clerical workers. Male clerical workers appear to occupy a contradictory class location, where their earnings are low in relation to those of manual workers, and out of line with their educational level and occupational status compared to other occupations. Accounts of this situation that accept the apparent discrepancy as a valid description of the location of clerical workers in the class structure, because they accept clerical work as a unitary category, fail to analyze the diverse career routes into and out of clerical employment. Stewart and his colleagues argue that through such an analysis the "discrepancy" between class and status disappears:

> The mistake implicit in the general formulation is one that identifies the market circumstances of individuals with the particular occupations they hold. Individuals at very different career stages may be gathered under one occupational title and, in addition, many different types of career may be developed from some general occupations (Stewart et al. 1980: 201).

Stewart and his colleagues demonstrate the strength of an occupational career approach, sensitive to the precise nature of the relationship between occupations and their incumbents. In their distinction between occupational categories and life course stages the authors demonstrated an integrity in career experiences lost or mishandled by a series of studies assuming the unity of occupational and social location (Stewart et al. 1980). So, in the case of social mobility:

> rather than seeing individuals as moving between positions in a fixed structure, crossing and re-crossing boundaries as they change occupations, we need to look at occupations and incumbents together. It is not a matter of one's position at a given time, b*ut of that position in relation to past and anticipated future experience.* Thus, typical patterns of occupational movement represent not change, but stability (Prandy 1986: 146; my emphasis).

Here, then, statements of "downward mobility" on entry in the workforce, or of counter-mobility, where a "lost" position is regained, are argued to be an artefact of a measurement procedure that neglects to analyze the processes by which occupational routes, over the life course, represent standard, class-related careers. Stewart and his colleagues have been criticized for overstating the strength of standard processes through which individuals move into promoted positions and higher status occupations as they age (Erikson & Goldthorpe 1992). The latter authors stress that by no means all sons who are downwardly mobile achieve counter-mobility, and they maintain that a higher degree of uncertainty characterizes individuals' work-life mobility chances than suggested by Stewart and his colleagues. This uncertainty, they argue, is not likely to be unappreciated by the individuals involved. Nevertheless, the authors also point to the significance of counter-mobility in creating inter-generational stability in social class arrangements. It should be noted, too, that "downward mobility" on entry into the workforce, where this is defined in relation to father's current class position, is not likely to be interpreted by those involved as a "loss" of position, as it appears to be by its theorists.

Clearly, what Erikson & Goldthorpe describe as mobility strategies may be undertaken, yet the distribution and propensity to take, for example, a part-time education route to occupational mobility is hardly, itself, incidental to the class structure. Further, the "loss" by sons, relative to their fathers, of position on entry into the workforce, is a misnomer if the standard expectation is one of economic and status improvements over their working lives. Erikson & Goldthorpe, in their cross-national comparative analysis, assess mobility rates against fathers' class at the time of respondents' early adolescence. It seems implausible to suppose that young adults expect to achieve the occupational position of their fathers, at the time they enter their first permanent job. It also seems unlikely that, if young adults leave their parental home to set up a household and commence a family, they should expect to reproduce the living standard currently achieved in their parental home. This is not to say that they are uninfluenced by customary living standards in their orientations to adequate standards in new households of their own making. No doubt this dynamic may contribute to a secular increase in levels of expectations about "adequate" material standards for resourcing new households. However, the life course dynamic of earnings and familial obligations, and the expectation of relative wealth and poverty over the life course, is no more likely to be lost on young adults than that which Erikson & Goldthorpe see as the uncertainty of their class position. In fact, available evidence, explored in the next chapter, suggests that there is a perception of fairness in societal resource allocation where higher rewards accrue to those with greater material obligations to dependents, that is, resource adequacy is seen to have an important life course element.

Both Goldthorpe and Jones see life course processes as having some relevance for understandings of class but for both it is only a partial statement. For Goldthorpe, different lifetime opportunities obtain across different social classes, yet by arguing that class-related patterns of job mobility, at an individual level, are irrelevant to class location, he appears to argue also that the life course, and family-related processes, are irrelevant to the reproduction of class-related inequality. For Jones, patterns of job mobility are problematic for describing the circumstances of youth, but not of adults. *However, a trajectory, or life course, approach to understanding inequality is salient not because life course processes sometimes encroach on the efficacy of measuring inequality, but because they are integral to its organization.* The operation of these processes is taken up in detail in the next chapter. Here I will be concerned principally with the relation between socio-economic inequality, orientations and patterns of early life course event timing.

Occupations are inadequate as measures of inequality where they are not analyzed in relation to the particular circumstances and material obligations of their incumbents. For example, just as we may accept that a female part-time shop assistant married to an unskilled manual worker has a differing class position than one married to a manager (after Erikson & Goldthorpe 1992), so it would be curious to suppose that a young single man and an older married man with dependent children, working in an identical occupation, necessarily share more than do the female shop assistants. We should be cautious too, in supposing that similar entry occupations will channel their incumbents into similar employment careers. Clearly there is a need for caution over straight divisions, based on current occupation, as a basis for assuming homogeneity and difference in social action. In the case of young adults we do not know the precise shape of their future careers, and to group them on the basis of conventional class divisions would impose a homogeneity of experience that may be inappropriate. A preferred approach is to develop a means of identifying social groups that are cohesive with respect to the processes that structure and differentiate the attainment of adult status, rights and obligations. Individuals within similar occupations may be on different career paths and have differing social reference groups. To explore the orientations and expectations of these young adults will not allow a privileged understanding of their future but it may accommodate a more detailed understanding of their current social location. In this way it is possible to explore event timing in relation to prospective careers, as they are reflected in the perceptions of the respondents, rather than assume the shape of future careers on the basis of current occupation. Such an analysis is undertaken in the subsequent sections, and patterns of actual and anticipated life course event timing amongst respondents are considered in relation to an index of social location that includes prospective careers as well as current occupation.

Gender and careers

In Chapter 4 I argued that there has been an increase in the significance of female financial contributions to household resourcing and that, in recent decades, this trend is integral to patterns of deferral in the timing of family formation. The trend is suggestive of a change in the gendered division of labour in the reproduction of households and family formation, that is, in the reproduction of a new generation of children, as well as in the maintenance of day-to-day living standards. Female earnings within conjugal households generally comprise a secondary, component, wage, but it is one that appears, for many, increasingly necessary to resource an "adequate" living standard. This dynamic calls into question the adequacy of measures of inter-household inequality based on head's occupation (cf. Goldthorpe 1983, 1984) for elucidating changes in the organization of inequality. It is, however, still clearly the case that male earnings tend to constitute the major component of household financial resourcing. Nevertheless, a consideration of careers and orientations, and their relation to patterns of family formation, require a greater sensitivity to the necessarily joint nature of female and male decisions around marriage and family formation than is conventionally the case in studies of the transition to adult status. It would be valuable to compare gendered earnings relativities, at the household level, prior to the birth of the first child, across generations. To my knowledge there is little data available on this. In this and the subsequent section, I address gendered relations to career routes, amongst the respondents, and across their employing sectors more generally, and explore respondents' perceptions of gendered responsibilities for household income maintenance.

The youth sample covered respondents aged between 16 and 35. While there is a corresponding variation in the career stages of the respondents, the most difficult issue to establish is the extent to which they are embarked on significantly different career trajectories. The sectors within which the survey was based serve as rough indicators, but they are approximate and may cover a wide range of circumstance in respect of income and career expectations, marriage and parenting patterns and social networks. The most obvious dissimilarity here is with respect to the gendered variation in such circumstance, since young men and women in the same occupations are not necessarily social peers. In this section I consider gender and the distribution of promotion chances and expectations across the insurance and retailing sectors. In the subsequent section I develop an analysis based on an index of the circumstances of reference groups, in exploring the timing of, and attitudes towards, family formation. Rooted as it is in a measure of material resources, the index reflects a gendered pattern of inequality in the level of resources associated with married status amongst women and men. In consequence, reflecting a greater salience of male earnings than female earnings to household income maintenance around family formation, it is more effective as a framework for exploring the expectations of young men than of young women. For this reason, some of the female responses to questions about family formation are considered separately below.

Respondents to the Main Survey were asked why they decided to work in their employing sector. The distribution of responses is shown in Table 5.1. The male respondents show some similarity in their responses over all three sectors, although clearly men in insurance are the most positive about their reasons for entering the sector. Twice as many men as women saw their current employment situation as the outcome of a positive choice on their part, rather than as a constrained choice, or one forced by circumstance. The percentage of

Table 5.1 Perceptions of choice as reflected in respondents' stated reasons for entering current employment sector.[20]

| Sector | Perceptions of choice | | |
	Constrained	Positive	Missing
Men			
Construction	10	14	9
Insurance	2	7	5
Retailing	4	7	3
Women			
Insurance	6	5	7
Retailing	10	3	0

women in the retailing sector who saw their circumstance as the product of a "constrained" choice is particularly high. These gender differences may reflect differing expectations concerning employment prospects.

All respondents were asked what work they expected to be doing five years hence. Of the 13 men interviewed in insurance, 8 named an internal occupational grade that they expected to be holding, and in seven cases this involved promotion to at least one grade up the career ladder. Of the men interviewed in retailing 2 were butchers and 2 were bakers. These trades were better paid than any other jobs held by age equivalents in retailing, and held a different relationship to the career structure than sales and supervisory jobs, but they could still feed into managerial positions. Of the 14 men in retailing, 9 named a retail occupation they expected to hold in five years. One of these men expected to continue as a baker, the other eight all expected promotion to a higher occupational grade. The remaining five men either named different types of work they expected to hold or were not able to say what they expected to be doing. In contrast, of the 15 women in insurance, 3 named an insurance-related grade they expected to achieve within five years, of which 2 expected promotion, 7 expected to be full-time parents and 5 said they did not know what they would be doing. Of the 13 women in retailing only 1 named a (promoted) grade she expected to achieve within five years, 2 expected to be full-time parents and 10 said they did not know. Amongst those in insurance and retailing the oldest current age of male respondents who said they did not know what they would be doing was 24, whereas amongst women it was 32. The level of uncertainty amongst women is substantially related to their expectations of departure from the labour force during family formation but even amongst those who do expect to be in the labour force in five years there is a high level of uncertainty.

These figures compare with those of two other studies that addressed expectations of promotion within the same occupations. Amongst male workers in my own survey 8 of 14 (57%) sales workers and 7 of 13 (54%) insurance workers expected to remain in their sectors and to achieve promotion. Amongst female workers the respective figures were 1 of 13 (8%) and 2 of 15 (13%). In the Young Adults in the Labour Market Survey conducted by Ashton and his colleagues, the authors found that 75% of men in both sales and clerical occupations responded affirmatively to the question "Are there any chances of promotion in your current job?" (Ashton et al. 1990). The higher figures of their study may be a consequence of the relative openness of the question, which by focusing on the chances of promotion would seem to invite a larger positive response than a question on expectations of its achievement. Amongst women in Ashton's study, 41% of sales workers and 63% of clerical workers responded affirmatively to the question on promotion chances.

Crompton & Jones presented data on expectations of promotion amongst men and women in clerical work. From their interview data they found expectations of promotion to be especially high amongst younger age groups, ranging from 77% amongst men aged under 25 to 87% amongst men aged 25 to 34 (Crompton & Jones 1984). This figure presumably increases between these ages because younger men not expecting promotion may have less commitment to the sector, and those with higher expectations would still be found there in the higher age group. In Crompton & Jones's survey, of the 85% of men (overall) and 62% of women who expressed interest in promotion, 79% of the men, but only 47% of the women, expected to achieve it. The authors suggest that this is partly a consequence of the gendered age differences in their sample, and of women's higher concentration in jobs with fewer promotion prospects. However, in general, women at the beginning of their working lives are argued to be positively oriented to promotion and a career but, controlling for domestic circumstances from marriage onwards, the authors note a decline in complaints of sex discrimination and in the level of interest in promotion, "particularly when aspirations at work are perceived as being in conflict with domestic responsibilities" (Crompton & Jones 1984: 163–4).

Census figures reflect the gendered pattern of inequality in promotion chances in the retailing sector. Of all women in retailing employment in 1981, 14.4% were shop managers and 49% were sales assistants. In contrast, 39.1% of men in retailing were shop managers and 12.6% were sales assistants (Distributive Trades EDC 1985).

The stark gender differences in expectations described above reflect general sexual inequalities in promotion chances. Significant promotions are frequently made at the ages at which women are either out of the labour force, rearing children, or constrained to taking part-time jobs for the same reason. Expectations of domestic time commitments amongst women, by employers, and the failure of institutional support for a career that can accommodate these terms, severely compromise women's promotion chances (cf. Craig et al. 1983). It is possible, of course, that some women will ascend career ladders and there is evidence that women who have limited domestic commitments through their labour force histories may follow career routes more similar to men. This is not to say that continuity of employment allows women to realize the promotion expectations that are held for men, but it does improve their chances. For example, Stewart & Greenhalgh, in their study of work history patterns amongst women surveyed in the National Training Survey, in 1975–6, found that 25% of women aged 45 to 54 with an unbroken employment record were in managerial, professional and technical occupations, in contrast to 13% of the age group with two or more breaks from employment (Stewart & Greenhalgh 1984). Dex & Shaw, in their analysis of the Women in Employment Survey, traced patterns of occupational movement over women's work histories, focusing in particular on the consequences of breaks from employment around family formation. The common pattern of downward occupational mobility following parenthood is explained by the significance of part-time work for female returners, and its prevalence in low paying and low status occupations, and by length of time spent out of employment. Recovery of pre-parenting employment status may be achieved but it is only the standard experience amongst professionally qualified women (Dex & Shaw 1986).

The following quotes, drawn from the Main Survey, illustrate some perceptions amongst female respondents of their particular relations to employment and family formation. Such statements of course are illustrative, but they indicate the significance of relative female and male earnings in decisions about family formation, and differences amongst women in their expectations about squaring the commitments of childcare with employment. The responses to the questions about family formation that were cited earlier, in Chapter 4, are not repeated but are similarly illustrative of the variety of concerns, including joint strategies for household resourcing, identified by the young adult respondents. One of these was a female senior clerk in an insurance company, aged 26. She had lived with her partner since she was 21, and married him at 25. Her husband was a supervisor in an insurance company. She was earning an annual salary of £8,500 before tax, her husband was earning £12,000 before tax. She expected to have her first child at 28 or 29. She explained the reasons for this:

My husband is a bit older than I am. He doesn't want to be too old before having another kid. He has a son already. Financially, in a year or so, we will be a lot better off and it will make it easier for me to stop working. I couldn't stop working now as we would not be able to manage. We couldn't manage on one salary and with him being married before and paying support for his son.

When I asked what she expected to be doing in five years' time she replied: "I expect hopefully to not be working and be at home with a child. I would take a part-time job if we needed the money, but I wouldn't like someone else to look after the child all day."

Another senior clerk in insurance appeared to have more mixed feelings about the conflicts she felt over parenthood and a career. She was 25 and living in a flat she bought at 23, cohabiting with her partner, although he was in the Navy and often away. Her annual salary was £7,400 before tax, and she estimated that her partner was earning £8,000 per annum before tax. She planned to marry at age 26, and expected to have her first child at about 28. She explained:

I think I will be ready then, I would have the time and patience. We would be financially stable. I don't know that I would give up work, I suppose I am quite selfish . . . I hate housewife type things. I would like to do part-time work, and to keep the cars that we've got. I wouldn't want our standard of living to drop, I think that's the reason for the later age.

I asked her when she expected to return to work after having children. She replied:

Waiting until I am 28 . . . I would worry about cheating on a kid a bit, by saying that my career comes first . . . But I would come back part time as soon as time allows. Not full time but the minute it gets into school I would be straight back into full-time work.

The following account is by a female retail worker. She was a checkout operator, aged 23 and living with her parents. She got engaged at 22, and planned to marry at 24 and to buy a flat or house. She worked a 32½ hour week but did up to 15 hours' overtime, earning £80–90 weekly net, including overtime payment. Her fiancé was a security guard, on £84 weekly net earnings, and he was looking for another, better paid, job, preferably as a heavy goods vehicle driver. She explained the reason for the timing of their forthcoming marriage: "Just really that we are not getting any younger." She anticipated having her first child at 25 or 26. When asked to explain her reasons she replied: "I don't know. I wouldn't like to be 29 say before the first as I think it is too old."

When I asked what she expected to be doing in five years' time she replied:

> Not working anyway. I suppose I would still be here in five years. About children, if [her partner] has a good job I wouldn't work, if not I suppose I would have to come back. I would work anyway until I have children. If [he] is on a decent wage, say £150 to £200 a week, if he's a long distance driver, if he is earning that I can just retire.

In descriptions of patterns of household and family formation, there have been few analyses of the integrated structure of gendered relations in the organization of household resourcing. In part this is a consequence of the young ages of respondents to small-scale surveys set up to investigate patterns of transition to adulthood. Analyses of large data sets tend to consider male and female transitions separately. General statements of gender inequality in transition, as described earlier, have stressed the gender specificity of adult status at the expense of an analysis of the interrelatedness of male and female relations to employment and parenthood. The necessarily joint and gendered enterprise of family formation, reflected in the above quotes, is taken up in detail in the next section.

Occupations, careers and adult wage jobs

This section addresses the relation between respondents' current social location and the patterning of their actual and expected ages at family formation. The description of social location attempts to move beyond a simple, cross-sectional measure of class, derived from current occupation, by incorporating an index of respondents' orientations to the future derived from their perceptions of the circumstances of salient reference groups. It therefore allows us to dispense with the crude assumptions about class differences in orientations to the future, which characterize descriptions of class-related patterns of transition to adult status. The questionnaire was not designed with this sort of analysis in mind, so certain assumptions need to be made, but, as a bottom line, the framework developed is a useful one for ordering some of the attitudinal data collected. However, the index developed is more effective in predicting life course event timing than are occupational divisions because, it is argued, it builds in a measure of potential careers that is derived from the perceptions of respondents. The index, which I call the adult wage index, is drawn from a series of answers by respondents to questions about the earnings structure of their employing sector, and about the marital status of typical incumbents in differing occupational grades. It turns out that the distribution of respondents' perceptions of "the normal" economic circumstances under which to be married, indexed by their perceived "adult wage" adheres roughly to their employment sectors, but that the perceived adult wage index is itself a much more effective means of ordering the available data on the timing of family formation.

The index is influenced by Siltanen's work, outlined in Chapter 2, on the structuring of positions and rewards in employment in relation to household financial obligation. Siltanen demonstrates the theoretical incoherence of undifferentiated gender categories in explanations of gender inequality in employment. A more effective explanation recognizes such inequality as a standard but not general nor uniform feature of employment processes. The distribution of people (within particular socio-economic strata) to jobs with differing levels of reward is patterned in relation to financial need and obligation. In classifying the relationship between rewards to employment and household circumstances, Siltanen distinguishes full and component wage jobs, which reflect the differing obligations of their incumbents to household resourcing. Full-wage jobs are ones that enable their incumbents to take principle responsibility for household income maintenance, in contrast to component-wage jobs, whose incumbents contribute, but cannot maintain a household single-handedly (Siltanen 1986). Any *particular* definition of the level of a full and component wage would, then, need to be derived from the circumstances of people within similar socio-economic strata, who can be grouped in relation to a broadly similar level of consumption at a household level. In the following analysis, however, I am using a measure akin to the concept of a full wage in order to index relative differences between socio-economic groups in their evaluations of the adequacy of material resources for family formation, evaluations that are expected to vary in relation to social location and perceptions of life chances. The adult wage index provides a measure of the earnings associated with married status, amongst men and women, derived from respondents' perceptions of the circumstances of incumbents in a range of occupations in their employing companies. Consequently it allows for differing perceptions of "a normal" level of earnings that attaches to adult status, without making prior assumptions about class-related orientations to future earnings prospects, of the middle-class deferred gratification, and the working-class fatalism, kind. The aim of the following analysis is to explore the relationship between individuals' economic and employment prospects and the way they organize early life course transitions. Orientations and lifestyle aspirations are integrated within the analysis through a framework that utilizes reference groups, in differing life course stages, and that considers perceptions of "normal behaviour" and potential employment prospects amongst respondents.

In the youth interviews a set of questions concerning the structure of their employing companies were asked of respondents. A series of job grades between junior and managerial levels were named to each respondent who was asked to identify, for each grade in turn, the attributes of a typical employee.[21] For each job named, respondents were asked whether it was done mostly by men, mostly by women, or by both. Then, for each grade and sex, respondents were asked what age groups(s) that employee would fall into and what their marital status would be: whether they would typically be single, married or either. Respondents were then asked what they considered to be the earnings bracket associated with each job. The midpoint of the first earnings bracket associated with sex-specific married status provides the adult wage estimate for each respondent. For example, if the grades named were clerk, senior clerk, supervisor and so on, for each of these the respondent would be asked to identify the attributes of a typical employee in each of these grades. In the resulting data, at the lowest job grade associated with married status, say clerk for a woman and supervisor for a man, the corresponding earnings bracket is used as an index for the adult female wage and adult male wage. Both measures were calculated for all respondents and represent the earnings they perceive to be associated with early married status, for women and men, within their employing sector.

The adult wage index does not resolve some of the problems of other life course studies. By tying the question of earnings levels and married status to career structures within current employment sectors, the adult wage index assumes the salience of this structure to the respondents, both as a referent for their prospects and for older, but socially similar, peers. The measure will be most meaningful for those who expect to progress through the specified career routes. Further, because male earnings become increasingly important to household income maintenance where women leave employment to have children, so a measure rooted in relation to employment and earnings is less useful for identifying the relationship between women's employment position, their orientations and life course transitions. It might be objected that the adult wage index assumes too much about the significance of employment over and above other salient circumstances, for example, obligations to family of origin, access to resources more generally, other significant reference groups, relationship to social networks and so on. However, while not all the respondents expected to remain in their current employing sector, the adult wage measure proves effective as a way of disaggregating the sample in relation to life course transitions.

Standard processes that move individuals across occupations and earning levels have clearly gendered consequences, with a divergence of male and female rewards from employment structured in relation to the division of labour within the household. The pattern is reflected clearly in respondents' expectations of earnings associated with male and female married status. Aggregated over all respondents, the distribution of these perceptions is shown in Table 5.2.

Table 5.2 Distribution of adult wage estimates made by all respondents to the Main Survey.

| | Respondents' estimates of adult wage | | | |
	Male adult wage (%)	N	Female adult wage (%)	N
£5500 or less	31.0	27	54.4	31
£5501–£7500	23.0	20	28.1	16
£7501–£9500	21.8	19	15.8	9
Over £9500	24.1	21	1.8	1
		87		57

Table 5.3 Distribution of adult wage estimates disaggregated by sex and employment sector.

	Male respondents		Female respondents	
	Male adult wage	Female adult wage	Male adult wage	Female adult wage
Insurance				
£5500 and under	2	4	4	10
£5501–£7500	4	6	6	4
£7501–£9500	4	3	5	2
Over £9500	3	1	1	1
Retailing				
£5500 and under	9	9	6	8
£5501–£7500	0	2	4	4
£7501–£9500	2	3	2	1
Over £9500	3	0	1	0

The distribution of adult wage estimates shown in Table 5.2 reflects a division in expectations over gendered earnings levels at marriage. While 54% of respondents suggested a man might be married at an income of £7,500 or below (1988 incomes), 83% suggested that a woman would be married at below this level. A disaggregation of these estimates by sex and sector is shown in Table 5.3, which considers employees in insurance and retailing only, in order to compare male and female responses.[22]

The majority expectation amongst respondents, in both the insurance and retailing sectors, is that women will be married at lower than male earnings levels. The lowest grade in retailing is sales assistant and, given its standard incumbency by married women, it is not surprising that the "female adult wage" is so low in this sector. It is interesting that the male adult wage is similarly seen to be so low, and by a majority of male respondents in the sector. While responses vary across the sectors in a fairly predictable manner, it is clear that within the sectors there is a good deal of variation in expectations of the typical earnings that attach to married status.

In studies of the gendered patterning of employment the expectation is that men in white-collar work are attached to career routes that underwrite an age-related progression and promotion through occupational categories. In retailing with its high employment levels of young people and its reliance on high turnover to maintain flexibility, many of its young incumbents will leave the sector. Sales work is low paid and its attachment to career routes is more tenuous than in clerical work. Young people in retailing are likely to hold a very diverse set of careers. It may or may not be a starting point of a "progressive" career. Ashton and his colleagues identify the risk of unemployment associated with early starts in this low paying sector and illustrate the high levels of movement between jobs in the "lower segments", training programmes and unemployment (Ashton et al. 1990). While the survey on which their mobility analyses are based is limited to 18–24 year-olds, and therefore a narrow slice of their respondents' early careers, it also demonstrates the uncertainty of their position.

The Main Survey questionnaire collected responses to a series of attitude statements that interviewees were asked to read and to indicate whether or not they agreed or disagreed with them. Interpretations of these sorts of data tend to assume that the statements invoke a common interpretation, but it is important to exercise caution about the nature of variation in meaning. In response to the statement "earning a wage makes a young person independent", 66% of male respondents agreed, in contrast to 90% of female respondents. The breakdown by sector is as follows: of men, 70% in construction, 79% in insurance and 43% in retailing agreed. Amongst women, 89% in insurance and 92% in retailing agreed. The relatively low level of agreement amongst men in retailing is suggestive of an inadequacy of earnings in supporting early independence. The high level of affirmation amongst construction workers is consonant with the expectation that manual workers standardly achieve independence at an early age. However, the even higher agreement amongst insurance employees, many of whom expect promotion within the sector and would, at young ages, still be some way from achieving their potential earnings expectations, suggests that the question may have been interpreted with an emphasis on independence in the more personal sense of autonomy from parents, and novel social freedoms. Responses to a statement that is more explicit about independence as a resource related status shows a different pattern of responses across construction and insurance sector employees. In response to the statement "by the time you are 19 you should be able to support yourself financially", 42% of male construction workers agreed, as did 29% of men in insurance and 14% of men in retailing. , In contrast to 85% of women in retailing, 22% of women in insurance agreed with the statement. A disaggregation by level of qualification,

Table 5.4 Attitudes towards independence in relation to qualification level attained at school: percentages agreeing that "By the time you are 19 you should be able to support yourself financially."

Qualification level	Females		Males	
	%	N	%	N
None	100	5	46	13
CSE	100	4	31	10
"O" level	46	13	30	26
Higher	0	9	25	12

shown in Table 5.4, indicates an association between no or low qualifications and a positive evaluation of financial independence by the age of 19, an association that is particularly clear-cut amongst women.

Amongst men in white-collar occupations the relatively low levels of agreement might be seen as a consequence of their expectations of increasing income over the life course and the perceived inadequacy of earnings at the age of 19, relative to advantaged employment careers, but this appears to hide an important source of heterogeneity. The particularly low figure amongst male retailing employees, in conjunction with their low qualification levels, suggests that resource constraints to independence are not uniform, but rather entailed by differing life course trajectories and thereby suggestive of differing social location and life course behaviour. The socio-economic indices above do not coincide exactly with employment sector and ostensible social peers may be on differing lifetime career and resource trajectories. It is these trajectories that are essential to understanding patterns of household and family formation and "adult" forms of inequality. These trajectories are explored using the adult wage index in the next section.

Employment trajectories, orientations and transitions to adult status

It is useful to combine the available survey data in order to achieve a summary measure of the timing of marriage and parenthood without breaking up an already small sample. Only some respondents are married or cohabiting, and only some are parents. To combine expectations about the timing of marriage and parenthood amongst some respondents with their actual timing amongst other respondents is not an ideal solution. However, it is worth recalling that expectations do not need to be accurate predictions for our purposes here. Rather, the point of including expectations is to obtain a better understanding of current circumstances and orientations of the respondents. What is important is that there is no systematic bias across respondents in the accuracy of their prediction. Only respondents aged 19 and over are included in the following discussion since amongst the youngest groups the questions on marriage and parenthood clearly had less salience.[23]

The distribution of current household status by whether or not the respondent has achieved his or her adult wage shows a clear patterning across male respondents. Amongst both male and female respondents there is a greater probability that those who are independent and living with a partner are at or above their "personal" adult wage. As we have seen, the divergence in earnings between women and men over the life course is associated with the particular relations of each to household resourcing and childcare. The perceived adult wage index is more strongly associated with domestic circumstances amongst men than amongst women. This may be a consequence of the greater importance of male earnings to household income maintenance at the point at which couples become parents. The association between respondents' household circumstances and the relation of their current earnings level to their "adult wage" is shown in Table 5.5. Their association illustrates, particularly amongst men, that those earning less than their adult wage are much more

Table 5.5 Relation of current earnings to own adult wage estimate by household status.

Current earnings	Household status	
	Dependent/ single	Independent/ with partner
Males		
Less than adult wage	30	9
At, or above, adult wage	6	10
Females		
Less than adult wage	8	7
At, or above, adult wage	7	10

likely to be single and dependent than to be independent.

Of the parents amongst the sample, 4 of the 6 fathers had children at an earnings level *below* their adult wage level, as did 1 out of the 4 mothers. The circumstances of these parents will be discussed later on. In general, their circumstances are disadvantaged. The salience of consumption aspirations implicit within the hypothesized association between adult wage levels and the timing of family formation appears to be lower amongst these men. For the moment though it is useful to broaden the sample under consideration to include those who are not yet independent nor parents. The rest of this section considers only male respondents, since here the adult wage index is more strongly associated with the timing of family formation than is the case among female respondents. It is apparent that the adult wage index is more effective in differentiating the sample with respect to ages at parenthood than ages at marriage. The questionnaire did not collect data on perceptions of employment structure and attributes of incumbents in respect of parenthood. While the adult wage measure is related directly to married status it is treated more generally as an index of the earnings associated with family formation. A more sophisticated measure would be one that could differentiate the different stages of family formation and allow for differences across groups in the relations between these stages.

The average expected or actual age at independent cohabitation (referred to as marriage whether or not this is formally the case) is very similar in both white-collar employment sectors. Actual and expected age at the birth of the first child amongst men varies very little across the white-collar employment sectors, yet for the reasons indicated we should be suspicious of a conclusion of similarity in respondents' social position and circumstance.[24]

Average ages at actual and expected ages at parenthood together are very similar across the two employment sectors. This is illustrated

Table 5.6 Average ages at parenthood (actual and expected combined), amongst men aged 19 and over, by employment sector (means and standard deviations).

Employment sector	Mean	SD	N
Insurance	28.3	4.2	9
Retailing	28.1	4.5	8

Table 5.7 Average ages at parenthood (actual and expected combined), amongst men aged 19 and over, by male adult wage (means and standard deviations).

Male adult wage:	Mean	SD	N
£7500 or less	26.9	3.7	11
Over £7500	31.9	3.4	5

in Table 5.6. However, a very different pattern is revealed where these ages are examined in relation to the perceived adult wage measure. Summarizing the latter into a dichotomous variable reveals a diversity that is lost to the employment sector disaggregation, and that is shown in Table 5.7.

The patterning over the adult wage brackets indicates a diversity of experience and expectations that cuts across the employment sectors. There is a relationship between the adult wage index and respondents' current ages. Those whose adult wage estimate was £7,500 or under had an average current age of 23½, those with the higher adult wage an average current age of 26. While the older men who are without children may have higher expected ages at family formation simply because of their age, there is no solely age-related reason why they should provide higher adult wage estimates. The pattern suggests that the relationship between the adult wage and ages at family formation is a substantive one.

The tables presented above suggest an association between the timing of family formation and the adult wage estimates. While the latter assumes much about respondents' perceptions its principal objective is to incorporate an index of career trajectories. It still assumes the salience to respondents of sector specific occupational career routes, and that others within the employing sectors provide reference groups that are salient to the respondents. Despite these assumptions the index appears more effective in differentiating the sample with respect to household circumstances than other, "cross-sectional", measures of current socio-economic location. The adult wage measure is used below as a way of ordering responses to open-ended questions that addressed respondents' expectations and attitudes towards marriage and parenthood. Part of the strength of the index, albeit as a proxy, was that it appeared to be patterned also in relation to this "qualitative" information. Responses to the questions on why respondents thought they would marry and become parents at the ages they specified, as well as retrospective questions on the same issues were diverse, and indicated different levels of decision-making and planning around family formation. An examination of responses of those who were married, cohabiting or engaged to be married, and those who were parents, reveals an association between the apparent salience to respondents of decision-making and the proximity of their current earnings to their adult wage. Where they have achieved a level of earnings close to their adult wage and the level of both is low, so this associates with a lower reported relevance of planning, and with early ages at marriage and/or parenthood. Where the adult wage is higher and respondents have not achieved a proximity to it, so planning and longer-term orientations appear to be more salient.

The following two quotes are from two men who married at a level of earnings below their adult wage. They both refer to income and living standards in their plans for family formation. The first respondent was a senior insurance clerk, aged 26, who married at 24 on an annual gross income of £6,500 and bought a flat on getting married. His partner is a shop assistant on an income of £5,500. His current annual income is £8,000 and his adult wage estimate is also £8,000. When asked why he married when he did he referred to a desire for independence, and said he found it hard to articulate other reasons. I asked him when he thought he would have children, and he was ambivalent. I asked him then what he thought a good age would be:

About 30; to be financially stable. Maybe my wife would not be able to work. These days when you are working off two salaries and got a bit of money . . . if that is halved I would want my own salary to be reasonable to pay the mortgage and bills, and other luxuries . . . if you are used to them.

The second respondent was a retail store department manager, aged 34, who married at 27 on an income of £6,600, living in private rented accommodation for a few months before and two years after they were married and then bought their own house. His wife is a clerical assistant earning £8,000. His current annual gross income is £7,800, and his estimated adult wage is £10,000. This "shortfall" parallels a perceived gap between his current household living costs and aspirations for a living standard he wishes to achieve for his future children. Reasons for the timing of living with his partner he related to inconvenient living arrangements prior to getting independent accommodation. He thought he would have children from the age of 36, explaining:

> The biggest reason I haven't started yet is money and the commitments I've got with the house. You have to take into account whether you can afford to start a family. I would expect, then, in a few years' time to have a promotion in hand and maybe afford to start a family. We probably could afford them now . . . I keep being told that, but I'm not one hundred per cent sure myself. It is whether you can bring them up in the fashion you want them brought up in.

The following quotes are from respondents who were engaged to be married. Of 6 engaged men in the sample, 3 were on incomes above their adult wage and 3 on incomes below it, although of the latter, 2 were on the Community Programme, and therefore on particularly low earnings. The adult wage estimates are not cited since, as labourers, the assumption of an apprentice route to crafts status is inappropriate. The apparent lack of salience of decision-making for the following man corresponds with his disadvantaged circumstance. A labourer working on the Community Programme, aged 20, his fiancée was a secretary earning an annual gross salary of £6,700. He was earning an income of £4,500. He expected to get married when he was 22 or 23 and when I asked him why, he replied: "I don't know. We'll wait until she gets a better job. I'm a bit young now, I like going out with my mates at weekends." He was similarly reticent about when he expected to have children.

The next two quotes are from men who both expected to marry within a year and who were both on earnings over their adult wage estimates. They were in very different employment positions, yet they were both making trade-offs, their relative "needs" being structured within very different resource circumstances. The first, on a low income and with a low adult wage was uncertain over his plans for children. He was a sales assistant, living with his parents, and he expected to be married at 21. His fiancée was an assistant manager at a café on an income of approximately £4,000. He was 20, on an income of £5,400, with an adult wage estimate of £5,000. When asked what sorts of things were important in the decision to marry (at 21) he replied: "We both decided by that time we would have saved up quite a bit of money. We want to try and get a mortgage for a house and get it done up before, with any luck". I asked him if he expected to have children at some stage, and he replied: "She says yes. I'm not a parent. I would like to later on." I then asked: "When, would you say?" and he said: "I've no idea. I would like to be in my thirties. It will probably happen sooner."

When I asked, later on, whether he and his fiancée's joint income had affected their decision about when to marry, he described how they were going to buy a flat the previous year but could not afford the surveyor's fee, and also that he was now selling his car as he could not afford to keep it. In contrast, the next respondent was a supervisor in an insurance company, who was living with his parents, and who expected to marry at 26. His fiancée was a bank clerk on £6,000. He was 25, earning £10,500, his adult wage was low at £4,500. He was therefore on an income substantially above his adult wage, but in what he says it is apparent that he felt relatively well off: "I was always quite highly paid in relation to what I did, that is, outside of work, it was easy to go abroad on holidays". He expected to have his first child at 28: "Money is only important when you haven't got any. I am aiming to be financially stable so I don't have to change my way of life." Asked whether he and his fiancée's joint income had affected their decisions he discussed their plans for children:

> In say three years my wife can pack in working and start a family. Over the next three years my salary will increase, maybe not up to the £6,000 she earns at the moment but by enough so that we can live comfortably on my individual salary.

In contrast to the apparent significance of the question to the above respondent was that of a sales assistant, engaged to be married and living with his fiancée at her parents, he was hoping to buy a house after learning of the length of the waiting list for council housing. His partner works part-time as a demonstrator in a retail outlet. He was 21 and on an income of £5,500, aged 21 at the birth of their child and on the same income. His adult wage estimate, also, was £5,500. The pregnancy, he said: "just happened, it wasn't planned or not planned." He expected to marry later in the same year. When asked why he replied: "I couldn't say. Why not?"

The fact that the question seemed impertinent may still be revealing. It is, of course, difficult to distinguish whether it is the case that decision-making had no particular relevance in the experience of this respondent, or whether he simply wished to retain his privacy. It is interesting to note the correspondence between his earnings and his low adult wage. When asked what he expected to be doing in five years' time he replied that he would probably still be working for his current employer. He currently expected to be promoted to a supervisory position. There is, then, some evidence from the responses that the salience of planning relates to the gap between current earnings and respondents' adult wage estimates. If the gap is large, and respondents are earning substantially less than their adult wage, there appears to be a greater salience of long-term planning, and a relatively late age at family formation. In contrast, low earnings and a low adult wage tend to correspond with relatively young ages at family formation and, at least as reflected in the responses, a lower perceived salience of planning. What is clear from the responses is the variety of levels of resource adequacy seen as appropriate to family formation, and the variety of orientations towards the salience of long-term planning.

Summary

The adult wage measure has been designed and used as an index of the "normal" circumstances under which to be married, as these are reflected in the experience of "typical" workers, as seen by the respondents, within their employment sectors. The adult wage is drawn from the data available on respondents' perceptions of the structure of their employing companies, and assumes the relevance to respondents of the associated career structures. It is for this reason that the index reflects more accurately on male, than on female, experience. As we saw earlier, it was the expectation amongst the majority of male respondents in insurance and retailing that they would remain in their current employment sector for at least the next five years, but clearly this was not the case for all respondents, some of whom were placed differently in relation to internal career routes. A more sophisticated index would require more detailed study of salient reference groups. Thus, the adult wage index provides a rather rough proxy for orientations to the future, for what respondents saw as the "normal" circumstances under which to be married. However, it is a step forward from assuming that orientations attach simply to current occupational class. It also builds in an understanding of norms as these attach to variable material circumstances and prospects, rather than assuming that norms and values about the "appropriate" age at which to marry and parent are more relevant to patterns of event timing in the latter part of the twentieth century than they were hitherto (cf. Hareven 1981). It is clear, from the respondents' descriptions, that patterns of, and decisions about, life course event timing reflect the salience of material resources and employment prospects, and any statement about the importance of age norms in life course event timing can be made meaningfully only in relation to the material circumstances through which transitions to adult status are organized.

In the context of the above discussion on orientations and their relation to social circumstances, it is appropriate to comment again on recent research into the life course related consequences of particular groups facing new forms of labour force disadvantage. Studies that have addressed the relationship between unemployment and the transition to adult status (e.g. Wallace 1987a; Hutson & Jenkins 1989) have not fully located the experience of particular groups in relation to general processes of change. Part of the problem, identified at the start of the chapter, is the difficulty of reconciling the traditional expectation that the most disadvantaged groups will attain independence and become parents at the youngest ages, with the hypothesis of deferral as a consequence of "new forms" of disadvantage, particularly mass youth unemployment. The latter hypothesis suggests that societal developments are at odds with individual expectations. Thus the youngster expecting to get a secure job at 16 will be quickly disabused of this notion on leaving school. If he or she holds on to prior expectations, however, a "deferral" in the timing of independence and family formation may be a consequence. The difficulty here, of course, lies in knowing what would have happened otherwise: the question of deferral, relative to what? (Amongst youth researchers the answer seems to be relative to what an age-equivalent peer would have done in the context of full employment. However, since deferral relative to previous cohorts is a general trend there is no constant basis for comparison.) If, for the youngster leaving school at 16, employment seems a distant and uncertain prospect, there is little to distinguish "old" from "new" forms of disadvantage, and no reason why the former should lead to early adult status and the latter to a deferral in its attainment. In short, it is not plausible to expect any single general consequence of unemployment, say of deferral in the timing of family formation, for the simple reason that we cannot treat unemployed youth as a uniform group. Any specific consequence of unemployment for the organization of life course transitions will reflect the diverse experience of those affected.

The significance of class-related lifetime income and employment prospects for the organization of transitions to adult status requires an understanding of how orientations "translate" potential future careers into class-related patterns of event timing. An understanding of the structure of orientations may itself enable a more sophisticated understanding of the particular social circumstances of youth than do assumptions of a determinate relationship between current class and the salience, or otherwise, of planning for the future. An understanding of orientations would allow a more complex understanding of class location than that achieved by equating it with current occupational position. This, then, has a bearing on the argument that life course processes are important to understanding inequality because standard, occupationally-based measures of class are insensitive to those lifetime careers that move people across occupational categories. However, as I suggested earlier, life course processes are also important to understanding the reproduction and restructuring of inequality across generations. In conventional statements of class-related inequality, life course related processes tend to be seen as a distinct micro-level concern (if they are acknowledged at all) contained within, and having little bearing on, the macro-level issues of class and the reproduction of social inequality (Goldthorpe 1984; Erikson & Goldthorpe 1992). Erikson & Goldthorpe maintain that life course processes, like issues of gender inequality, are marginal to the concerns of stratification theory, at the level of analyzing and understanding macro-level, historical changes in the class structure. However, what is not addressed in their replies to the criticisms of their treatment of gender, is the issue of the adequacy of treating the occupational structure as "the backbone of the reward system" (cf. Garnsey 1982). This criticism, however, would seem to present a fundamental challenge to "the conventional view". It suggests that the latter, by marginalizing issues of gender, and, it should be added, life course processes, fails to explain the dynamics of the occupational structure, as a system of rewards, in relation to the organization of social reproduction. As we saw in Chapters 3 and 4, there is strong evidence to suggest the salience of the latter, through gender and life course related processes, to inequality in employment and to the historical reproduction and restructuring of social inequality. These processes are explored further in the next chapter.

Chapter 6

Age-related distributive justice

Introduction

A number of writers have identified age-related social processes and the succession of generations to be increasingly salient to the structuring of socio-economic inequality, and to present a challenge to theories of class and stratification (e.g. Foner 1974, 1988; Kohli 1988; Riley 1988; Turner 1989). Age-related social claims and conflict are seen in such arguments to underlie a new dynamic of social change. Several authors, in identifying the variation in resource availability and political power across different age groups, have emphasized dimensions of injustice, and a growing potential for social conflict, along age-related lines (e.g. Preston 1984; Thomson 1989; Turner 1989). These arguments appear as an aspect of the more generally perceived crisis in the Welfare State. Two characteristic concerns of the literature addressing "the problem of ageing" are of interest here. The first issue concerns the relationship between age, or life course related processes, and theories of class and stratification, a problem seen to be increasingly salient to sociological theory given the growing numbers of those, particularly the aged and the unemployed who cannot be straightforwardly classified by an occupational schema. The second issue concerns the definition of age-related interests and associated theories of the nature of conflict over the societal distribution of resources.

Some versions of the age stratification approach entail an understanding of conflict over welfare that operates around the perimeters of the productive sphere. Excluded groups appear to be at odds with one another and with the working population, as they make their own claims over welfare resources, claims which, in the case of the elderly, are argued by some to be successfully achieved to the detriment of other age groups, particularly the young. The division between the working population and a dependent "welfare" population is stark in this argument, where the latter struggle over their share of the welfare pie. The welfare "crisis" is seen to lie along conflict axes running between welfare groups and between these and the working population. *The claims, then, of particular (welfare) groups appear as problematic while other aspects of resource distribution (rewards from employment) do not.*

The division between work and welfare in these arguments is only sustainable because of the conceptual separation of class- and age-related processes. While class theories are criticized for their partiality, and the failure to elucidate the experience of those outside paid employment, the age stratification framework sets up as supplementary a set of social relationships that leave intact the premises of production based theories of inequality. It is an argument of this chapter that age-related processes do not "add on" to socio-economic inequality but rather, like gendered processes, are an integral part of it. Age- and gender-related processes should be central to explanations of the structuring and reproduction of inequality.

As argued earlier, poverty and inequality amongst "dependency" groups, and the structuring of dependency itself, cannot be separated from the social organization of access to, and rewards from, employment for different social groups. The age stratification literature neglects the way in which these processes are themselves the outcome of social claims (cf. Peattie & Rein 1983; Rainwater et al. 1986). So, for example, as argued previously, claims to economic resources by women and young adults cannot be separated from the historical "success" of claims to a family wage by adult men. Differing rewards to men and women in employment, including claims to forms of welfare protection and pension rights, are very important to patterns of inequality in old age (e.g. Arber & Ginn 1991; Falkingham 1989). The relationship between experience in, and outside, employment speaks of a structural coherence that is lost in the particularism of the conflict models.

The authors of the age stratification and generational conflict approaches share the assumption that contemporary changes in the population structure and the organization of resource distribution to the "dependent" population are polarizing the wellbeing of different age cohorts and consequently feeding a nascent sense of injustice that will crystallize into novel dimensions of social conflict. These writers fail to describe the processes by which they insist that the changing demographic structure will engender increased age-related conflict. They point instead to aggregate level changes in the welfare of different age groups, and assume that the combination of demographic change and economic retrenchment will increase age-related inequality, that this in turn will be perceived as unjust, and that conflict will ensue, jeopardizing the stability of a welfare project that requires a contract of reciprocity across generations. However, authors of the age stratification framework have not demonstrated that members of age cohorts share interests that are consonant with their cohort experience, or perceive their interests to be at odds with those of members of other age cohorts or generations. As it is, we appear to know more about these writers' views on distributive justice than we do about the views of their subject populations. The literature offers little evidence on social actors' perceptions of inequality over the life course or on their evaluations of just claims by different age groups. Age, as we have seen, is a proxy for more fundamental sets of social relationships, importantly for life course stage and domestic circumstances. My survey included a number of questions designed to elicit attitudes towards the appropriate distribution of economic rewards in relation to domestic circumstances. In respondents' perceptions, claims to resources are bound up with the organization of household resourcing, and the associated division of household labour, between men and women and across generations. Evaluations of claims reflect the salience of life course stage and domestic circumstance to perceptions of distributive justice. This evidence is discussed in the latter part of the chapter.

The structure of perceptions of distributive justice indicates that age inequalities are a stable aspect of social relationships. Social change may entail, and be entailed by, a re-ordering of age inequalities. We have seen, in the example of change in the relative earnings of young men and women and new patterns of family formation, evidence of the ways in which a restructuring of age inequalities is bound up with broader social changes. However, the complexity and coherence of these processes is occluded by models that assume that inequalities straightforwardly engender conflict.

Age stratification and the question of generational conflict

The debate on age stratification has grown over the last decade, reflecting increasing concerns about the social problems expected to ensue from a growing non-employed population. The relative position of the young and the elderly has been particularly important in discussions about the changing age profile of wellbeing. Some writers maintain that changes in the circumstances of different age groups are directly linked, and that conflict will ensue as a result of historical changes in their relative social position (e.g. Turner 1989; Thomson 1989). Theories of change in the age profile of wellbeing would appear to have potentially important consequences for "conventional" (production based) theories of class and stratification. This section commences with a discussion of the arguments of two writers, Turner and Foner, who have made this issue central to their descriptions of age-related processes and social change (Turner 1989; Foner 1974, 1988).

Turner points to the absence of a coherent sociological theory of ageing and age groups as aspects of social stratification. In developing an argument of the significance of age-related processes to the organization of inequality, he proposes an alternative approach that relies on a model of conflict between age groups:

> Given the current recession which characterizes the world economy, the ageing of the human population poses not only serious economic implications for economic growth, but also raises the spectre of significant political conflict between age groups . . . we can refer to such struggles as a politics of resentment between welfare clients (Turner 1989: 603).

The politics of ageing is conceptualized here as a series of conflicts around economic class, political inequality and cultural lifestyles (Turner 1989). The stigmatization of the elderly, a state of affairs which he takes as axiomatic, is to be understood in terms of an age-related model of varying reciprocity and social exchange over the life course. In this argument, stigmatization is a consequence of a lack of social reciprocity and long-term dependency. Turner's initial assumption of age as a meaningful dimension of social and welfare antagonism is reified in a model of direct conflict between the young and the old:

Because compulsory retirement creates a condition of extended and in principle probably unlimited dependence on welfare, the aged become stigmatized as parasitic recipients of social benefits in a situation where they are forced to compete for scarce resources with unemployed youth (Turner 1989: 600).

Turner argues that the problems of ageing cannot be analyzed independently of their economic context, but he argues simultaneously that age groups, as status blocs, cannot be assimilated analytically to economic class analysis. The question of the relationship between age strata and conventional understandings of socioeconomic stratification is set up in terms of conflict between the old and the young as "dependency" groups. Turner's argument of stigmatization may speak more of the evidence of poverty amongst the elderly than a politics of resentment. The argument of stigmatization as a consequence of "low reciprocity" is merely postulated by Turner, and is at odds with the arguments of others writing on age and inequality, studies that are not addressed by Turner (e.g. Taylor-Gooby 1985, and those reported by Preston 1984; Minkler 1986). These studies suggest that claims by the elderly achieve a high level of popular support, for a variety of reasons, and will be addressed later on.

Other writers also maintain that age inequalities will engender conflict over the societal distribution of resources (Johnson 1989).[25] This model, of latent antagonism, or overt conflict between age groups, appears to stem from an analogy between age inequality and class inequality:

Age inequalities occur because age is used as a criterion for assigning people to roles that are differentially rewarded. "Age strata" are formed as people of similar ages fill similar sets of age related roles . . . In this sense, age forms the basis of a stratification system (Foner 1988: 178).

Like Turner, Foner argues that conventional theories of inequality pay insufficient attention to age-related processes. She maintains that:

age inequalities cannot be understood solely in class terms because dynamic processes related to age contribute directly to age inequalities; and, therefore, understanding how these age processes operate is important for grasping the roots of inequality (Foner 1988: 176).

Class analysis, Foner argues, is inadequate for dealing with the structuring of inequality outside the occupational sphere. She suggests that scholars interested in age and class stratification have tended to focus on the impact of class on age stratification and on class differences within age strata but not on the impact of age stratification on the class system. This argument is important, yet it has not been developed very far in the literature. Foner poses two questions: do age inequalities lead to age conflicts and, if so, how do they affect the relationship between classes? Part of the significance of a theory of age stratification is seen, by Foner, to lie in its emphasis on a structural potential for political conflict between the young and the old. However, while such age groupings may be important to conflict over "idealistic" issues, she argues, political conflict over the distribution of material resources, implicit in the structure of age inequality, is defused by "age conflict reducing mechanisms", specifically "age mobility" (ageing) and socio-economic heterogeneity within age groups (Foner 1974), both somewhat begging the question of whether conflict is an appropriate model with which to approach these issues. In her more recent paper, Foner returns to the question of why age is not a *standard* dimension of social conflict. However, she attempts to reclaim the argument that age stratification affects class relationships by pointing to specific examples of age-related behaviour or conflict that she sees as undermining class cohesion, such as youth subcultures diverting working-class youth from class-related activities, or age-related disputes within the workplace reducing class solidarity (Foner 1988).

Kohli suggests that the relationship of the age stratification approach to the question of class is mostly metaphorical (Kohli 1988). I would suggest further that the age stratification model rests on an analogy with class divisions, an analogy that is overdrawn. "Age mobility", for example, is a cumbersome term for ageing. Why should it be presented as a "conflict-reducing mechanism" given its uniformity and inevitability? Foner recognizes that career trajectories are bound up with class, but sees the latter as constraining the way in which social benefits change over the life course rather than seeing this ordering of resources and opportunities over the life course as part of the substance of class-related experience. Her general argument fails to demonstrate, indeed points to evidence against, a systematic patterning of age-based conflicts over material resources. By adhering to a theory of age-based conflict despite her difficulty in demonstrating its validity in practice, class takes on a static quality. Age-related processes may be as much an aspect of confirming class identity as undermining it, but more important is the possibility that age-related processes influence patterns of socio-economic inequality, with ensuing consequences for class processes. There is a potentially productive parallel here with gender theorists' critiques of stratification theory described earlier: that age-related processes are central to the reproduction, and restructuring, of socio-economic inequality. Theories of stratification that are rooted in a narrow conception of the economic sphere are not simply incomplete, they misrepresent the processes by which unequal rewards accrue to different social groups (cf. Garnsey 1982; Humphries & Rubery 1984). Before returning to this question it will be useful to consider further how issues of resource distribution and inequality in societies with ageing population structures have been constructed as a problem of age, and generational, conflict.

A great deal has been written on "the problem of ageing" in the United States where there has been something of a backlash against the perceived success of the grey lobby. Similar arguments have been published in Britain, however, suggesting an unfair redistribution by the Welfare State in favour of the elderly. In the United States, Preston argued that the relative wellbeings of the young and the elderly have diverged over recent decades. Transfers from the working-age population to the elderly are, in effect, transfers away from children and youth (Preston 1984). Preston points out the significance to this pattern of, for example, the rise in numbers of lone-mother-headed households, and cutbacks in federal expenditure on welfare that benefits the young, for example in entitlements to Aid to Families with Dependent Children (AFDC), and he argues that a series of public and private choices has dramatically altered the age profile of wellbeing (Preston 1984). In 1970 the incidence of poverty among the elderly in the United States was twice the national level, but by 1982 the proportion of elderly living in poverty had fallen below the national average. Over the same years the incidence of poverty amongst children aged under 14 increased from 37% below that of the elderly to 56% above (Preston 1984). The success of the elderly in pressing welfare claims appears, in his argument, to have undermined the position of the young, a group with little political support or lever-age. There is a suggestion here that the young are relatively weak as a political group, and the elderly relatively strong, but the structural relation between these groups is acknowledged to be more complex, and less direct, than that posited by Turner (1989). In Preston's argu-ment the success of the elderly is born of their numbers and conse-quent political influence, and further by a wide constituency of support, comprising the elderly themselves and the working-age population favouring public welfare for the elderly who might other-wise need family support, and simultaneously voting on behalf of themselves when they reach old age (Preston 1984).

The publication of the argument of Preston, then President of The Population Association of America, and a report by the US President's Council of Economic Advisors stating that the elderly were finan-cially better off than the general population, and the accompanying media attention in the United States have been cited as part of the background to the development of AGE, Americans for Generational Equity, an organization that attacked the US government for creating a situation in which "today's affluent seniors are unfairly competing for the resources of the future elderly" (Hewitt, quoted in Minkler 1986: 541). This statement assumes that increased poverty amongst children and youth is directly related to improvements in the relative economic standing of the elderly population. Entitlement pro-grammes for the latter are seen, consequently, to "mortgage our chil-dren's future", to jeopardize their life chances as a consequence of meeting "excessive" claims by the elderly population (Minkler 1986). Such arguments are criticized by Minkler as a new form of victim blaming.

According to Thomson, who focuses on New Zealand but claims his arguments to have a much wider salience: "a prevalent image of the elderly is still of impoverishment, but in the 1980s this no longer accords with the facts" (Thomson 1989: 52). He argues that there will be a change in perceptions of the affluence of the elderly, as the mem-bers of the first welfare generation, now approaching retirement, reach old age. Members of this generation have been the prime beneficiaries of the Welfare State through their adult lives. As they have aged the Welfare State has shifted from one that was oriented to programmes benefiting the young to one that favours the elderly. By cutting welfare expenditures to the young in the 1970s and 1980s, the State has, he suggests, undermined the incentive to maintain the implicit social contract between generations on which the welfare system largely depends, since welfare insurance is underwritten by an intergenerational contract in which current pensions are financed by current employee taxes. Why, Thomson asks, should today's young people honour a welfare contract that has not benefited them and which will require them increasingly to subsidize the "welfare generation" in its old age (Thomson 1989)?

In the United States, while it appears that the elderly have defended their position more effectively than other welfare claimants, it is not clear that their claims have undermined the position of those other groups. Pampel & Williamson, in their study of the determinants of social welfare spending across 18 advanced industrial nations, argue that population age structure has been largely neglected in studies of Welfare State development, yet, they suggest, the strongest influence on the rise in spending from 1950–80 has been the size of the elderly population, whose political efficacy has resulted in increased expenditure per head of the elderly population. However, the authors also argue that the percentage of elderly in the population has no effect on age-standardized spending for programmes not directed to the aged, such as public assistance, family allowance and unemployment benefits (Pampel & Williamson 1989).

The generational equity framework, and the theory of competition between generations from which it derives, has been strongly criticized for presenting a new form of victim blaming, and for advocating cuts in support to the elderly to restore justice between generations. Minkler outlines her objections to the generational equity arguments in terms of the implied homogeneity of "the elderly", in terms of the measures of poverty used and through survey evidence that suggests cross-generational consensus rather than conflict in attitudes towards government spending.[26] However, the latter point, critical of arguments for reduced expenditure for the elderly, appears to sidestep Preston's point that this consensus is part of the problem in so far as it is not matched by support for the young. Minkler does not directly address the possibility that a large cohort with a broad constituency of support and political power may detract attention from the extent of poverty elsewhere. Most authors appear to concur that the elderly are well placed with respect to popular affirmation of state expenditure and pension maintenance, achieving a level of support not attained by some other "dependency" groups. However, this situation is simultaneously described as unjust because of a public failure to acknowledge the legitimate claims of the young. This raises questions concerning the structuring of evaluations of justice. There is evidence that the processes underlying such judgements are more complex than suggested by arguments of age-related self interest.

With respect to claims amongst the non-working population, Heidenheimer points to an historically clear demarcation in the United States between social insurance and welfare programmes. He argues that the concept of contributory insurance benefits has permeated the politics of social security so that any alterations to these programmes are resisted since they represent individually earned rights to income. In contrast, public assistance programmes have no similar legitimacy and consequently are much more vulnerable to demands for public spending cuts (Heidenheimer 1990). Taylor-Gooby notes a similar distinction in Britain, where his survey evidence revealed general support for services directed towards the elderly, sick and disabled, and education and the National Health Service, and much less general support for benefits for the unemployed, the low paid, single parents and children (Taylor-Gooby 1985). This evidence suggests that children and young adults are not so well placed as the elderly in general perceptions of the legitimacy of their claims. However, the relationship between the young and the elderly does not hold the symmetry that is implied by a theoretical dichotomy between work and welfare, where the young and the old are seen to hold a parallel social location simply on the grounds of their exclusion from the productive sphere.

The emphasis, by class theory, on employment-based relationships has neglected the structuring of rewards and life chances over the life courses of men and women, and neglected patterns of continuity and change as people move through different life course stages (Arber & Ginn 1991; Rainwater et al. 1986; Kohli 1988). Writers on age stratification have argued that inequalities across age groups present a challenge to class theory, and have substantive consequences for social change. By extending this analogy between age and class they suggest that age divisions, in conjunction with a growing welfare burden, also entail age-related conflict. In turn this is seen as significant to class theory. In Foner's model, age-related conflict undermines the potential for conflict between classes; in Turner's model, age conflict appears to be fought out around the perimeters of the productive sphere. Claims in the latter are not treated as problematic, but "problem groups", dependent on state or family, struggle over their rights to welfare resources. Questions about distributive justice then, appear as claims about welfare distribution, but not about the distribution of wellbeing more generally, and not about the relation between the experience of "dependency" groups and the productive sphere (cf. Holmwood 1991; Arber & Ginn 1991). In the next section some of the problems that arise from separating claims by the "dependent", or non-employed population from claims to rewards in employment are discussed.

Age, cohort and inequality

I have already argued that explanations of the historical development of the modern life course require an understanding of its social and economic construction, and that access to, and rewards from, employment do not operate independently of more general social relationships. Rainwater and his colleagues similarly criticize the autonomy of "market" processes in explanations of inequality, and develop a conceptual framework around claiming:

> to reject the placing of claims from work ("earnings") in a special status given by national economic processes, but rather to develop a language within which "earnings" may be seen as quite as institutionally determined as claims on consumption arising out of kinship relations or through the welfare system (Rainwater et al. 1986: 12; see also Peattie & Rein 1983).

The following considers some problems that arise from theories of age stratification and conflict that separate the claims of welfare groups in the "political" arena of redistribution from claims to rewards in employment. The examples point to the joint nature of life course and class-related processes in ordering resource distribution and in the reproduction of inequality.

The intersection of biography and history is frequently documented and has been the subject of research into the life chances and experiences of broadly adjacent birth cohorts (e.g. Elder 1974; Hogan 1981; Riley 1988). The convergence of severe economic recession in the early 1980s and entrance into the labour force by cohorts born in the 1960s had not only dramatic age-related consequences, manifest in the level of youth unemployment and in related government policy, but may leave a substantial proportion of people in affected cohorts disadvantaged over their lifetimes, relative to previous and subsequent cohorts. The experience of the 1980s suggests that such a convergence is inseparable from the incidence of long-term unemployment and socio-economic polarization. The intersection of life course stage and economic slump, where employment structures heighten the vulnerability of youth, is an aspect not simply of age inequality but of lifetime opportunity and constraint. Youth employment could not be so disrupted at no cost to the future absorption of a large section of the population into "standard" employment trajectories.

The representation of unemployed youth as a group located in a structurally determined antagonism with the elderly (e.g. Turner 1989) appears to be a consequence of the perception of their joint claims on a finite level of welfare resources. This is a peculiar argument, given that the issue for unemployed youth is more fundamentally an issue of employment! Claims to security amongst young unemployed adults and retired workers are quite distinct elements of the welfare project. Social security amongst the unemployed is about underwriting the risk of insecurity in the labour force. The British obsession with scrounging and work disincentives, seen as particularly problematic for young unemployed adults, is significant in setting benefit levels and rights of entitlement. Many arguments about restructuring the social security system are principally concerned with the issue of work incentives amongst unemployed people (e.g. Cooke 1987; McLaughlin 1989). In contrast, pensions to retired people are organized precisely to be a disincentive to employment. It is therefore not clear how claims amongst these groups can be construed as antagonistic.

Age inequalities hold contrasting meanings over differing, class-related, life course trajectories. Greater income inequality over an individual's life course is a standard aspect of white-collar careers, where expectations turn on job security, promotion and a rising earnings profile over the life course. A flatter, and possibly interrupted, earnings profile attaches more clearly to male manual work and female employment trajectories. In the context of individual life course trajectories, age equality is an aspect of relative disadvantage and age inequality an aspect of relative advantage. It would seem extraordinary, then, if age inequalities were to engender conflict between young adults and older workers.

The separation of claims to welfare from employment processes further neglects the ways in which inequalities amongst the non-employed are structured in relation to claims to rewards in employment. The claims of children are entailed in adult claims to a family wage, and in gender inequalities in earnings. In turn these relationships are essential to understanding patterns of poverty and inequality in old age. The description of structured dependency of the elderly has been criticized for suggesting an unwarranted notion of independence during their working years. The elderly with the lowest pensions are typically those who held low paid and precarious employment careers. Retirement means more control over their incomes than such individuals may have experienced for large parts of their economically active years (Kohli 1988). To this can be added the gendered pattern of employment rewards, economic dependency within the "economically active" years, and differences in pension rights and in life expectancy. These are fundamental to the gendered patterning of poverty in old age (Arber & Ginn 1991; Ginn & Arber 1991). A pensioner who lives alone is at higher risk of poverty than pensioner couples, and is more likely to be female than male (cf. Millar & Glendinning 1987).

Heidenheimer presents data describing the risk of poverty amongst different household types over a number of countries. Examples of some of these international differences are shown in Table 6.1. All countries except Sweden show a higher risk of poverty amongst lone elderly women. Such women in Britain are at a particularly high risk of poverty, although Britain is also unusual for the extent of poverty amongst elderly married couples, a circumstance that Heidenheimer explains as a consequence of minimum, uniform levels of income security in Britain (Heidenheimer 1990; see also Hedstrom & Ringen 1987).

The gendered patterning of poverty in old age has several causes: the longer life expectancy of women, diminishing savings over the post-retirement years, and the greater probability that a female pensioner will be living alone, in a situation where risks of poverty amongst the single elderly are much higher than amongst elderly couples. Pensioner couples comprise 9.7% of all households and 14.7% of all poor households, single male pensioners comprise 2.7% of all households, and 4.9% of all poor households, and single female pensioners comprise 10.9% of all households and 23.6% of poor households (Millar & Glendinning 1987; their poverty line is set at 140% of supplementary benefit levels).

Table 6.1 Percentage of children and elderly in poverty by family type and country (1979-82).

| | Children | | | Elderly | |
	Single parent families %	Two parent families %	Male living alone %	Female living alone %	Married couple %
Britain	39	10	55	70	24
Germany	35	5	19	24	9
United States	51	9	26	31	8
Sweden	9	5	7	3	0

Source: Heidenheimer 1990, after Palmer et al. 1988. Poverty is defined in terms of the official US poverty line, converted to other currencies using OECD purchasing power parities and adjusted for family size.

The poverty of the elderly is clearly partly rooted in their employment experience. While this continuity in inequality is broadly recognized (e.g. Pampel & Williamson 1989; Kohli 1988) it does not sit comfortably with a model of conflict between welfare "dependency" groups. The salient issue for claiming seems more appropriately addressed to inequalities in retirement as these are rooted in the organization of income support on the basis of past employment contributions. These inequalities cannot be reduced to claims in employment, but nor should explanations neglect the extent to which such claims are significant to the structuring of poverty and inequality in old age.

Table 6.1 also shows the risk of poverty amongst single- and two-parent families. Heidenheimer argues that the differences illustrated in the table are consistent with the structure of income maintenance programmes. It is the high minimum benefits and broad entitlement approach of Sweden, for example, which is consistent with the low poverty rates amongst children and the elderly there. Presumably this can only be the case if employment policy is considered to be an aspect of income maintenance policy. In Sweden the labour force participation rate of lone mothers is 85% in contrast to 67% in the United States and 39% in Britain (Lewis 1989). Lewis suggests that the high rate in the United States is a consequence of many states treating lone mothers as workers under their workfare programmes. In Britain, changing patterns of household dissolution have contributed to the significant rise in the number of lone parent families, from 570,000 in 1971 to 940,000 in 1984 (Lewis 1989). The history of policy debate and formulation has been characterized by uncertainty over the treatment of women heading such families as workers or mothers (Lewis 1989; see also Lewis 1980). The comparison between Britain and Sweden illustrates the constructed nature of the division between work and welfare statuses, and the range of experience that characterizes "dependency" statuses as these relate to structures of claims to, and within, paid work.

Evidence of change in these claims structures has been demonstrated in earlier chapters, importantly the restructuring of female employment over the life course, and of claims to employment by youth. Another problem for the age conflict models is the failure to take on issues concerning the changing employment composition of the population aged 16–64, with respect to levels of unemployment and to changes in female labour force participation, especially the extension of labour force continuity over the female life course. These changes are not addressed in any detail in accounts of the impending "demographic timebomb". The dependency ratio has been widely quoted in relation to this problem, and used in guiding pension policy formulation. It measures the ratio of the population of non-working age to the population of working age and does not take into account changes in levels of unemployment and non-employment amongst the latter, nor does it consider the relative value of social activity that is not accorded a market value, nor the level or structure of private transfers across the population (cf. Falkingham 1989; Arber & Ginn 1991). Changes in the patterning of female employment have been discounted as unimportant for the dependency ratio because they are equated with the growth of part-time work, a situation seen to have negligible consequences for the system of tax accounting and social transfers (e.g. Thomson 1989). However, changes in the lifetime participation of women in employment must be significant to the balance of the dependency ratio. As we have seen, such changes appear significant to extended periods of dependency amongst youth. Furthermore, they may be important to the resources that families accrue and carry into old age. The lifetime experience of different cohorts is essential to understanding the resourcing of those outside paid employment, and changes in living standards amongst the elderly, children, youth and the unemployed.

The age conflict approaches focus attention on distributive justice, yet their emphasis on the circumstances of age groups and "welfare" or "dependency" status neglects the historical structuring of claims in the "productive" sphere, and the relationship of the success or fail-ure of such claims to people's circumstances as they move between work and "dependent" statuses. In consequence, the arguments of the conflict theorists tend to understate the significance of inequality within age cohorts and overstate the extent of shared interests on the basis of cohort experience (cf. Ryder 1965). The attempt by Foner to move beyond this aggregation of cohort experience by considering the articulation of age and class presents the related processes in terms of distinct dynamics. Class factors "constrain" the way in which benefits vary with age (Foner 1988). This position maintains some autonomous basis for age-related rewards, yet offers no in-dependent explanation of their dynamic. As we have seen, age has limited meaning outside its social context. The age stratification approach distinguishes the experience of dependency groups from the structures of access to, and rewards from, employment, and from the structuring of dependency itself. The division reifies the tendency to present issues of distributive justice around the fringes of employ-ment. Questions are raised about where the boundary should be drawn and "what counts" as social participation (e.g. Turner 1989; Minkler 1986), but they are still framed in a way that encourages a view of welfare and processes of secondary redistribution as political in the realm of claiming, and distinct from processes of "primary allocation" seen to reside within a distinct economic sphere (see Holmwood 1991).

Arber & Ginn have also suggested that age conflict models fail to take into account the social and economic value of unpaid work (Arber & Ginn 1991). They emphasize the ways in which dependency is a socially constructed and, importantly, gendered, concept. Like Land (1989) they suggest that interdependence is a preferable frame-work for understanding social interaction, although they stress how only certain forms of dependence (those typically associated with women, children and the elderly) entail a loss of power and status, in contrast to other forms of dependence (for example, of men on women, for caring services). I will return to this question of depend-ence and independence, and the division between them, as value-laden concepts, in the final chapter. It is, however, clear that social evaluations of dependence and independence are reflected, and embodied, in the structuring of rewards to different types of labour. The next section considers the relationship between claims to em-ployment and earnings, and domestic divisions of labour, as it is reflected in perceptions of fairness across the life course. Data from my survey are consistent with more general evidence, and suggest that the patterning of inequality over age groups is an aspect of stability in the social structure, rather than its undoing.

Attitudes to dependence, independence and the resourcing of households

Life course structure and claims to employment

The definition of transitions to adult status in terms of the inter-relatedness of claims and obligations has been discussed in detail. This section explores this relationship through empirical evidence concerning obligations in the resourcing of dependence, the attain-ment of independence, and gendered responsibilities in household income maintenance and childcare. While empirical evidence is short on these questions of distributive justice, and much of the literature on age-related conflict has turned more on speculation than on empirical analysis, some questions, relating to transitions from youth to adult status, can be explored through data collected in the Main Survey. In order to locate these questions it is useful to address empirical evidence from other, secondary, sources.

In a study of perceptions of distributive justice in the United States, Jasso & Rossi make a distinction between distribution rules, which refer to "what is", or the current structure of resource allocation, and their legitimacy, or perceptions of "what ought to be". They question whether judgements of justice relate to actual distributions of resources or some Utopian referent. (The relationship between actual distributions and perceptions of distributive justice is an important issue, to which I will return.) In their survey, the authors required respondents to rank, on a scale of over- or under-payment, a series of individuals with various attributes: sex, marital status, number of children, education and occupational level, and earnings, as de-scribed in a series of vignettes. The authors conclude the salience of both need and merit to their respondents' justice evaluations (Jasso & Rossi 1977). In a similar, but larger-scale, survey, Alves & Rossi revise the earlier argument of the existence of a consensus over just distri-bution rules. In the modified argument, need and merit aspects are again demonstrated to underlie evaluations of just earnings, but respondents' own social location influenced their relative importance (Alves & Rossi 1978; cf. Stewart & Blackburn 1975). Higher occupational status groups placed greater emphasis on merit, proposing higher earnings for those with higher qualifications or occupational position, and lower status groups placed greater emphasis on need considerations, proposing more earnings for households with more children (Alves & Rossi 1978). Evidence from my survey suggests that there is a patterning also of attitudes towards claims that relates to respondents' own life course stage. Before looking at this evidence it is of interest to examine the patterning of inequality by household type. Table 6.2 compares the average total income of different types of household (after Rainwater et al. 1986), and Table 6.3 reproduces an analysis by Millar & Glendinning (1987) on the relation between household circumstance and risk of poverty.

The data presented by Rainwater and his colleagues, reproduced in Table 6.2, is aggregated, and it is therefore not possible to distinguish in detail the contributions of different household members, or family life course stage. "No children", for example, includes young couples prior to family formation and older couples in the "empty nest" stage of the family life course. Married couples without children presumably comprise two wage earners, whereas those with children are probably more reliant on male earnings. Rainwater points out that in families with children, husbands contribute a higher proportion of aggregate household income than is the case for couples without children. The median reliance on husbands' earnings for couples with children in Britain is 85%.[27] However, such families still have an average income slightly above the national mean. This pattern reflects not only the particular significance of male earnings to such families but also a structure of earnings that rewards men with dependent children more highly than other groups. This pattern of earnings over household types is reflected also in the data presented in Table 6.3, which demonstrate a similar structure of inequality, with respect to risk of poverty. Married couples without children, in both sets of evidence, are the best placed in respect of household income, followed by couples with children, and lone female parents are the worst placed (Millar & Glendinning 1987).

The patterning of varying needs and claims over the life course is broadly reflected in responses to two questions in my survey where respondents were asked to assess claims to resources by people in different household circumstances. In a question concerning access to

Table 6.2   Inequality by household structure.

Household type	Ratio of mean household income to national mean income
Single men	0.804
Single women	
No children	0.650
Children	0.501
Married couples	
No children	1.123
Children	1.007

Source: Rainwater et al. 1986; estimated from 1973 GHS.

Table 6.3   Extent and risk of poverty by household type, Britain 1983.

	All households %	Poor households %	Risk of poverty (% in each group in poverty)
Pensioners			
Couple	9.7	14.7	42%
Woman	10.9	23.6	61%
Man	2.7	4.9	51%
Non-pensioners			
Single woman	3.9	4.6	33%
Single man	5.1	5.5	30%
Couple, no children	17.2	7.3	12%
Couple, children	28.2	20.7	20%
Lone mother	3.6	7.7	61%
Lone father	0.4	0.6	43%

Poverty is measured as net weekly income minus net housing costs below 140% of ordinary rates of supplementary benefit; Family Expenditure Survey data. After Millar & Glendinning 1987.

employment, respondents prioritized the claims of adults with dependent children over the claims of young single adults without similar obligations. Respondents were asked to imagine that there is a job vacancy for which six different people apply, to assume that they are all equally qualified, and to rank their preferences of who they would most like to get the job. The potential worker "types" were defined in terms of household circumstance. The question, therefore, assumes the legitimacy of need and the salience of circumstances of dependency and obligation in ordering claims to employment, and describes individuals only in terms of domestic

Table 6.4   Ranking of claims to work by individuals in differing household circumstances by respondents to the Main Survey and the Parents' Survey.[28,29,30]

| Individual described in vignette: | Rankings given to vignette individuals | | | |
| | Young adults | | Parents | |
	1st	2nd	1st	2nd
Young single man, living at home	5	5	2	2
Young single man, living away from home	3	5	0	5
Young single woman, living away from home	2	8	0	3
Married man, young, with children, wife not working	48	28	29	4
Married woman, no children at home, husband not working	3	21	0	6
Woman with no husband, young children	33	23	4	13

circumstance. The respondents were asked to rank all six individuals described. The question was designed in part to examine the hypothesis that youth would be more inclined to favour their age peers. Within the confines of a fixed-choice question this was the minority response and most gave priority to those with family obligations. The majority of respondents ranked first either the married man with dependent children or the single mother. Only nine out of 92 young respondents ranked first any of the young single adults as described in the exercise. The incidence of first and second place ranking is shown in Table 6.4.

The lower preference given to young single people in the responses suggests the salience of household obligations to perceptions of the value of differing claims to resources. The low number of respondents prioritizing youth over and above adults with dependent children may in part attach to the voluntary nature of residence in, or departure from, parental homes amongst the majority of respondents. It is clearly "non-standard" household transitions that are the most problematic, transitions that are not well represented in the data, and that might encourage a higher level of preference for young, single adults. Age conflict models posit self-interested claims made on the basis of age, but this sort of age-related identification of interest is not evident in the structure of responses. Their pattern is consistent with the findings of those studies reported above which

Table 6.5 Highest ranking of claims to employment by respondents' own status.[31]

Individual described in vignette:	Respondents to Main Survey			
	Men		Women	
	Dependent	Married	Dependent	Married
Married man	18	12	7	11
Lone mother	18	4	6	5
Youth	4	3	2	0

suggest that perceptions of earnings justice involve judgements about relative need. The ranking, by respondents, of the relative claims to the job by the individuals described in the vignette suggests the significance of social obligations and responsibilities towards dependents in perceptions of distributive justice.

There is some evidence of a relationship between responses and individuals' own household circumstances. Amongst the older generation, of parents to the youth sample, there is a strong majority preference for the married man with a young family. The limited priority for single mothers amongst the older generation is not necessarily evidence of an historical change in preference for positive discrimination for this group, however, since amongst the youth sample those who were themselves cohabiting or married favoured the married man more than the sample as a whole. The division between dependent young adults and those who are independent and cohabiting is strongly associated with the division of preference for the married man and the lone mother, a division that is quite clear-cut amongst the male sample.

Table 6.5 shows the patterning of first preferences for the individuals described by respondents' own household circumstance. "Youth" groups the three young and single individuals described because of the small number of respondents giving them top priority. Where the *relative* ranking of the single mother and the married man are considered, regardless of their relationship to the other individuals described, the ratio of the former to the latter is 18 : 22 amongst dependent men and 4 : 15 amongst family men. Amongst women the equivalent ratios are 6 : 9 and 5 : 11. That is, and especially amongst men, their own life course stage appears to be quite strongly associated with their responses.[32] There is no similar relationship apparent over employment sector or qualification level. This pattern of responses is associated, not directly with age, but with household

status, an important distinction that is often conflated in age stratification theories. For example, 47 male respondents are aged 25 or
below, of whom seven are independent and living with a partner.
While those who are young and single are evenly divided in their
giving priority to the single mother or married man, all seven of those
aged 25 and under who live independently with a partner favour the
married man. The questionnaire did not ask respondents the reasons
for their preferences, although some explicitly stated that "positive
discrimination" lay behind their prioritizing the lone mother. Across
the sample, those who are themselves independent and living with a
partner are more likely to favour the married man over the single
mother. Relatively high levels of need, or anticipated need, characterize the family formation period as households face higher costs, and
the probability of losing much, if not all, female earnings contributions, at least in the early years of childrearing. The significance of
male earnings to family living standards at this stage in the life course
is reflected in the stronger preference by similarly placed respondents
for the "male breadwinner" claim to employment.

The majority of cohabiting men and women, like the parent
sample, prioritize the claims of married men over those of single
mothers. The sample size is very small here, but it is worth noting
that a more substantial minority of young adults favour the claims of
single mothers than do respondents amongst the parental generation.
It is an interesting question whether in later years, in a more affluent
stage of the family life course, members of the younger generation
would reveal a different structure of priorities.

The lower priority given to the claims of young, single adults
deserves comment. Millar & Glendinning's data demonstrate a higher
risk of poverty amongst single adult households than is the case in
families with children or, by extension, the circumstances of young
adults living with their parents. It is clear in the case of married men
with young children that not to give them work would probably drop
their families into poverty. This would not be a standard consequence
in the case of young adults dependent on their parents. Some comments made by respondents in the course of answering the question
indicated an expectation that young adults living away from home
had attained their independence voluntarily. This suggests that the
claims of young men living at home were ranked first more than any
other group without obligations to children, because they were seen
to hold a particular form of personal, as opposed to household,

disadvantage, as might be entailed, for example, in being unemployed and (still, perhaps) dependent on their parents.

The significance of respondents' own life course stage is associated not only with claims to work amongst different groups, but also with stated preferences for organizing family formation decisions around earnings and career opportunities. Respondents were read the following vignette: "John and Maggie are a young married couple, and are both working. Maggie is offered another job that pays less than the one she has now, but it has better prospects. However, they hope to have children over the next few years. What should she do?" Of the 92 young adult respondents 37 replied "She should stay in the old job"; 36 that she should "take advantage of the potential career prospects and delay having children", and 13 that she should "take the new job and quit when she gets pregnant". Amongst the 36 respondents to the Parents' Survey, the corresponding responses were 9, 15 and 8. The other respondents suggested some alternative course of action. Again, amongst the young adult sample, domestic circumstance is strongly associated with the pattern of responses, which are shown in Table 6.6.

The different salience of the question to young adults in different circumstances may be important to the pattern of responses. However, the greater preference for the woman described in the vignette to remain with her old job, amongst cohabiting respondents, appears to reflect the importance of earnings in a period of relative need. A substantial proportion, over one third of the sample of those who are cohabiting, suggest she should take the new job. That a minority advocates delay does not contradict the evidence that contemporary cohorts of young adults are deferring parenthood relative to previous cohorts. Such delay is not necessarily a consciously formulated decision, but rather it is embedded within *contemporary* social relationships. Amongst respondents to the Parents' Survey it is notable

Table 6.6 Preference for career and family decisions, as described in vignette, amongst respondents to the Main Survey.

| Respondents' circumstances: | Preferred solution to problem | | |
	New job and quit	Old job	Delay
Dependent	7	18	30
Married	6	19	6

173

that a higher percentage advocates moving to the new job than staying in the old, and as in the youth sample around half advocate delaying the start of childbearing. This relatively high sympathy to female claims to careers cannot be separated from the older generation's perceptions of better employment opportunities for contemporary cohorts of young women (described in Chapter 4).

To summarize, the evidence presented in this section suggests the significance of life course related circumstances, specifically relations to household resourcing, is reflected in respondents' attitudes towards the relative strengths of employment claims by different groups. Further, the perceived salience of particular needs itself varies in relation to respondents' own household circumstance. In Chapter 2 we saw how some researchers maintain that the attitudes of their respondents are often at odds with their behaviour (Wallace 1987a; Cockburn 1987). Cockburn looked specifically at gender role attitudes and suggested that "liberal" attitudes were taken over by "traditional" employment roles (Cockburn 1987). However, the evidence presented here suggests that people's attitudes are not at odds with their circumstances, so long as the latter are located within a longitudinal, life course perspective.

Claims to independence and the patterning of social obligation

In Chapter 5 a set of interview questions was described, where respondents were asked to describe the attributes of a typical employee in a series of job grades and to indicate the earnings they thought to be typical of each grade. Respondents were also asked whether or not they would choose to reward any job grade more highly (even though it would mean rewarding another one less), or whether they would reward any grades less. Considering here only the lowest grade, that is the ones associated with the youngest employees, the majority of respondents said they would keep the earnings level the same, that is, not reward it more highly at the expense of higher paid jobs further up the career ladder. This result was the same across all companies. Unfortunately, for those men interviewed who are perhaps the worst placed in respect of potential employment chances, on the Community Programme and Special Measures YTS, there was no question on earnings that related directly to their own experience, rather than apprentice-based career routes. In general, such men kept the level of apprentice earnings the same in this exercise. In the other two sectors, women were more inclined to increase the earnings of the lowest job grades than were men. Thirteen women suggested the lowest grade should be paid more highly, while 15 said they would leave it the same; amongst men the respective figures were 8 and 18. There is no clear association of responses with qualification level, employment sector, company or respondents' age, or expectations concerning their own employment circumstance, including promotion, five years hence. Men were less inclined than women to alter the age structure of earnings in their sector. The higher level of dissension amongst female respondents may reflect the lower salience to them of an age-graded earnings profile that is a standard aspect of male white-collar career structures. However, it is worth underlining that the majority of respondents, and over two thirds of male respondents, did not rearrange the age structure of earnings, which were uniformly seen to have an age-graded profile.

Harris, in his discussion of the dependency assumptions built into social security policy, suggests that families now desire and expect young people to have more independence than they did in the past (Harris 1988). Responses to the attitude statements in the survey suggest, however, that while the ability to achieve independence is viewed positively, the expectation of parental obligations to youth is also high. Rites of passage to adulthood are partly structured by the expectation that the underwriting of continued dependence is more a family affair than a public responsibility. The statement "it should be easier than it is for young people to get their own place and live independently" revealed a high and almost identical pattern of agreement amongst parents and youth: 52/69 young adult respondents agreed, 22/28 parents agreed (21/28 young adult children of interviewed parents agreed). However, in response to the statement "young people should be content to stay with their parents until they are earning enough to support themselves financially", the majority also agreed (60/79 young adults; 24/34 parents and 23/34 young adult children of interviewed parents).[33]

Most of the young adults in the survey were either living at home or had left voluntarily. The majority of parents with young adult children at home indicated that the board money they received from their children at most covered costs and was rarely seen as a significant contribution to household resources. Most parents accepted their role in supporting their young adult children as a "natural"

Table 6.7 Attitudes to obligations for household income maintenance.

		Young adults	Parents	Young adults (paired)
A husband works to support his family and a wife works for the extras	disagree	21	11	2
	agree	10	23	10
A husband and wife both need to work to keep up with the cost of living	disagree	12	13	4
	agree	16	19	7
A mother of young children should work if the family needs the money	disagree	7	13	3
	agree	25	19	8

"Paired young adults" refers to respondents to the Main Survey whose parents were interviewed.

thing to do. Again this may in part be a consequence of the relative advantage of those parent–child pairs interviewed, but it is consistent with other evidence, including the experience of many unemployed youth (see Hutson & Jenkins 1989). Both of these examples, where parents support young adults who are working but living at home, and where parents help to carry the costs of unemployment even though they may be poorly placed to do so, suggest that the structural relationship between generations is one of mutuality and not one of conflict.

Another set of cross-generational comparisons reveals interesting differences in attitudes towards gendered divisions of responsibility in household income maintenance. Responses to a series of statements relating to such divisions are shown in Table 6.7. The table includes only independent, cohabiting young adults since the statements may have a different, and abstracted, meaning to youth who are single or living with their parents. The majority of young respondents disagree that "a husband works to support his family and a wife works for the extras". These responses suggest the salience of female earnings to household income maintenance and contrast with the responses of the parental generation. These differences are consistent both with a life course effect and with structural changes through the post-war decades in female contributions to household resourcing. The majority of respondents believe that both partners need to work to keep up with the cost of living. The higher level of disagreement that "a wife works for the extras" suggests that more respondents see a woman's wages as significant to maintaining lifestyles than necessarily to "getting by" as implied by the cost of living statement. The similarity of responses over the generations with respect to employment and the cost of living, and the generational difference in responses to the statement concerning whether or not a wife works for extras is consistent with a life course interpretation. "Extras" amongst the older generation may contribute to the ability to sustain a particular lifestyle. Young adults, most of whom are in, or entering, the family-building stage, are likely to interpret female financial contributions as more basic to household resourcing than to describe them as "extras". The structure of responses is suggestive of the greater value to young adults of female contributions to household income maintenance.

The available empirical evidence points to the significance of both life course and period effects in structuring attitudes. There is no evidence, however, that standard processes place different age groups or generations in an antagonistic relationship to one another, or that age-related claims engender conflict. Relationships over the life course and between age groups and generations are essential to explanations of structures of inequality, but the organization of such relationships is not a precursor to crisis, rather it is an aspect of a coherent social structure.

Summary

This chapter has described some of the processes that give coherence to the relationships between age groups and generations. These processes point to problems that ensue from supposing that the relationship between those in paid work and those who are not so employed is one of structural antagonism. One such problem that is embedded within age stratification and conflict approaches is the conceptual distinction between claims amongst different age groups, or between the claims of work and "welfare" groups. It is as if thought becomes trapped in the particularity of the experience of different social groups.[34]

The organization of social claims is central to understanding the mutuality of relationships between "dependency" groups and those in paid employment. For example, the claims of children and dependent youth cannot be separated from the high rewards of adult men relative to other groups of workers, nor from gendered inequalities in rewards to employment and ensuing patterns of inequality in old age. The extent to which financial rewards are structured in relation to economic and social obligations, as these are standardly carried by certain groups, underlies the material problems that characterize the experience of "non-standard" circumstances, for example amongst lone mothers and their children, and amongst dependent youth with unemployed parents. Either way the structuring of rewards to different groups is inseparable from the relationships through which these groups are linked in the resourcing of individual and household reproduction.

The stability of "horizontal" inequality, that is intra-class inequalities over the life course and across different household structures, is reflected in perceptions of distributive justice. The empirical evidence on attitudes to this inequality suggests that people perceive it to be just, partly because it reflects differing levels of need over the life course. Most respondents prioritized the claim to work amongst individuals with dependents over the claims of individuals without similar obligations. The majority of young adults preferred not to rearrange the age hierarchy of earnings in their employment sector. These responses suggest that a profile of earnings graded in relation to age and domestic responsibilities is seen as a legitimate ordering of claims to economic resources. Evaluations of claims amongst different age groups appear, then, to incorporate understandings of horizontal equity, where some continuity in living standards is seen as appropriate, yet where the burden of household income maintenance is spread unevenly over the life course. These evaluative judgements are made in relation to a structure that rewards certain groups more highly and regards others as, at least partially, dependent. In this sense fairness judgements, or evaluations of claims, are structured in relation to "what is", to an actual rather than a Utopian referent (cf. Stewart & Blackburn 1975; Alves & Rossi 1978). Age-related inequalities cohere with expectations of varying economic obligations over the life course. Changes in the structure of inequalities between age groups are seen in age-stratification and age-conflict models to engender a restructuring of social claims. These claims are simultaneously assumed to result in conflict between different welfare groups or between welfare groups and the working population. However, the claims of "dependency" groups are not separable from the experience of, and rewards to, those who are active in paid employment. Perceptions of fairness reflect the stability of these processes, and the coherence of age-related processes and social structure.

Stability, however, is of course commensurate with social change. The reorganization of life course processes, as we have seen, reflects changes in the relative position of different groups in the resourcing of social reproduction. In this way, the processes shaping "horizontal" inequality and "vertical" inequality are not distinct. For example, the incidence of economic vulnerability, such as unemployment amongst youth and amongst workers approaching retirement, and amongst single mothers, has significant implications for general structures of inequality. The undermining of claims by youth to an adult wage, and to independence at early ages, may exacerbate the risks of poverty amongst those who are poorly placed to make claims on other family members. The convergence of life course related vulnerability with economic insecurity and recessionary and structural economic change may result in some groups being permanently disadvantaged relative to others. Location with respect to the organization of social reproduction, then, is of central importance in the distribution of risks of poverty, and in the structuring of inequality. Change in the ways in which reproduction is organized, and the position of different groups in relation to these processes, is essential for understanding the organization of inequality. Proponents of the age stratification framework claim to challenge economically based stratification theories by pointing to their partiality, specifically their failure to take on issues of inequality outside the "economic" sphere. However, a more convincing challenge to stratification theory lies in recognizing the ways in which age- and gender-related processes hold general importance in the structuring and reproduction of socio-economic inequality.

Chapter 7

Conclusion

The transition from the partial dependence of youth to the independence associated with adult status is both a stage in the life course of individuals and an aspect of the general social arrangements through which dependence and independence are resourced. This book has offered an analysis of recent developments in the organization and experience of the transition from youth to adulthood in relation to general changes in the structure of employment and of households. The mutuality of arrangements in employment and in the family reflects the structure of claims and obligations through which people resource their everyday lives. There have been significant changes over recent decades in the location of different groups with respect to these claims and obligations. It has been argued that the associated processes have given rise to changes in the contours of transitions from youth to adult status. I suggested earlier that it may be appropriate to describe the transition from youth to adulthood as having a moral character. This is because the organization of social reproduction embodies evaluations of the social worth of different groups, different circumstances and different activities. I will say more about this shortly, but first it is appropriate to review the main arguments and consider their implications for understanding life course processes and social structure.

Transition has been treated as labelling individual life course trajectories through the partial dependence of youth to the independence associated with adult status. A series of significant life course events have been considered as valuable in describing the transition from youth to adult status, specifically leaving the parental home, forming an independent household, cohabitation, marriage and parenthood. Many writers, as we have seen, have addressed the relation between the timing of these domestic life course events and labour force circumstance, with a view to responding to the hypothesis that recent economic retrenchment and the decline in employment opportunities and rewards to young people have undermined the resource basis through which earlier generations of youth secured independence and adult status. Research in the area has furnished detailed insights into the experience of recent cohorts of youth and young adults, but it has been less successful in elucidating the processes giving rise to change in the shape of transitions from youth to adult status. The difficulties have been acknowledged by a number of those writing in the area, in the complaint that research has not fully located youth and transition in their social context. It seems that this problem has arisen for two related reasons, one to do with the emphasis on the developments of the 1980s, the other to do with the tendency to prioritize life course stages over the relations through which they derive shape and meaning.

In respect of the first reason, the stress on the 1980s has foreshortened the sorts of questions that can be asked about processes underlying change in transitions from youth to adulthood. The very high levels of youth unemployment, the extension of youth training programmes, most notably the YTS, and changes in social benefits that gave youth fewer claims against the state were amongst developments that led many writers to suggest that the period was something of an historical turning point in the fortunes of youth. However, definitions of youth as an age group, and the methodological focus of qualitative research set up to explore the domestic, life course consequences of economic restructuring, gave rise to difficulties in locating transitions from youth to adulthood as an aspect of more general, and longer-term, changes in life course and employment structure.

The second, and related, reason for difficulty in elucidating structural change in the organization and experience of transitions from youth to adulthood relates to the definition of the statuses that transition is supposed to bridge. Conventional approaches have treated the partial dependence of youth and the independence associated with adulthood as distinct statuses. In such approaches independence is seen to be secured through direct access to earnings from employment and, in consequence, the transition to adult status becomes an issue of access and constraint in the securing of "adult" rights and responsibilities. However, dependence and independence are not independent categories. Both indicate sets of claims and obligations present in the conduct of social life and articulated through the structure of rewards to employment and people's differing relations to household resourcing. Independence, as it is achieved by young adults, signals a progression through an employment structure in which a form of family wage system is operating, and where earnings careers, of both women and men, are patterned in relation to the accumulation of financial and caring obligations towards those without direct access to a wage. It is for this reason that the question of the impact of employment restructuring *on* particular life course transitions is less straightforward than it might at first appear, because the statuses that transition is seen to bridge are already implicated in the employment structure, that is in patterns of demand for, and structures of rewards to, different labour force groups. As we have seen, the composition and relative position of such groups are not constant. Long-term changes in the organization of household and family structure, and changes in the contributions of different members to the resourcing of households, are essential to understanding change in the shape and substance of life course trajectories. In conjunction, changing relations to household resourcing cannot be separated from changes in the structure of employment. Treating employment as a form of social, rather than individual, provisioning, enables a combined analysis of change in its reward structure and change in the relations between different social groups.

These processes are essential to understanding contemporary transitions from youth to adulthood. The reversal of long-term trends to younger ages at marriage and parenthood from the early 1970s, after which successive cohorts of young adults have manifested a pattern of deferral in the timing of family formation, coincided with changes in the gender- and age-related structure of earnings in employment. From the early 1970s the earnings of young women have improved relative to the earnings of young men, and the earnings of the latter have declined relative to the average earnings of men in the highest earning age group. The analysis of demographic and economic evidence over the longer term suggests that the economic and political developments of the 1980s were not quite such a radical shift in the circumstances of youth and young adults as conventionally suggested, since the claims of young people to independence and adult lifestyles at an early age were already being undermined by general processes.

There are two principal, and linked, ways in which these processes have underlain change in the transition from youth to adulthood. First, over this century there has been an increase in the affluence of families with children approaching adult status that has been increasingly independent of the material contributions of the latter. The increasing importance of paid employment amongst women through the post-war decades is integral to changes in gendered and generational divisions of labour in household resourcing. There is a sense, then, in which young adults in such family circumstances can "afford" not only to stay in full-time education to older ages, but also to take relatively low paying jobs. Secondly, the available evidence suggests that the general patterns of delay in household and family formation by young couples are, in part, a consequence of the increased importance of the earnings of young women, relative to those of young men, in resourcing new households and becoming parents at a standard of living commensurate with orientations towards general, societal, levels of consumption.

The improvement in the earnings of young women relative to young men deserves emphasis since it would seem to contradict the convention that there has been continuity in the level of gender earnings inequalities. It seems that such statements follow from consideration of aggregate level earnings data. However, since female-to-male earnings ratios are improving amongst successive age cohorts, a comparison of gender-related earnings inequality amongst all working-age people will underestimate the magnitude of such change. The analyses presented in this study indicate that patterns of delay in family formation are bound up with changes in gender-related inequalities. However, the decline in the earnings of young, relative to older, men suggests that change in gender-related earnings inequality has as much to do with a decline in the relative sufficiency of male earnings as with a "levelling up" of female earnings. This seems hardly surprising. If male earnings are predicated on some version of a breadwinner wage, where men are rewarded in relation to the claims of those who are at least partly financially dependent, then we might expect that the achievement by women of greater earnings would be matched by a decline in the relative worth of "breadwinner" earnings. The growth in the earnings of young women relative to young men corresponds with other evidence of an increase in co-dependence between spouses in the financial resourcing of new households and young families. These developments indicate significant changes in the relation of women and men to household resourcing and paid employment. Further, the compression of the childbearing period, the increasing speed with which women return to work after childbirth, and the increase in employment participation by women over their lifetimes suggests a female family-related life course structure that is becoming more similar to that which has held only for men.

In contrast to those who maintain that changes in gender-related inequality are merely an aspect of longer-term historical continuities, other writers are forthright in claiming the significance of a recent historical transition in the structure of social conduct. Beck, for example, suggests that women are increasingly achieving freedom from the ties of the family, as a consequence of the extension of capital and "full" market relations in the realm of employment. In this argument the family wage, and hence the family itself, appears to be undermined as capital constructs all adults as workers. According to Beck, as people become less constrained by traditional social forms, particularly the family, so they are increasingly free to "make" their own biographies (Beck 1992; and cf. Chisholm & du Bois Reymond 1993). However, it is not clear why, over the period in which capital is supposed to have constructed all adults as workers, it has also presided over the exclusion of children, the elderly and, increasingly now, youth from paid employment.

The argument of a transformation in the nature of social action is paralleled in recent debates about the declining salience of traditional class distinctions for describing the structure of social inequality or contributing effectively to an analysis of social action (e.g. Turner 1988; Pahl 1989). These writers call into question the "productionist bias" of conventional analyses of class and inequality, which take people's relations to the productive sphere, and most typically occupation, as a principal indicator of class position. They maintain that such analyses are increasingly irrelevant, failing as they do to elucidate the cultural and political underpinnings of inequality. In such arguments, status is seen to have become more salient as a concept for analyzing contemporary capitalist society since, for example, gender, age and consumer groups are seen to better describe the structure of social inequality and the social divisions around which people organize and act than do "traditional" social class distinctions.

While the emphasis on gender- and age-related processes by mainstream sociological theorists is to be welcomed, the movement away from the "traditional" concerns of class and employment inequality is unfortunate. Gender- and age-related processes pose an important challenge to production based theories of inequality. However, those who stress the importance of age-related processes for understanding new dimensions of social cleavage and conflict tend to treat these issues as operating independently of the productive "sphere". I have argued that this distinction misrepresents the relationship between life course processes and social change. I will say more about this shortly, but first it is pertinent to recall those critiques of "the conventional view" of class and stratification by a number of gender theorists. These writers challenge the particularity of production-based theories of class but, rather than leave intact the premises of the latter, they argue that the project of mapping out and explaining class-related inequality and its reproduction needs to be rethought in the light of gender processes. There are important parallels to be drawn here in considering life course related issues. However, it is important that gender, and particular life course stages, should not be taken as primary categories.

Some gender theorists, then, argue that gender inequalities present an important challenge to stratification theory (e.g. Garnsey 1982; Stanworth 1984). In such arguments, the employment structure is not to be treated as the baseline for mapping out the structure of inequality, as in the "conventional view" (e.g. Goldthorpe 1983; Erikson & Goldthorpe 1992). This is because the latter treats as secondary the circumstances of the large part of the population that is not engaged in paid employment, or that supposedly holds a tangential relation to paid employment and hence to the class structure. Further, the conventional view neglects the way in which the marginality of certain groups with respect to employment is itself important in shaping the structure of employment. The structure of social reproduction, and the associated domestic division of labour, through which men are constructed as principal earners and women as secondary earners, means that men and women can be hired at different wage levels. This variation in labour costs influences the structure of occupations and the nature of change in the employment structure (e.g. Garnsey 1982). That is, the structure of occupations and employment inequality is not given by "economic" processes but is shaped also in relation to social divisions.

It has been an argument of this book that such divisions are a central aspect of employment inequalities. However, the category gender, like the category youth, does not provide a sufficiently detailed description of the salient social divisions as these relate to employment processes. This becomes clear when we consider that gender and life course related inequalities are themselves subject to change. A more general and inclusive description of differences across groups is to be drawn from the processes that give rise to such differences. Change in household and family structure, and changes in domestic divisions of labour between women and men, and across generations, have altered these groups' relations to one another in the resourcing of everyday life, and have changed their identities in important ways. These relational changes are inseparable from change in the structure of rewards to employment and in the structure of households and people's differing relations to household resourcing.

The distinctions between life course and employment processes are drawn both by "conventional" class theorists and by those who maintain a new salience of status distinctions in the structuring of social inequality and social action. We have seen how, amongst social class theorists, there is a tendency to treat life course processes, like gender, as incidental to their main task of elucidating the structure and reproduction of employment-based inequality. However, like gender-related processes, and overlapping with them, life course processes are basic to understanding the organization of employment inequality, and the nature of employment restructuring. Furthermore, it is not simply that the availability of labour for different costs influences the ways in which employment, and hence class-related, inequalities change. The analysis of earnings data, and divisions of labour in household resourcing, illustrates changes in the respective social positioning, and costs, of different labour force groups. Variation in claims and obligations that are reflected in the life course structure, then, are not incidental to employment processes, but integral to them. This coherence of employment and family-related processes has been described through an analysis of aggregate level changes, specifically change in the timing of family formation by successive cohorts of young people, and its relation to change in the structure of rewards in employment. It has been addressed too, in relation to survey respondents' descriptions of their own experience and expectations, and their perceptions of distributive justice. The first of these analyses has a direct bearing on the issue of occupation as an adequate indicator of class location, or the problems that arise from treating life course processes as incidental to the class structure in relation to individual careers. The second analysis bears on the problems that arise from treating status (age and gender) related distinctions as independent from the employment structure.

Much literature on class-related patterns of life course event timing amongst young people shares the assumption that current occupational position serves as a satisfactory indicator of class location. Class-related differences in the ages at which people attain independence from the parental home, set up a household and establish a family are explained in terms of class-related differences in orientations and expectations. The "logical" relationship between lifetime earnings profiles and the timing of family formation can only be explained in terms of individuals' expectations for the future. However, the nature of such expectations is often deduced from current social class position, which is in turn deduced from current occupation. In analysis of the survey data an index of orientations to future earnings was derived from a consideration of the circumstances of salient reference groups, as perceived by respondents. The analysis explored variation in social circumstance amongst respondents by using the index of their perceptions of the "normal" circumstances in which to marry as an aspect of their current social location, rather than merely "modelling" their orientations on their current social class location. The index proved more effective in differentiating patterns of event timing amongst respondents than did a straight, cross-sectional, occupation-based measure, and provided a useful framework for exploring their experience of, and attitudes towards, the timing of marriage and family formation.

The issue of the relation between orientations and material circumstance has a bearing on research into the consequences of unemployment for the timing of household and family formation amongst young adults: whether people "drift into" parenthood regardless, or whether people delay as a consequence of new forms of disadvantage. Unemployment could presumably encourage a deferral in the timing of family formation for those who would plan it in relation to their orientations towards adequate living standards. Similarly, unemployment could undermine the salience of any such orientations to the future. It seems implausible that there would be any single consequence of unemployment on the timing of independence from the parental home, or the timing of family formation. Any comprehensive elucidation of the relationship between the timing of such transitions and the experience of unemployment would have to locate developments in relation to the general patterns of deferral in family formation that have obtained since the mid 1970s. It is by their relations to general social arrangements that the circumstance of particular groups can be understood.

Life course processes then, in terms of lifetime careers and prospects, need to be considered in descriptions of current occupational position. This too has an important bearing on statements concerning the reproduction of class inequality across generations. While it is common to characterize lifetime occupational movement in terms of class mobility, many class-related career trajectories standardly move people across different occupational categories. The characterization of such movement as "class mobility" signals how standard class measurements obscure the importance of life course trajectories in shaping the structure of resource distribution across the population.

The shaping of employment structure in relation to life course related claims and obligations is important too, in reconsidering theories of new forms of status conflict. The age conflict theorists, who envisage significant societal changes as a consequence of changes in the age profile of wellbeing, set up welfare claims as problematic, in contrast to the organization of rewards to employment, which are effectively taken as given. It is clear, however, that this organization of rewards itself reflects a structure of claims and obligations in the reproduction of social life. The extent to which "welfare" claims are embedded within the employment structure was reflected in survey respondents' attitudes towards distributive justice, in terms of who should get and do what, as their obligations and claims vary with life course circumstance. Not only did the content of responses to a range of attitudinal questions suggest the importance of such considerations in respondents' judgements about entitlement, but the structure of responses too indicated an important life course dimension in the ordering of perceptions of social justice. I have argued that the coherence of family and employment-based claims and obligations is consistent with, and reflected by, respondents' judgements on distributive justice. Perceptions of justice are framed in relation to the current structure of resource distribution, and the patterning of such perceptions illustrates how people are differently located with respect to this structure.

In tracing the mutuality of "productive" and "reproductive" processes I have stressed the importance of the social organization of dependence and obligation. The latter term has been a device for exploring the social construction of "independence", challenging its taken-for-granted nature as a consequence of employment security. Dependence and independence, or obligation, refer to different circumstances in the resourcing and organization of social reproduction. They simultaneously provide a framework for exploring employment inequalities as *social* processes. Some writers, however, maintain that dependence and independence are value-laden concepts, and prefer to replace them with a theory, and terminology, of interdependence (Land 1989; Arber & Ginn 1991). This preference is part of an attempt to foreground the social and economic value of unpaid, particularly domestic, labour. While my own terminology, of the interaction of dependence and obligation, is a little clumsy, the more "streamlined" concept of interdependence would not necessarily add anything to the analysis, and risks taking away something valuable. In part, the objective of its proponents is no different from my own, where the concern is to explore the social construction of differing forms of obligation and dependence, and the ways in which their organization reflects the social nature of all human activity. However, it is important to retain dependence and obligation as distinct concepts, while acknowledging that both refer to financial and care-related resources, precisely because through them it is possible to articulate broader social evaluations of the worth of different activities. That some work is paid, and other work is unpaid, could not provide a clearer reflection of such evaluations. To speak of interdependence then is appropriate at one level, but as a general concept it is not detailed enough to elucidate the ways in which social activities are evaluated. It is important to maintain distinctions that are fine enough to reflect the complexity of evaluations of different activities, to elucidate the arrangements by which different social values and the activities of different groups are associated, and to analyze the processes underlying continuity and change in such arrangements.

As we have seen, standard arrangements place groups differently in the resourcing of their daily livelihoods. Some are dependent on other family members, or on the state, for maintaining themselves; others have "independent" access to earnings from employment, as these are patterned in relation to claims for resourcing dependents.

There is, however, no straightforward relationship between dependence and disadvantage, or between independence and advantage. In assessing particular arguments for a more equitable distribution of social resources and opportunities it is useful to distinguish between two different aspects of inequality, although they are closely related, one shaped by the other. The distinction I wish to draw is between inequality and poverty as a consequence of non-standard circumstances, which place people at a particular disadvantage, and inequality as implicit within the arrangements by which social reproduction is organized. The former might be seen as a particular instance of the latter, that is, standard arrangements place particular groups at risk of poverty, and at risk of social exclusion. Examples of the former, non-standard circumstances, are unemployment, and single parenthood. Examples of the latter can be seen in claims that counter standard arrangements, such as arguments for resources sufficient to support independent living amongst young people. Youth research has been conducted in relation to the latter, particularly in its arguments of an undermining of "traditional" claims by youth to independence and employment security. However, the methodological focus of much youth research has been with the former, that is with youth in particular, and often problematic circumstances. In short, it has failed to locate its arguments in relation to general processes of change in the arrangements by which youth, and transitions to adult status, are reproduced.

I have been concerned with changes in the social processes through which the transition from youth to adult status is organized. Any concern with the claims of young people must be placed against an understanding of such processes. That over the long term many households are better placed to support their dependent young adult children clearly means that those that are not so placed face particular problems, especially where government policies are encouraging greater "privatization" in the resourcing of material dependence. Any claims by, or on behalf of, young people, or other groups without independent access to material resources, are claims against the relations of dependence and obligation through which social reproduction is organized. Potentially, then, such claims would be part of a more general challenge to the practices, beliefs and policies that place particular groups at risk of, or in, poverty, and at the margins of society. The circumstances of such groups speak about the broader social morality.

Appendix 1

The survey context: Scotland and England compared; YTS and the employers

The survey was conducted in Scotland. Interviews with young adults in the insurance and retailing sectors were conducted in Edinburgh. Young people in the construction industry were interviewed in Edinburgh and Glasgow. Most respondents to the Parents' Survey lived in Edinburgh, or in other parts of Lothian. Those living further afield were sent postal questionnaires. Because of the importance attached throughout the analysis to locating the data in relation to more general evidence, the Scottish base of the sample need not compromise the salience of the evidence to understanding patterns of transition across Britain more generally. Edinburgh itself is probably closer to the socio-economic make-up of parts of England than it is to the rest of Scotland. Further, it may be no more appropriate to point to the particularity of a Scottish base of the survey than to question the national representativeness of any regional or local base for empirical research. With respect to national differences in youth employment opportunities between Scotland and England and Wales, it appears that the similarities outweigh the differences (Raffe & Courtenay 1988). The evidence indicates that the occupational and industrial structures across Scotland and England and Wales are broadly alike, and have very similar labour markets (Raffe & Courtenay 1988).

There are two key areas of contrast between Scotland and England identified by Raffe & Courtenay. First, there is a more staggered entry into the labour force amongst youth cohorts in Scotland, in contrast to the more clearly defined transitions at ages 16 and 18 in England and Wales, the latter associated with the completion of "A" level courses. In contrast, the Scottish students who stay beyond the minimum school-leaving age standardly sit the Higher grade of the Scottish Certificate of Education. Highers are usually taken over one year of study although the flexibility of the system means that a number of Highers are often spread over a two-year period. For this reason, along with school-leaving arrangements which differ to those in England and Wales, the age 17 is a more significant transition stage in Scotland (Raffe & Courtenay 1988). The second key difference is described by Raffe & Courtenay as the weaker labour market in Scotland. Data comparing the Scottish Young People's Surveys of 1985 and 1986 to the England and Wales Youth Cohort Study indicate that two years after the minimum school leaving age, by April 1986, rates of employment stood at 61% in Scotland and at 72% in England and Wales. Where YTS trainees were excluded from the analysis the rates stood at 68% and 76% respectively (Raffe & Courtenay 1988).

The YTS was slightly more extensive in Scotland where, of the year group who were eligible to leave school in 1984, 42% had entered YTS by 1986 compared with 37% of their English and Welsh peers. A demand for young male employees which is more depressed than that for young females is mirrored in YTS participation rates of 39% and 46% amongst girls and boys respectively in Scotland, and of 35% and 39% respectively amongst girls and boys in England and Wales. Trainees in Scotland had more difficulty entering employment at the end of their schemes. Of those on YTS in April 1985, one year subsequently 56% in Scotland were in full-time jobs compared with 65% in England and Wales. Amongst males the respective percentages were 57% and 67%, and amongst females, 56% and 63%. By April 1986, 49% of full-time employees in the surveys had been on YTS (Raffe & Courtenay 1988).

YTS was always principally an employer-based scheme, where trainees were provided with work experience and on-the-job training, and a 13-week component of off-the-job training. Such (Mode A) schemes, organized by managing agents (employers or groups of employers), operated between 1983 and 1986 and were complemented by Mode B schemes, which ran as community projects, training workshops or information technology centres, where employer-based schemes could not provide sufficient training places. When YTS was extended to a two-year scheme in 1986 there was an attempt to tackle what had become a two-tier system, with the most disadvantaged youngsters concentrated in the Mode B schemes. New funding arrangements meant that extra funding would be available for those trainees with particular needs, but within a uniform system of provision. Because of the employer-based nature of the scheme it does not seem surprising that YTS reproduced prior patterns of entry into employment, whether these followed patterns of gender segregation across occupations, or whether post-YTS employment chances were patterned in relation to prior educational qualifications.

The three employment sectors in which the Main Survey was conducted held differing relationships to YTS. In summary, construction and insurance industries are characterized by an extensive period of training, structured around standard career routes within the sectors. Retailing is characterized by a low level of training, with requisite skills for performing job tasks learned quickly, and by high levels of turnover and temporary employment. Construction and retailing sectors were both very important YTS participants, while large insurance firms made limited use of YTS. The sectors therefore covered a diverse set of training practices. Construction and insurance observed high levels of skills training and high and low participation in YTS respectively. Retailing observed low levels of skills training and high participation in YTS. It is suggested that the form of linkage of YTS to these sectors is dependent upon their longer-term recruitment and promotion strategies, and their respective employment structures. Both the construction and the insurance sectors have long periods of training involved in career routes that are available to a significant proportion of workers who remain employed in the sector.

Clearly there is a great deal of variation in the level of promotion achieved in insurance, especially across male and female employees. However, promotion within internal labour markets is a standard (though not uniform) employment route for those with continuous participation. YTS was not avoided by insurance companies, but nor was it taken up extensively, and interviews with employers revealed their ambivalence towards its value. Reasons for lack of participation were explained by different employers in terms of levels of qualifications required for entry, set by some companies at five "O" grades or above, by the burden of administration required by running YTS, by the desire to offer "real career jobs", and because of the low pay associated with YTS. Reasons given for discontinued participation, a feature of one of the companies in the sample, related to its administrative burden, the desire to avoid pressure to recruit trainees, and dissatisfaction with the trainees' ability. This pattern of temporary participation characterized a number of the companies visited. YTS trainees could not normally progress to take Chartered Institute exams, which require a minimum of five "O" grades. While not explicitly raised by employers, the structure of a one- and subsequently two-year training scheme may not sit easily with existing training practice and promotion policies within the insurance sector. The frequent reference to the heavy administrative load associated with running YTS suggests that it could not be incorporated within existing practices to employers' satisfaction.

In the building industry completion of a time-served apprenticeship is a prerequisite to attaining skilled craft status. Approximately 90% of apprentice starts achieve full craft status (Construction Industry Training Board (CITB), in discussion). YTS was taken up by CITB to augment their apprenticeship training programme. Immediately prior to YTS the apprenticeship period stood at three years' duration. When the survey was undertaken, training for craft status began with one year YTS which fed into a three-year apprenticeship in Scotland and a two-and-a-half-year apprenticeship in England. In Britain 60–70% of apprentices then came through the YTS route (CITB, in discussion). The ability to fit YTS within the apprenticeship system also met a desire by the CITB and building employers to lengthen the apprenticeship period (CITB and employers, in discussion). None of the building workers interviewed in the survey were self-employed, but the significance, and recent growth, of labour only subcontracting on the structure of the industry has been an area of some concern, particularly in industry specific research on labour force segmentation (e.g. Winch 1986; Moore 1981; Bresnen et al. 1985. See also Austrin 1980).

In the retailing sector the proportion of young to older employees has fallen dramatically. Under-18s employed in the sector declined as a percentage of total retail trade employment from 10–5% between 1961 and 1981. This change is partly accounted for by the raising of the school-leaving age in 1972. Retailing is still an extremely important employer of young people, with over 20% of school-leavers entering the distributive trades in 1983 (26% of girls and 18% of boys; figures from Distributive Trades EDC 1985). Turnover in the sector is very high with interviewed employers commonly reporting annual rates of 30–40%. Moves out of the sector by young people are as typical an employment route as internal career progression. Around 10% of the total British workforce is employed in the retail sector, compared to around 20% of school leavers. Of the former, 55% of employees are part-time (Distributive Trades EDC 1985, figures for 1984) and unlikely to be attached to career routes. It is suggested that the ease of attaching YTS as a training programme within existing recruitment criteria (16 year-old entry and limited school qualification requirements) and existing employment structures underlay the breadth of its take up in the retail sector.

The relation of YTS to the employment structures of these sectors illustrates the sorts of continuities we might expect, in respect of both their take up of YTS, and in respect of the labour force careers of YTS participants. The extension of YTS through the 1980s was part of the changing structure of youth employment opportunities and rewards, and it was to an understanding of these more general developments that the questionnaire survey was directed.

Within the three employment sectors the sample of organizations in which employees were interviewed turned simply on access. I interviewed senior management personnel about their company's employment structure, recruitment and training programmes in several companies across the three sectors. After detailed discussion of my research design a number of organizations agreed to allow me to interview a number of their employees. In most of the survey organizations potential respondents were identified and approached by a manager with whom I had discussed the criteria for selecting a sample of respondents. The principal criterion was to organize a sample that covered a variety of occupational grades, ages and domestic circumstances, "up to" those who had recently become parents, but including also older, single or childless respondents. In two companies I was permitted to identify the sample of respondents directly. In one of the insurance companies I was provided with an anonymized list of employees that identified their occupational grade, age, sex and marital status, and interviews were scheduled with the sample I identified. In the supermarket I was permitted to approach staff directly, through department managers. In all organizations I was provided with a private room in which to conduct interviews. Current workloads on staff appeared to be the main criterion by which respondents were "filtered" in the other organizations. However, the level of access granted allowed me to interview a range of respondents that appears representative of the available spectrum of employee "types" within the organizations.

Appendix 2

Questionnaires

Appendix 2a: Youth and adulthood:
a survey of young adults in employment and training

Section 1

1. What is your current job/training scheme title?
2. Please describe the work that you do.

I'd like to ask you now about educational qualifications. Could you tell me first:

3. When did you leave school? (month and year).
4. What qualifications did you get at school?
   (a) No qualifications
   (b) SCOTVEC National Certificate (modules)
   (c) SCOTEC/SCOTBEC Certificate
   (d) SNC, ONC or equivalent
   (e) SCE "O" grades or GCE "O" levels
   (f) CSEs
   (g) SCE Highers
   (h) Certificate of Sixth Year Studies (CSYS)
   (i) GCE "A" levels
5. Have you ever started any courses after leaving school?
6. Please describe these.
7. Have you obtained any qualifications since leaving school?
   (a) City and Guilds
   (b) YTS Certificate

(c) SCOTVEC modules

(d) Other qualifications (describe)

8. What is your date of birth?

Section 2

I am interested in your experience of work and training from when you left school to the present. You said you left school in . . . , can you tell me what training schemes and jobs you have done since then, and the pay that you received in each one? Say if there were any periods when you were unemployed. I would also like you to tell me the dates that you were doing each of these things.

So, starting with when you left school, when did you start your first training scheme, job or apprenticeship? (*Establish if unemployed before that. Record labour force history to present day*)

9. Do you work any overtime? How much? Why?

10. Do you get any company perks? (*Describe*)

11. Do you do any other paid work?

Now, I would like you to think over the period since you left school again, and tell me about your household circumstances during this time, and if and how they have changed. I want you to tell me about whether you have ever moved where you live, if you are engaged or in a steady relationship, or if you have ever married or had a child. Starting off with when you left school:

– Where were you living then? (*If not with parents, establish background and situation*)

– Who else was living in the house at the time?

– Did your parents own the house or rent it?

IF RENTED

– Did they rent it from the council or was it private rented?

– Have you ever left your parents home?

(*Domestic histories recorded alongside labour force histories*)

IF IN FIRST JOB OR TRAINING SCHEME

12. How did you hear about your present training scheme/job?

(a) Careers office

(b) School careers officer

(c) Advertisement

(d) Applied direct

(e) Job Centre

(f) Told about it by relative or friend

ALL

13. Why did you decide to do this particular scheme/job/work in ... (sector)?

14. Did you have any alternatives? (Please describe these)

I would like you to think back to when you started on YTS/your first job after leaving school. (*If YTS and job ask about both, in sequence*)

15. Did you feel any different about yourself after you started your first scheme/job? (*Both if relevant*)
    In what ways?

16. (a) Did you feel that people treated you any differently after you started your scheme/apprenticeship/working? (e.g. parents, friends, adults in general). (*Scheme and work if relevant*)

    (b) Did your social life or your personal circumstances change in any way after you started your scheme/apprenticeship/first full-time job?

Section 3

IF STILL SINGLE/NOT LIVING WITH PARTNER/LIVING IN PARENTAL HOME

If living with parents

17. Do you pay any money for your food and keep?

18. (a) How much do you pay?

    (b) Do you help out with other things at home, e.g. looking after anybody?

All

I would like now to talk about your ideas on marriage and having children.

19. First, could you tell me if you think you will marry at some stage? (*If no, ask why not*)

20. How old do you think you will be when you do get married?

21. Why then? (*Probe with: what sorts of things do you think are important in deciding when to get married?*)

Now, thinking about children:

22. Could you tell me if you expect that you will have children at some stage? (*If no, ask why not*)

23. How old do you think you will be when your first child is born?

24. Why then? (*Probe with: what sorts of things do you think are important in deciding when to have children?*)
25. Are you currently engaged or going steady with someone?

If engaged

26. Is your fiancé(e) working?
27. (a) What does s/he do?
    (b) What are his/her earnings?
28. Do you think that your (joint) income has affected, or will affect, your decision about when to marry?

IF MARRIED/LIVING WITH A PARTNER/DIVORCED

29. Why did you marry/move in together when you did?
30. (a) Have you had any children?
    (b) How many?

If has child/ren

31. Did you plan when to start having children?

If planned

32. Why did you have your first child when you did?
33. Would you say that you were financially prepared for having a child at that point? (*Detail*)

If did not plan

34. Did having a child then make things difficult for you?
    IF YES: In what ways?
    IF NO: Did you have to adapt your lifestyle in terms of work, housing or organizing your finances in any way?
35. How many children do you expect to have?

If living with a partner, not married

36. Do you have any plans to get married?

If plans to marry

37. When do you think that will be?
38. Why then?

If has no plans to marry

39. Could you say why not?

If has not had children

40. Do you expect to have children at some stage? (*If no, ask why not*)
41. What age do you think you will be when you have your first child?
42. Why then?
43. How many children do you expect to have?

44. Is your husband/wife/partner working?

If partner working

45. What job does he/she do? (*Detail*)
46. What is his/her pay? (*Ask if its full- or part-time*)
47. (a) If he/she were not earning do you think you would look for a different job? Why?
    (b) Did your social life change in any way after you got married/moved in together?

ALL

Thinking now about your work and the future, could you tell me:

48. What do you expect to be doing in five years' time?
    (*Record expectations on*)
    (a) Work/position/pay?
    (b) Household circumstances?
    (c) Partner to be working?
    (d) Your joint income?
49. How would you compare it with what you are doing now? (*Probe: will this level of income allow you to do things you can't afford to now?*)

Now I would like to ask you some questions about your family:

50. How old were your mother and father when they left school?
51. How old are they now?
52. (a) Were they both working when they got married?
    (b) What were they doing?
53. What year did they get married?
54. (a) Are they working now?
    (b) What are they doing?
55. Do you have any brothers or sisters?
56. (a) How old are they?
    (b) Single or married?
    (c) Age at married?
57. (a) (When) did your mother go to work after having children?
    (b) Did she work between children?
    (c) What as?
    (d) Full- or part-time?

If she worked after having children

58. How old were you/your youngest brother/sister when she started working again?

Section 4

Now I would like us to think generally about employment:

59. Imagine there is a vacancy for a job and six people apply. Assuming that all are equally qualified, which of the people on these cards would you most like to see given the job? Who would you next most like to see? (*Can rank side by side*)

    (a) Young single man, living at home.
    (b) Young single man, living away from home.
    (c) Young single woman, living away from home.
    (d) Married man, young, with children, wife not working.
    (e) Married woman, no children at home, husband not working.
    (f) Woman with no husband, young children.

[For the following set of questions respondents were handed show cards with a list of options from which to choose in making their responses. Job titles were listed as follows. For respondents in the insurance sector job titles listed on the show card covered the range of clerical, through supervisory to senior official grades. For those in retailing, jobs listed covered the range from general/shop assistant through supervisory and management grades up to branch/store manager. Job titles matched those within respondents' employing organizations. For those in construction, jobs listed ranged through first and third year apprentice, tradesman/craft operative, charge-hand, foreman, site agent, projects manager.]

60. I would like you to answer the following questions thinking about work in . . . (sector)

    Some jobs done in . . . (sector) are done mostly by men, some mostly by women and some have about the same numbers of men and women. Which of the following jobs is most likely to be done by men, by women or by about the same numbers of men and women? (*Show card*)

    Now I would like us to consider the ages of people doing jobs. Some jobs are done by people of any age, some are usually done by younger people, some by older people and others by those in the middle of their working lives. (*Show card*)

    First of all, thinking only of those jobs that might be done by women:

    – Will you go through the jobs one by one and say whether you think the job would be done by women of all ages or

> women in particular age groups (it may be more than one group). (*Show card*)
> – Are there any jobs where a women doing the job would be more likely than usual to be single?
> – Are there any where she would be more likely to be married? (Say if you think it would be equally likely.)
>
> Now, thinking only of the jobs that might be done by men:
> – Will you go through the jobs one by one and say whether you think the job would be done by men of all ages or men in particular age groups (it may be more than one group.) (*Show card*)
> – Are there any jobs where a man doing the job would be more likely than usual to be single?
> – Are there any where he would be more likely to be married? (say if you think it would be equally likely).
>
> Could you tell me how much you think an average person in each of these jobs earns? (*Show card*)
> Thinking through these jobs again, could you consider whether there need to be such differences in earnings or, on the other hand, whether they need to be greater in particular cases?
> (a) Are there any jobs that you think could be paid more, even though others would then have to be paid less?
> (b) Are there any that could be paid less?

[Amongst construction workers the questions were asked as relevant for men only.]

Section 5

61. People tend to think of different things as being important in their decisions about when to get married, have children and so on. Here are some cards – which of these things would you say is the most important to achieve before getting married? Which is the next important? (*Rank all*)
    (a) Having a secure job.
    (b) Having a place of your own to share with your spouse.
    (c) Your partner having a secure job.
    (d) Having some savings put aside.
    (e) Having good career prospects.
    (f) Your partner having good career prospects.
    (g) Being able to afford home ownership.

62. Thinking through these again, which would you say is the most important to achieve before having children? Which is the next most important? (*Rank all*)

63. I would like you now to think of four friends. I will ask you some questions about them – what they are doing, how old they are, what their living circumstances are and so on. So, thinking of the first one:
    (a) Male or female?
    (b) How old is s/he?
    (c) What does s/he do?
    (d) Who does s/he live with?
    (*As relevant:*)
    How old was s/he when s/he
    (a) Left school?
    (b) Got a place of his/her own?
    (c) Got married?
    (d) Had his/her first child?

Section 6

64. I am now going to read out some dilemmas that people might find themselves in, and ask you to say what you think they should do under the circumstances.
    Iain and Lynn intend to get married but they don't have a place of their own to move into yet. What should they do?
    A. Marry and stay with Lynn's parents until they can get a place of their own?
    B. Delay getting married until they can get a place of their own?
    C. Do something else? (What?) Why?
    John and Maggie are a young married couple and are both working. Maggie is offered another job that pays less than the one she has now, but it has better prospects. However, they hope to have children over the next few years. What should she do?
    A. Take the new job and quit when she gets pregnant?
    B. Stay in the old job?
    C. Take advantage of the potential career prospects and delay having children?
    D. Do something else? (What?) Why?

Duncan and Sue have two children aged 1 and 3. They do not intend to have any more. Duncan is working, and Sue is offered her old job back, which she can take on a full- or part-time basis. Her mother has offered to look after the children while Sue is at work. Should Sue:

A. Go back to work full-time?
B. Go back to work part-time?
C. Stay home and look after the children full-time?
D. Do something else? (What?) Why?

Sue actually decides to go back to work part-time. Things work out well for a year and Sue's boss has told her that if she was available to work full-time she could expect good career prospects. Then Duncan loses his job. Sue's mother has become ill and cannot look after the children now. What should they do:

E. Should Sue give up her job and look after the children so that Duncan is free to look for work?
F. Should Sue work full-time, and Duncan look after the children?
G. Should they do something else. (What?) Why?

Jean is 19, unemployed and pregnant and she intends to keep the child. She is not seeing the father of her child and she lives with her mother, two sisters and a brother-in-law. If she stays at home her mother can help with the baby. However, she will get a council house now if she applies for one, but it will be in another part of town. Should she:

A. Get a council house and have a place of her own in which to bring up her baby, by herself?
B. Stay at home and have her mother help her with the baby?
C. Do something else? (What?) Why?

Section 7

65. I should now like to ask your opinions on a number of things about young adults, employment and so on. I shall give you a list of statements that people often make and I should like you to say whether you agree or disagree with them. I have tried to make the statements representative of a wide range of views so you should find some that you agree with and some that you don't. Please remember I am interested in your own personal view. Take your time in answering them.

RESPONDENTS' SELF-COMPLETION SCHEDULE
[Responses: strongly disagree, disagree, neither agree nor disagree/
don't know, agree, strongly agree.]

- Young people should not expect to leave home until they have been working for a few years.
- Young people entering their first job should not expect to be able to save money.
- People on YTS should get more money than they do.
- Earning a wage makes a young person independent.
- You're not really an adult until you have left home.
- A single woman can get ahead in work in the same way that a man can.
- People who are working are more mature than those who are not.
- Teenagers these days need to think about the future more than they used to.
- By the time you are 19 you should be able to support yourself financially.
- Working wives help to raise family living standards.
- Everyone doing the same job should be paid the same regardless of their age.
- A woman cannot expect to raise a family and get ahead in work.
- Young people should be content to stay with their parents until they are earning enough to support themselves financially.
- Everyone doing the same job should be paid the same regardless of their sex.
- A husband and wife both need to work in order to keep up with the cost of living.
- Work skills that are in demand now need longer periods of training than they used to.
- A mother of young children should work if the family needs the money.
- There should be more provision for childcare so that a woman with young children can work.
- Everyone needs to work these days: being a wife and mother is by itself not satisfying enough.
- It should be easier than it is for young people to get their own place and live independently.

- A husband works to support his family and a wife works for the extras.
- A woman should not expect to work while she is bringing up children.
- There should be provision for temporary leave from work so young fathers can share in looking after their baby.
- If a woman can earn more than her husband then he should stay at home and look after their young children.

[At end of interview, I explained that I wanted to interview respondents' parents about their experience of youth and early adulthood, and took parents' names and addresses/'phone numbers where respondents were willing. Asking respondents to mention the survey to their parents may have helped the response rate to the Parents' Survey.]

Appendix 2b: Youth and adulthood: a survey of parents

As you know I interviewed . . . , and we discussed his/her experience of work since leaving school and his/her thoughts about being a young adult in the 1980s, and attitudes towards work, and towards leaving home, starting a family and so on. I would like to talk to you about your own experience of being a young adult and the sorts of decisions you made at the time, as well as your ideas about work and family now.

Section 1

Could you tell me:
1. Are you currently working?
2. What (work) do you do?

I would like you to think back now to your own experience of youth and early adulthood, what work you did at the time, when you left home, when you got married and so on. Lets start at the point at which you left school:
3. How old were you when you left school?
4. What year was that?
5. What is your date of birth?
6. Did you have any qualifications when you left school?
   IF YES: What qualifications did you get?

7. Did you study at all after you left school – either in full-time education or while you were working?
8. Did you get any qualifications after you left school?
9. What was your first job after leaving school (college etc.)? (*Establish employment status, e.g. apprentice*)
10. When did you start that?
11. How much did you earn when you started? (i.e. what was your first wage?)
12. Who were you living with at the time? (*If not with parents establish background and situation*)
13. When did you leave your parents' home?
14. Why did you leave when you did?
15. What type of housing did your parents live in:
    (a) council rented?
    (b) private rented?
    (c) owner-occupied?
    (d) other?
16. Whereabouts was this (which town)?
17. What type of housing did you move into:
    (a) council rented?
    (b) private rented?
    (c) owner-occupied?
    (d) other?
18. Whereabouts was this (which town)?
19. Were you still working as . . . at this time?
    IF YES: Had you changed your job or grade within this employment? (Please describe any changes made)
    IF NO: What were you doing? Did you do any other types of work up to this point?
20. What were you earning at this point?
21. (a) When did you get married?
    (b) Was this to your current partner?
22. What was your work at this time? (*If different: trace through changes up to this point*)
23. How much were you earning when you got married?
24. Was your husband/wife working at the time?
25. What work was s/he doing?
26. How much was s/he earning when you got married?
27. Did you have any savings put aside when you got married?
28. Did you get any significant loans or gifts of money from family

210

to help you get started in married life?

29. Where were you living when you got married? (*Clarify any moves, and housing circumstances when married*)
self:
partner:

30. Did your considerations for getting a place of your own to live affect you when you married in any way?

31. Did you both continue to work after your marriage?
IF NO: Why was that?

32. Were you both working full-time?
IF NO: Why was that?

33. When did you have your first child?

IF MOTHER (YOU/YOUR WIFE) WAS WORKING

34. At what point did you (she) give up working?

35. What was your/your husband's work at this point? (*Check if had changed grade*)

36. What was he/were you earning when your first child was born?

37. How many children did you have altogether?

38. In what years were they born?

39. Did you/your wife do any paid work between having children?
What did you/she do?
Why did you/she (not) work? (*Probe: Would you have worked if you didn't need the money?*)

40. (When) did you/your wife work after you/she finished having children?

IF DID NOT WORK
Could you say why not?
IF DID WORK
    (a) When did you (she) start work again?
    (b) What work did you (she) do?
    (c) Was this full- or part-time?
IF PART-TIME
    (a) Did you (she) go back to full time-work at any point?
    (b) Was this with the same job?

41. Was it an option, whether or not you (she) went back to work?

42. Why did you (she) go back to work *when* you/she did? (*Probe*)

43. What job changes, if any, have you made since then? (*Dates/ year*)

211

44. What job changes, if any, has your husband / wife made since then? (*Dates/year*)
45. What are you earning at the moment?
46. What is your husband/wife earning at the moment?
47. Have you ever changed the type of housing tenure that you live in, since getting married?
48. Did you move house at all before or when you were having children? (*Explain*)
49. Have you/your partner ever been unemployed? (*If yes, establish when, and for what periods*)
50. Have there been any other significant changes in household/ family circumstances since having children? (*Confirm where children are/age at leaving. Check: divorce; new household; changes in people living in household; children leaving; relatives etc. moving in*)

Section 2

51. What is your husband's/wife's date of birth?
52. How many brothers and sisters does s/he have?
53. (a) How old are his/her parents?
    (b) If dead, when did they die?
    (c) How old were they when they died?
54. (a) How old are your own parents?
    (b) (If dead), when did they die?
55. Do you have any brothers or sisters?

For each of them, I would like you to tell me whether they are married or single, whether they have children, and what ages they were when they did these things.

(a) Brother or sister?
(b) Married or single?
(c) Age at marriage?
(d) Age at which children were born?

I would like you to think back now to when you had your first child. You said you had your first child in 19 . . .:

56. Did you make a conscious decision to have him/her when you did?

IF NO CONSCIOUS DECISION MADE

57. Did having a child then make things difficult for you?
    IF YES: In what ways?
    IF NO: Did you have to adapt your lifestyle in terms of work,

212

housing or organizing your finances in any way? (*Probe: e.g. husband more overtime? Any less able to afford things?*)

IF CONSCIOUS DECISION MADE

58. What sorts of things were important in this decision?
59. Would you say that you were financially prepared for having a child at that point?
60. Did you have to adapt your lifestyle in terms of work, housing or organizing your finances in any way? (or other) (*Probe: e.g. husband more overtime? any less able to afford things? etc.*)

ALL

61. Did you make plans early on over how many children to have?
   IF NO: Why did you stop having children when you did?
   IF YES: Did you change these plans at all after you started a family, or did you have the number of children you had hoped for? (*If changed plans, ask how and why*)
62. Looking back now, do you feel you got married at the right time? (*Detail*)
   IF NO: How would you change it?
63. Looking back now, do you feel that you had children at the right time? (*Detail*)
   IF NO: How would you change it?
64. I would like you now to think of two or three friends (they might be relatives of your own generation or neighbours) and I am going to ask you some questions about them – about how old they were when they left school, married, had children and so on.
   So thinking of the first one:
   (a) Male or female?
   (b) How old is s/he?
   (c) What does s/he do?
   (d) Who does s/he live with?
   (e) How old was s/he when s/he
      – left school?
      – started working?
      – got a place of his/her own?
      – got married?
      – had his/her first child?
      – had other children?

Section 3

I would like us to think now about young people today.

65. Thinking of your children and their generation, which of the following would you say is the most important to achieve before getting married? Which is the next most important? (*Rank all*)

   (a) The man having a secure job.
   (b) The woman having a secure job.
   (c) Having a place of their own to move into.
   (d) Having some savings put aside.
   (e) The woman having good career prospects.
   (f) The man having good career prospects.
   (g) Being able to afford home ownership.

Do you think that any of these things have become any more important or less important since the time you got married?

   IF YES: Which? Why do you think that?

Thinking through these again, and thinking again of your children and their generation, which would you say is the most important to achieve before having children? Which is the next most important? (*Rank all*)

Do you think that any of these things have become any more important or any less important since the time that you had children?

   IF YES: Which? Why do you think that?

66. Thinking still of your children and their generation, and firstly thinking of young men, what would you think of as being a sensible age to:

   (a) leave home?
   (b) get married?
   (c) have a first child?

   Now thinking of young women, what do you see as a sensible age to:

   (a) leave home?
   (b) get married?
   (c) have a first child?

67. Do you feel that the ages you have suggested are different to the ages at which you actually did these things?
   IF YES: Why is that?

Do you feel that things are different for young people nowadays in deciding when to leave home than they were when you were young?

- Why do you think that? (*Probe: e.g. compare with own experience*) Do you feel that things are different for young people nowadays in deciding when to get married and start a family that they were when you were young?
   - Why do you think that? (*Probe: e.g. compare with own experience*)

Section 4

The following questions ask you about the ways in which you and your children help each other out with costs of living and so on.
IF ANY CHILDREN STILL AT HOME
68. How many of your children are living with you?
69. Have any of these children left school? (*Yes/No. How many?*)
IF ANY CHILDREN HAVE LEFT SCHOOL
70. Do they (s/he) pay board money? (*Be explicit on (youth respondent)*)
71. How much do they (s/he) pay?
72. How did you decide on the amount(s)?
73. How far do you think this goes to the cost of their (his/her) living here?
74. Have you changed the amount at all over the time since they (s/he) left school? How?
75. Do they (s/he) help out with other things at home? (say what)
76. Do you give or loan money to them (him/her) or help him/her out, for example buying them (him/her) clothes or anything?
77. Have you thought about when your children might leave home? (*Yes/No*)
    IF YES: At what point do you think that might be?
78. Do you think it will make any financial differences to you when they do leave home? (Give details)
    IF NO: Why not?
IF ANY CHILDREN HAVE LEFT HOME
Thinking about your children who have left home:
79. Did they (s/he) pay board money when they (s/he) were living at home? (*Yes/No*)
80. How much was s/he paying before s/he left? (*List individually and age at leaving*)
81. Did you change this amount over the period that they lived at home?
82. How did you decide on the amount?

83. How far do you think this went towards the cost of their (his/her) living here?

84. Did it make any financial differences to you when they (s/he) left home?

85. Do you get any contributions to the family from your children now that they (s/he) has left home (e.g. any help in paying for things, or helping out with family affairs)?

86. Do you give any support to your children now that they (s/he) has left home, again, say, in helping to pay for things, or helping out in anyway?

ALL

87. Do you think it is easier or harder than it used to be for young people to leave home and set up on their own?

88. Do you think that this has or will affect you in any way? (*Yes/No*)
    IF YES: How do you feel about it?
    IF NO: Could you say why not?

Now I would like us to think generally about employment.

89. Imagine there is a vacancy for a job and six people apply. Assuming that all are equally qualified, which of the people on this card would you most like to see given the job? Who would you next most like to see? (*Rank all*)
    (a) Young single man, living at home.
    (b) Young single man, living away from home.
    (c) Young single woman, living away from home.
    (d) Married man, young, with children, wife not working.
    (e) Married woman, no children at home, husband not working.
    (f) Woman with no husband, young children.

90. I am now going to read out some dilemmas that people might find themselves in, and ask you to say what you think they should do under the circumstances.
    Iain and Lynn intend to get married but they don't have a place of their own to move into yet. What should they do?
    A. Marry and stay with Lynn's parents until they can get a place of their own?
    B. Delay getting married until they can get a place of their own?
    C. Do something else? (What?) Why?

John and Maggie are a young married couple and are both working. Maggie is offered another job that pays less than the one she has now, but it has better prospects. However, they hope to have children over the next few years. What should she do?

A. Take the new job and quit when she gets pregnant?
B. Stay in the old job?
C. Take advantage of the potential career prospects and delay having children?
D. Do something else? (What?) Why?

Duncan and Sue have two children aged 1 and 3. They do not intend to have any more. Duncan is working, and Sue is offered her old job back, which she can take on a full- or part-time basis. Her mother has offered to look after the children while Sue is at work. Should Sue:

A. Go back to work full-time?
B. Go back to work part-time?
C. Stay home and look after the children full-time?
D. Do something else? (What?) Why?

Sue actually decides to go back to work part-time. Things work out well for a year and Sue's boss has told her that if she was available to work full-time she could expect good career prospects. Then Duncan loses his job. Sue's mother has become ill and cannot look after the children now. What should they do:

E. Should Sue give up her job and look after the children so that Duncan is free to look for work?
F. Should Sue work full-time, and Duncan look after the children?
G. Should they do something else? (What?) Why?

Jean is 19, unemployed and pregnant and she intends to keep the child. She is not seeing the father of her child and she lives with her mother, two sisters and a brother-in-law. If she stays at home her mother can help with the baby. However, she will get a council house now if she applies for one, but it will be in another part of town. Should she:

A. Get a council house and have a place of her own in which to bring up her baby, by herself?
B. Stay at home and have her mother help her with the baby?
C. Do something else? (What?) Why?

SELF-COMPLETION SCHEDULE

[Responses: strongly disagree, disagree, neither agree nor disagree/ don't know, agree, strongly agree.]

- Young people should not expect to leave home until they have been working for a few years.
- Young people entering their first job should not expect to be able to save money.
- People on YTS should get more money than they do.
- Earning a wage makes a young person independent.
- You're not really an adult until you have left home.
- A single woman can get ahead in work in the same way that a man can.
- People who are working are more mature than those who are not.
- Teenagers these days need to think about the future more than they used to.
- By the time you are 19 you should be able to support yourself financially.
- Working wives help to raise family living standards.
- Everyone doing the same job should be paid the same regardless of their age.
- A woman cannot expect to raise a family and get ahead in work.
- Young people should be content to stay with their parents until they are earning enough to support themselves financially.
- Everyone doing the same job should be paid the same regardless of their sex.
- A husband and wife both need to work in order to keep up with the cost of living.
- Work skills that are in demand now need longer periods of training than they used to.
- A mother of young children should work if the family needs the money.
- There should be more provision for childcare so that a woman with young children can work.
- Everyone needs to work these days: being a wife and mother is by itself not satisfying enough.
- It should be easier than it is for young people to get their own place and live independently.

- A husband works to support his family and a wife works for the extras.
- A woman should not expect to work while she is bringing up children.
- There should be provision for temporary leave from work so young fathers can share in looking after their baby.
- If a woman can earn more than her husband then he should stay at home and look after their young children.

Notes

1. The approach suggested by these arguments is distinctive from the "dual systems" approaches of much feminist theory, which has concerned itself with the historical articulation of capitalism and patriarchy as distinct, but interacting, spheres. At the level of relations between paid employment and the family, the explanation of gender inequality is generally constructed as an issue of causality from one to the other (cf. Barrett 1980; Walby 1986, 1992; Delphy & Leonard 1992). The use of the terminology of social reproduction in the present study is intended to help focus analysis on the way in which employment and family-related processes are integral to one another.
2. There are parallels between Humphries & Rubery's argument and Garnsey's critique of conventional approaches to class analysis that treat the occupational structure as "the backbone of the reward system". Proponents of the "conventional view" see the problem of class analysis as an issue of how labour comes to be allocated to particular positions in the reward structure, an approach that Garnsey criticizes for seeing the reward structure as determined by economic and technological exigencies (Garnsey 1982).
3. The questionnaire schedules for the Main Survey and the Parents' Survey are included in Appendix 2. The postal questionnaire, abridged appropriately for self completion, covered no information further to the face-to-face schedule, and is not included.
4. In addressing generational changes in patterns of transition, I hoped that attitudinal data would help in extending an understanding of young adults' social circumstances, given the limitations to socio-economic data gathered from their own, often short, labour force careers. One possibility would be to disaggregate the sample so as to explore co-variation between socio-economic circumstance, attitudinal data and life course event timing. This sort of analysis would provide a basis from which to consider differences in event timing across the generations. For example, would there be evidence that some socio-economic groups were deferring transition relative to their parents, in contrast to other

221

socio-economic groups? However, while elements of such an analysis are revealing, it became clear that as a general strategy, it relied too heavily on a small sample, whose diversity is better understood in relation to other available data. Further, the potential for comparison was reduced since the reporting of parental ages at marriage by respondents to the Main Survey are unreliable. Respondents were asked the ages of their siblings and the year in which their parents married, but where comparison with parents' self-reported ages at marriage is possible, it is clear that there is some inaccuracy in the reports of their young adult children. Across the sample as a whole, then, such reports of parents' ages at marriage are liable to be less accurate still. The sample allows at best a limited comparison of life course event timing across both generations. Where patterns of change in event timing are at issue, the strength of the survey data lies in a framework that locates such data in relation to aggregate level evidence and general processes.

5. The minimum school-leaving age was raised to 14 in 1918, and to 15 in 1947.

6. These cross-sectional rates will underestimate the cohort average.

7. The percentages are based on estimations for each yearly cohort, in order to control for the consequences of any imbalance in the age distribution (Penhale 1990).

8. Thompson's data refer to births within marriage because details on birth order and mothers' ages were not available for births registered outside of marriage.

9. It seems likely that this late twentieth-century turning point in trends from lower to higher ages at family formation will not be superseded by a new demographic transition for some time. OPCS projections of fertility, made in the mid 1980s, assumed that falling rates for women in their early twenties and rising rates for older women would level off. This had not happened by the end of the 1980s and OPCS now predicts that the overall mean female age at childbirth will rise from 27.3 years in 1989 and to 28.7 years by the end of the century and will fall back to 27.8 years by 2015. The mean female age at birth of the first child is predicted to continue to rise from 25.3 years in 1989 to 26.5 years by 2000 before beginning to fall (Shaw 1990).

10. Tables 3.5 and 3.6 treat the sample as a synthetic cohort (cf. Penhale 1990), that is, cross-sectional evidence of age-related experience is compared over age groups as if they formed a single cohort. The experience of older respondents at younger ages is treated as equivalent to the contemporary experience of younger respondents. Younger respondents, of course, are not bound to repeat the experience of older respondents.

11. I did not tape interviews, but relied on recording responses to questions directly onto the questionnaire schedule. There might be slight errors, then, in the exact wording of some responses where my own shorthand was less accurate than a transcribed tape recording of the responses to open-ended questions. I am confident, however, that most quotes are accurate, and those that are not verbatim transcripts correctly convey the detail of the responses given.

12. As we have seen, this is the case amongst recent youth theorists. It is also true of historical studies of demographic change and the timing of marriage and parenting (e.g. Hajnal 1965; Gillis 1985; Banks 1954; Gittins 1982) and amongst economists' explanations of fertility patterns (e.g. Easterlin 1968; Ermisch 1983).

13. McRae (1994) is centrally concerned with the impact of employers' maternity leave policies on women's labour supply decisions in the context of increasing lifetime labour force participation by women. In relation to this concern, it would be of particular interest to explore maternity leave policy decisions by employers and their relation to female employment duration prior to parenthood.

14. Another version of the significance of norms to employment patterns is provided by those interested in gender role attitudes and labour force commitment. Again, however, the significance of such norms is not located adequately with respect to material changes and, in consequences, norms and expectations acquire a static, ahistorical character. For example, Mott and his colleagues explore inter-generational influences in female labour force commitment (Mott et al. 1982). In their comparative analysis of mothers' and daughters' employment participation rates in the United States, they argue that the probability that young women work has a stronger statistical association with the attitudes of their mothers (described as gender role traditional or gender role liberal) than to their mothers' own experience of limited or extensive labour force participation. The writers argue that as gender role attitudes become more liberal, so women will be able to make more economically rational decisions about whether or not to work. They neglect the possibility of a "reverse" form of socialization, where mothers are more liberal in their attitudes to women working precisely because of the experience of their daughters. Neoclassical theory, they suggest, will become increasingly appropriate as a framework for analyzing female employment participation, as attitudes become less constrained by traditional gender role expectations (Mott et al. 1982).

15. The NES has been carried out in its current form since 1970, although the method of estimating average weekly earnings differs slightly from subsequent years. Also, from 1974 onwards, age was measured in the survey in terms of completed years at 1 January. For 1973 and previously, age was measured in terms of completed years at the time of the survey.

16. Data are not available from NES prior to 1968, and age-disaggregated earnings data were not included in the 1972 NES data.

17. The GHS is a national survey of households in Britain, from which Jones derived a subset of data on 12,000 people aged 16 to 29, combining the 1979 and 1980 surveys. The NCDS is a cohort study of all people born during one week in March 1958, with a current sample size of 12,500. Jones analyzed data from the 1981 sweep of the survey, whose respondents were then 23, which gathered information for the period since they were 16 years old (Jones 1987).

18. Further, one might question the definition of youth classes in relation to fathers' occupation in the absence of a theory of the salience of gender

processes to the reproduction of class inequality (cf. Garnsey 1982). Heath & Britten point to the inappropriateness of the Registrar General's social class groupings for classifying female non-manual jobs. Looking specifically at female clerical workers and shop assistants they argue that the manual/non-manual division is not a major break in the class structure and that women in sales work share more with female manual workers than they do with their relatively advantaged "peers" in clerical jobs (Heath & Britten 1984). The problems with the Registrar General (RG) scale, however, are far more serious yet. The Hope Goldthorpe scale provides a measure of the social desirability of occupations, drawing on a ranking exercise by a sample of the population for the Oxford Mobility Study (Goldthorpe & Hope 1974). In a comparison of occupations' RG classification and their scores derived from the Hope Goldthorpe scale, Bland examined the degree of overlap between classes, using this as a measure of their failure to meet the OPCS claim that each category is homogeneous. Rearranging the cross-classification to remove all overlap it is necessary to change the RG class definition for 33% of the male population. While the manual/non-manual distinction works more or less effectively in aggregate comparisons, within class III the division is ineffective, with only a 61% probability that any randomly chosen skilled non-manual occupation is ranked higher on the Hope Goldthorpe scale than a similarly chosen skilled manual occupation (Bland 1979). He argues that inferences made on such a distinction should be avoided.

19. The tables allocate respondents and their parents to Registrar General social classes on the basis of occupations recorded in the Main Survey of young adults. These include young adult respondents' current occupation at the time of their first marriage, as recorded by young adult respondents. There are several missing cases, where respondents were uncertain about their parents' occupation at their marriage. In addition, where parents are not currently in employment, or were not in employment at the time they married, they are excluded from the relevant tables. There are obvious limitations, then, in the comparisons offered, but the evidence is indicative of the importance of occupational change over the life course and of the problems such lifetime trajectories present for measures of class based on cross-sectional evidence. Problems inherent in measuring inter-generational reproduction of class positions are compounded where comparisons are made at different points in the life course.

The RG classification categories, as used in these five tables, are as follows:

I	Professional/managerial occupations
II	Intermediate occupations
IIINM	Skilled occupations, non-manual
IIIM	Skilled occupations, manual
IV	Partly-skilled occupation
V	Unskilled occupations

Tables N.1 and N.2 illustrate patterns of class mobility amongst the fathers and mothers of respondents to the Main Survey. Their class

Table N.1 Fathers to all respondents.

Social class at marriage	Current social class					
	I	II	IIINM	IIIM	IV	V
I	1			1		
II						
IIINM		4	2	1		
IIIM	2	5	4	13	1	1
IV		1		2	3	
V				1		2

Table N.2 Mothers to all respondents.

Social class at marriage	Current social class					
	I	II	IIINM	IIIM	IV	V
I						
II		1	1			
IIINM		5	9		3	1
IIIM		1	3			1
IV		1	4	1	2	4
V		1		1	1	2

position is based on their occupations as reported by their young adult children.

Both men and women experienced quite a high degree of occupational mobility over their labour force careers. Of 44 fathers, 21 are in the same class now as they were at marriage, 4 were "downwardly mobile" and 19 "upwardly mobile". Of 42 mothers, 14 are in the same class now as they were at marriage, 10 were "downwardly mobile" and 18 "upwardly mobile". A comparison of children's social class and that of their same-sex parent contrasts with a comparison based on parents' social class location at their marriage and indicates a higher degree of stability across generations when we compare their social class designations at similar points in their lifetimes. Table N.3 shows that of 28 father–son pairs, 10 sons are occupationally stable *vis-à-vis* their fathers, 7 are "upwardly mobile" and 11 are "downwardly mobile". However, the comparison with fathers' social class at his marriage shows a greater degree of stability, with half of the respondents in the same social class and only 3 out of 30 being "downwardly mobile". All daughters are classified as skilled non-manual. The comparison with mothers' social class (see Table N.5) shows that of 11 mother–daughter pairs, 3 daughters are occupationally "stable" *vis-à-vis* their mothers, 1 is "upwardly mobile" and 7 are "downwardly mobile". The comparison with mothers' social class at marriage shows 6 out of 11 daughters to be in the same social class, and only 2 out of 11 to be "downwardly mobile".

20. Reasons for entering current employment sector were classified as follows:

Table N.3 Inter-generational mobility: sons' class by fathers' current occupational social class.

Father's current social class	Son's current social class					
	I	II	IIINM	IIIM	IV	V
I				1		
II			5	3		
IIINM		1	2			
IIIM			4	7	2	
IV			1	1	1	
V						

Table N.4 Inter-generational mobility: sons' class by fathers' occupational social class at his own marriage.

Father's social class at marriage	Son's current social class					
	I	II	IIINM	IIIM	IV	V
I			1			
II						
IIINM			4			
IIIM		1	6	10	2	
IV			1	1	1	
V		1		2		

Table N.5 Inter-generational mobility: daughter's occupational social class by mother's current occupational social class and by mother's occupational social class at marriage.

Daughter's current social class	Mother's current social class					
	I	II	IIINM	IIIM	IV	V
IIINM		7	3	1		

	Mother's social class at marriage					
	I	II	IIINM	IIIM	IV	V
IIINM		2	6		2	1

Negative:
- better than unemployment/the dole
- I needed the money
- it was all I could get (I did not have the qualifications for anything else)
- it was the first job I was offered/it came up

Positive:
- I wanted to work in sector/area (interested in work)
- I wanted to get a trade/apprenticeship

- I wanted to further myself (or any reference to prospects and future)
- better money
- job seen to be more permanent/secure/better paid than previous job or alternatives

Missing values were assigned where answers were too vague to usefully classify, or where a combination of positive and negative reasons were given.

21. I am grateful to Professor Sandy Stewart for providing me with a questionnaire designed by him and his colleagues at the Cambridge School of Applied Economics, and from which I adapted this set of questions.

22. The male adult wage distribution amongst construction workers was six responses to each of the lower three adult wage brackets, and 13 responses to the highest (£9,500+) bracket. Tradesman was the status most typically associated with married status, and because this occupation is a standard long-term employment position for many men in the building industry, with highly varied incomes, respondents in this sector are excluded from subsequent quantifications using the adult wage index.

23. Nobody under 19 at the time of interview was engaged, married or a parent.

24. What is known about respondents' educational backgrounds is sufficient cause for caution in assuming similarity on the basis of current occupational location. It should be noted that there is no straightforward patterning of life course event timing in relation to level of educational qualification amongst respondents.

25. Riley provides a slightly different description of the relationship between age-related processes and social change (Riley 1988). She distinguishes between ageing within cohorts and changes in society as cohorts move through historical time. Historical changes mean that cohorts age in different ways (e.g. through increased longevity) and in turn these changes drive changes in the social structure (e.g. as people press for re-evaluations of age-related social roles). However, Riley maintains that a lack of synchrony between processes of ageing and social change results in a disruption, and "structural strain", as age-related roles and institutions outlive their original (positive) functions. Like the conflict theorists, Riley stresses inherent tendencies to disintegration within the social system. The third element in her argument, of asynchrony, appears to contradict her notion of a dialectical interplay between age-related processes and social change.

26. Two separate poverty lines were used in the United States for those aged 65 and over and those under 65. The 1984 poverty line for the latter group was 8.5% higher than that used for the elderly. If the same poverty cut-off had been used for both groups, 15.4% of the elderly would have fallen below the line, giving the aged a higher poverty rate than any other group except children (Minkler 1986).

27. The summary measure hides sources of variation. Rainwater and his colleagues note that around one quarter of their sample families have non-head earners, and in Britain such earners contribute 28% of their family's income. The analysis is based on 1973 data and subsequent changes in

structures of household income maintenance, as described, suggest that reliance on husbands' earnings may have declined, particularly at some periods of a household's lifetime. Such reliance, however, remains particularly high where the arrival of children is accompanied by loss of female earnings.

28. The term "parents" refers to the older generation, of parents to the young adults interviewed, unless otherwise indicated.

29. The ideas informing the questions on claims to work by individuals in different household circumstances were adapted from the Cambridge questionnaire (see note 21). (See Stewart et al. 1980.)

30. Two respondents in the Main Survey made a joint first ranking which are included, so the first column sums to 94, not 92.

31. The definition of young adults as dependent includes those who are living with their parents *and* those who are independent, but single. The description of young adults as married refers to those who have left their parental home *and* are living with a partner.

32. This compares with the evidence described in Chapter 5 where earnings levels manifest a stronger relation to patterns of family formation amongst men than amongst women, and is explained by the higher financial contribution of male earnings to household resourcing.

33. The denominator in these figures is the total number of respondents who agreed or disagreed. Those who said they neither agreed nor disagreed, or who responded "don't know", are excluded here. These latter two options were grouped together in the questionnaire, although it would be better to provide for these responses separately, given their differing meanings.

34. A similar process appears to characterize recent discussions of an under-class in Britain (e.g. Runciman 1990). The problems of understanding the experience of the unemployed through conventional class theory leads not to a challenge to the latter but rather to defining those outside as beyond the proper remit of class theory, literally under-class.

Bibliography

Alves, W. M. and P. H. Rossi 1978. Who should get what? Fairness judgements of the distribution of earnings. *American Journal of Sociology* **84** (3), 541–64.

Anderson, M. 1985. The emergence of the modern life cycle in Britain. *Social History* **10** (1), 69–87.

Arber, S. & J. Ginn 1991. *Gender and later life. A sociological analysis of resources and constraints*. London: Sage.

Ashton, D. N. & D. Field 1976. *Young Workers*, London: Hutchinson.

Ashton, D. N. & G. Lowe 1991. School to work transitions in Britain and Canada: comparative perspective. In *Making their way. Education, training and the labour market in Canada and Britain*, Ashton & Lowe (eds). Milton Keynes, England: Open University Press.

Ashton, D. N. & M. J. Maguire 1986. *Young adults in the labour market*. Department of Employment, Research Paper 55.

Ashton, D. N., M. J. Maguire, M. Spilsbury 1987. Labour market segmentation and the structure of the youth labour market. See Brown & Ashton (1987).

Ashton, D. N., M. J. Maguire, M. Spilsbury 1990. *Restructuring the labour market. The implications for youth*. London: Macmillan.

Atkinson, A. B., A. K. Maynard, C. Trinder 1983. *Parents and children: incomes in two generations*. SSRC/DHSS Studies in Deprivations and Disadvantage 10. Oxford: Heinemann.

Atkinson, P., T. L. Rees, D. Shore, H. Williamson 1982. Social and life skills: the latest case of contemporary education. See Rees & Atkinson (1982).

Austrin, T. 1980. The "lump" in the UK construction industry. In *Capital and labour: studies in the capitalist labour process*, T. Nichols (ed.). Glasgow: Fontana Paperbacks.

Banks, J. A. 1954. *Prosperity and parenthood*. London: Routledge & Kegan Paul.

Banks, M., I. Bates, G. Beakwell 1992. *Careers and identities*. Milton Keynes, England: Open University Press.

Barrett, M. 1980. *Women's oppression today*. London: Verso.

Bates, I., J. Clarke, P. Cohen 1984. *Schooling for the dole? The new vocationalism.* London: Macmillan.

Bazalgette, J. 1978. *School and work life. A study of transition in the inner city.* London: Hutchinson.

Beck, U. 1992. *Risk society. Towards a new modernity*. London: Sage.

Beechey, V. 1978. Women and production: a critical analysis of some sociological theories of women's work. In *Feminism and materialism. Women and modes of production*, A. Kuhn & A. Wolpe (eds). London: Routledge & Kegan Paul.

Benn, C. & J. Fairley (eds) 1986. *Challenging the MSC on jobs, training and education*, London: Pluto.

Black, B. 1990. Age and earnings. In *Portrait of pay 1970–1982. An analysis of the New Earnings Survey*, M. B. Gregory & A. W. J. Thomson (eds). Oxford: Clarendon Press.

Blackburn, R. M. & M. Mann 1979. *The working class in the labour market.* London: Macmillan.

Blake, J. 1968. Are babies consumer durables? *Population Studies* **22** (1), 5–25.

Bland, R. 1979. Measuring "social class". A discussion of the Registrar-General's Classification. *Sociology* **13**, 283–91.

Brenner, J. & M. Ramas 1984. Rethinking women's oppression. *New Left Review* **144**, 33–71.

Bresnen, M. J., K. Wray, A. Bryman 1985. The flexibility of recruitment in the construction industry: formalisation or re-casualisation? *Sociology* **19** (1), 108–24.

Brown, P. D. N. Ashton (eds) 1987. *Education, unemployment and labour markets*. London: Falmer Press.

Building Societies Association 1985a. House prices and earnings. *BSA Bulletin* **43**, July, 12–17.

Building Societies Association 1985b. An international comparison of housing tenure by age. *BSA Bulletin* **43**, July, 7–11.

Burchell, B. & J. Rubery 1989. *Segmented jobs and segmented workers: an empirical investigation*. The Social Change and Economic Life Initiative. Working Paper 13, ESRC.

Busfield, J. 1987. Parenting and parenthood. In *Social change and the life course*, G. Cohen (ed.). London: Tavistock.

Busfield, J. & M. Paddon 1977. *Thinking about children. Sociology and fertility in post-war England*. Cambridge: Cambridge University Press.

Bynner, J. 1991. Controlling transition. *Work, Employment and Society* **5** (4), 645–58.

Caffrey, J., S. McKellar, P. Woodhead 1986. More than just the waste of a generation. *Youth in Society*, January, 10–12.

Central Statistical Office. *Social trends*. London: HMSO.

Centre for Contemporary Cultural Studies 1984. *Unpopular education. Schooling and social democracy in England since 1944*. London: Hutchinson.

Chisholm, L. 1990. A sharper lens or a new camera? Youth research, young people and social change in Britain. In *Childhood, youth and social change: a comparative perspective*, L. Chisholm, P. Buchner, H. Kruger, P. Brown (eds).

London: Falmer Press.

Chisholm L. & M. du Bois-Reymond 1993. Youth transitions, gender and social change. *Sociology* **27**, 259–79.

Cockburn, C. 1987. *Two-track training. Sex inequalities and the YTS*. London: Macmillan.

Coffield, F., C. Borrill, S. Marshall 1986. *Growing up at the margins: young adults in the North East*. Milton Keynes, England: Open University Press.

Cooke, K. 1987. The withdrawal from paid work of the wives of unemployed men: a review of research. *Journal of Social Policy* **16** (3), 371–82.

Cooper, J. 1991. Births outside marriage: recent trends and associated demographic and social changes. *Population Trends* **63**, 8–18.

Craig, J, 1992. Fertility trends within the United Kingdom. *Population Trends* **67**, 17–21.

Craig, C., E. Garnsey, J. Rubery 1983. Women's pay in informal payment systems. *Employment Gazette* **91**, 139–46, 148.

Crompton, R. & G. Jones 1984. *White collar proletariat. Deskilling and gender in clerical work*. London: Macmillan.

Davin, A. 1978. Imperialism and motherhood. *History Workshop Journal* **5**, 9–65.

De Cooman, E., J. Ermisch, H. Joshi 1987. The next birth and the labour market: a dynamic model of births in England and Wales. *Population Studies* **41**, 237–68.

Del Mercato, A. P. 1981. Social reproduction and the basic structure of labour markets. In *The dynamics of labour market segmentation*, F. Wilkinson (ed.). London: Academic Press.

Delphy, C. & D. Leonard 1992. *Familiar exploitation: a new analysis of marriage in contemporary Western societies*. Cambridge: Polity Press.

Department of Employment. *Skills and Enterprise Network*. Moorfoot, Sheffield.

Dex, S. & L. B. Shaw 1986. *British and American women at work. Do equal opportunities policies matter?* London: Macmillan.

Distributive Trades Economic Development Committee 1985. *Employment perspectives and the distributive trades*. London: National Economic Development Office.

Doeringer, P. B. & M. J. Piore 1971. *Internal labour markets and manpower analysis*. Cambridge, Mass.: Heath Lexington Books.

Dollamore, G. 1989. Live births in 1988. *Population Trends* **58**, 20–26.

Dunnell, K. 1979. *Family formation 1976*. London: OPCS/HMSO.

Easterlin, R. 1968. *Population, labor force, and long swings in economic growth. The American experience*. New York: National Bureau of Economic Research/ Columbia University Press.

Elder, G. 1974. *Children of the Great Depression*. Chicago: University of Chicago Press.

Elder, G. 1978. Family history and the life course. In *Transitions: the family and the life course in historical perspective*, T. K. Hareven (ed.). New York: Academic Press.

Elias, P. & B. Main 1982. *Women's working lives*. Institute for Employment Research, University of Warwick.

Erikson, R. & J. H. Goldthorpe 1992. *The constant flux*. Oxford: Clarendon Press.

Ermisch, J. E. 1979. The relevance of the "Easterlin Hypothesis" and the "New Home Economics" to fertility movements in Great Britain. *Population Studies* **33**, 39–57.

Ermisch, J. E. 1981. Economic opportunities, marriage squeezes and the propensity to marry: an economic analysis of period marriage rates in England and Wales. *Population Studies* **35**, 347–56.

Ermisch, J. E. 1983. *The political economy of demographic change*. London: Heinemann.

Ermisch, J. E. 1988. Economic influences on birth rates. *National Institute Economic Review* **4/88**, No. 126, National Institute of Economic and Social Research.

Falkingham, J. 1989. Dependency and ageing in Britain: a re-examination of the evidence. *Journal of Social Policy* **18** (2), 211–33.

Finch, J. 1987. The vignette technique in survey research. *Sociology* **21** (1), 105–14.

Finn, D. 1982. Whose needs? Schooling and the "needs" of industry. In *Youth unemployment and state intervention*, T. L. Rees & P. Atkinson (eds). London: Routledge & Kegan Paul.

Finn, D. 1987. *Training without jobs: new deals and broken promises*. London: Macmillan.

Foner, A. 1974. Age stratification and age conflict in political life. *American Sociological Review* **39**, 187–96.

Foner, A. 1988. Age inequalities. Are they epiphenomena of the class system? In *Social change and the life course (vol. 3) Social structures and human lives*, M. W. Riley with B. J. Huber & B. B. Hess (eds). London: Sage.

Frith, S. 1984. *The sociology of youth*. Ormskirk: Causeway Books.

Furlong, A. & G. Cooney 1990. Getting on their bikes: teenagers leaving home in Scotland in the 1980s. *Journal of Social Policy* **19** (4), 535–51.

Garnsey, E. 1982. Women's work and theories of class and stratification. In *Classes, power and conflict. Classical and contemporary debates*, A. Giddens & D. Held (eds). London: Macmillan.

Gillis, J. 1981. *Youth and history. Tradition and change in European age relations, 1770–present*. New York/London: Academic Press.

Gillis, J. R. 1985. *For better, for worse: British marriages, 1600 to the present*. Oxford: Oxford University Press.

Ginn, J. & S. Arber 1991. Gender, class and income inequalities in later life. *British Journal of Sociology* **42** (3), 369–93.

Gittins, D. 1982. *Fair sex. Family size and structure, 1900–1939*. London: Hutchinson.

Goldthorpe, J. H. 1983. Women and class analysis: in defence of the conventional view. *Sociology* **17** (4), 465–88.

Goldthorpe, J. H. 1984. Women and class analysis: a reply to the replies. *Sociology* **18** (4), 491–9.

Goldthorpe, J. H. & K. Hope 1974. *The social grading of occupations*. Oxford: Clarendon.

Goldthorpe, J. H., D. Lockwood, F. Bechhofer, J. Platt 1969. *The affluent worker in the class structure*. Cambridge: Cambridge University Press.

Griffin, C. 1985. *Typical girls? Young women from school to the job market*. London: Routledge & Kegan Paul.

Hajnal, J. 1965. European marriage patterns in perspective. In *Population in history*, D. V. Glass & D. E. C. Eversley (eds). London: Edward Arnold.

Halsey, A. H. 1986. *Change in British society*. Oxford: Oxford University Press.

Hareven, T. K. 1981. Historical changes in the timing of family transitions and their impact on generational relations. In *Aging: stability and change in the family*, J. G. March (ed.). New York: Academic Press.

Harris, N. 1988. Social security and the transition to adulthood. *Journal of Social Policy* **17** (4), 501–23.

Haskey, J. 1987. Trends in marriage and divorce in England and Wales: 1837 to 1987. *Population Trends* **48**, 11–19.

Haskey, J. & K. E. Kiernan 1989. Cohabitation in Great Britain – characteristics and estimated numbers of cohabiting partners. *Population Trends* **58**, 23–32.

Heath, A. & N. Britten 1984. Women's jobs do make a difference. Reply to Goldthorpe. *Sociology* **18** (4), 475–90.

Hedstrom, P. & S. Ringen 1987. Age and income in contemporary society: a research note. *Journal of Social Policy* **16** (2), 227–39.

Heidenheimer, A. J. 1990. *Comparative public policy. The politics of social choice in America, Europe and Japan*. New York: St. Martin's Press.

Hogan, D. 1981. *Transitions and social change. The early lives of American men*. New York/London: Academic Press.

Holmwood, J. 1991. W(h)ither welfare. *Work, Employment and Society* **5** (2), 283–304.

Humphries, J. & J. Rubery 1984. The reconstitution of the supply side of the labour market: the relative autonomy of social reproduction. *Cambridge Journal of Economics* **8**, 331–46.

Hutson, S. & R. Jenkins 1987a. Coming of age in South Wales. In *Education, unemployment and labour markets*, P. Brown & D. N. Ashton (eds). London: Falmer Press.

Hutson, S. & R. Jenkins 1987b. Family relationships and the unemployment of young people in South Wales. In *The social world of the young unemployed*, M. White (ed.). PSI Discussion Paper no. 19.

Hutson, S. & R. Jenkins 1989. *Taking the strain. Families, unemployment and the transition to adulthood*. Milton Keynes, England: Open University Press.

Irwin, S. & L. Morris 1993. Social security or economic insecurity? The concentration of unemployment (and research) within households. *Journal of Social Policy* **22** (3), 349–72.

Jamieson, L. 1986. Limited resources and limiting conventions: working class mothers and daughters in urban Scotland c. 1890–1925. In *Labour and love. Women's experience of home and family, 1850–1940*, J. Lewis (ed.). Oxford: Basil Blackwell.

Jamieson, L. 1987. Theories of family development and the experience of being brought up. *Sociology* **21** (4), 591–607.

Jasso, G. & P. H. Rossi 1977. Distributive justice and earned income. *American Sociological Review* **42**, 639–51.

Johnson, P. (ed.) 1989. *Workers versus pensioners: intergenerational conflict in an ageing world*. Manchester: Manchester University Press.

Jones, C. 1991. Birth statistics 1990. *Population Trends* **65**, 9–15.

Jones, C. 1992. Fertility of the over thirties. *Population Trends* **67**, 10–16.

Jones, G. 1986. *Youth in the social structure: transitions to adulthood and their stratification by class and gender*. PhD thesis, University of Surrey.

Jones, G. 1987. Young workers in the class structure. *Work, Employment and Society* **1** (4), 487–508.

Jones, G. 1988. Integrating process and structure in the concept of youth: a case for secondary analysis. *Sociological Review* **36** (4), 706–32.

Jones, G. & C. Wallace 1990. Beyond individualization: what sort of social change? See Chisholm et al. (eds) (1990).

Jones, G. & C. Wallace 1992. *Youth, family and citizenship*. Milton Keynes, England: Open University Press.

Joshi, H. 1985. *Motherhood and employment: change and continuity in post war Britain*, OPCS Occasional Paper 34, British Society for Population Studies.

Joshi, H. 1990. The changing form of women's economic dependency. In *The changing population of Britain*, H. Joshi (ed.). Oxford: Basil Blackwell.

Kiernan, K. E. 1986. *Transitions in young adulthood*. National Child Development Study User Support Group, WP No. 16. SSRU, City University.

Kiernan, K. E. & I. Diamond 1983. The age at which childbearing starts – a longitudinal study. *Population Studies* **37**, 363–80.

Kohli, M. 1988. Ageing as a challenge to sociological theory. *Ageing and Society* **8**, 367–94.

Land, H. 1980. The family wage. *Feminist Review* **7**, 55–77.

Land, H. 1989. The construction of dependency. In *The goals of social policy*, M. Bulmer, J. Lewis & D. Piachaud (eds). London: Unwin Hyman.

Lee, D., D. Marsden, M. Hardey 1987. Youth training, life chances and orientations to work: a case study of the Youth Training Scheme. See Brown & Ashton (1987).

Leonard, D. 1980. *Sex and generation. A study of courtship and weddings*. London: Tavistock.

Lewis, J. 1980. *The politics of motherhood. Child and maternal welfare in England 1900–1939*, London: Croom Helm.

Lewis, J. 1986. The working class wife and mother and State intervention 1870–1918. In *Labour and love. Women's experience of home and family 1850–1940*, J. Lewis (ed.). Oxford: Basil Blackwell.

Lewis J. (ed.) 1986. *Labour and love. Women's experience of home and family 1850–1940*. Oxford: Basil Blackwell.

Lewis, J. 1989. Lone parent families: politics and economics. *Journal of Social Policy* **18** (4), 595–600.

McLaughlin, E. 1989. Work and welfare benefits. Social security and un/employment in the 1990s. Paper delivered to the Social Policy Association Annual Conference, Bath, July 1989.

McRae, S. 1994. Labour supply after childbirth: do employers' policies make a difference? *Sociology* **28** (1), 99–122.

Main, B. G. M. 1988. The lifetime attachment of women to the labour market. In *Women and paid work*, A. Hunt (ed.). New York: St. Martin's Press.

Main, B. G. M. & D. Raffe 1983. The industrial destinations of school leavers 1977–81. University of Strathclyde, Fraser of Allander Institute. Quarterly Economic Commentary, 8.

Markall, G. & D. Gregory 1982. Who cares? The MSC interventions: full of Easter promise. See Rees & Atkinson (1982).

Martin, J. & C. Roberts 1984. *Women and employment. A lifetime perspective.* London: HMSO.

Mayer, K. U. & U. Schoepflin 1989. The state and the life course. *Annual Review of Sociology* **15**, 187–209.

Millar, J. & C. Glendinning 1987. Invisible women, invisible poverty. In *Women and poverty in Britain*, J. Millar & C. Glendinning (eds). Brighton: Wheatsheaf Books.

Minkler, M. 1986. "Generational equity" and the new victim blaming: an emerging public policy issue. *International Journal of Health Services* **16** (4), 539–51.

Modell, J., F. F. Furstenberg, T. Hershberg 1976. Social change and transitions to adulthood in historical perspective. *Journal of Family History* **1** (1), 7–32.

Moore, R. 1981. Aspects of segmentation in the United Kingdom construction industry. In *The dynamics of labour market segmentation*, F. Wilkinson (ed.). London/New York: Academic Press.

Mott, F. L. (ed.) 1982. *The employment revolution: young American women in the 1970s.* Cambridge, Mass.:MIT Press.

Mott, F. L., A. Statham, N. L. Maxwell 1982. From mother to daughter: the transmission of work behaviour patterns across generations. See Mott (1982).

Murphy & O. Sullivan 1986. Unemployment, housing and household structure among young adults. *Journal of Social Policy* **15** (2), 205–22.

National Institute of Economic and Social Research 1986. *Young people's employment in retailing*, Distributive Trades Economic Development Committee. London: National Economic Development Office.

Office of Population Censuses and Surveys, Social Survey Division. *General household survey.* London: HMSO.

Office of Population Censuses and Surveys. *Population trends.* London: HMSO.

Oppenheimer, V. K. 1982. *Work and the family. A study in social demography.* New York/London: Academic Press.

Pahl, R. E. 1984. *Divisions of labour.* Oxford: Basil Blackwell.

Pahl, R. E. 1989. Is the Emperor naked? Some questions on the adequacy of sociological theory in urban and regional research. *International Journal of Urban and Regional Research* **13**, 709–20.

Pampel, F. C. & J. B. Williamson 1989. *Age, class, politics and the Welfare State.* Cambridge: Cambridge University Press.

Peattie, L. & M. Rein 1983. *Women's claims. A study in political economy.* Oxford: Oxford University Press.

Penhale, B. 1989. *Associations between unemployment and fertility among young women in the early 1980s.* SSRU, City University, Working Paper 60.

Penhale, B. 1990. *Living arrangements of young adults in France and England and Wales.* SSRU, City University, LS Working Paper 68.

Piore, M. J. 1975. Notes for a theory of labour market stratification. In *Labour market segmentation*, R. C. Edwards, M. Reich & D. M. Gordon (eds). Mass.: Heath and Company.

Prandy, K. 1986. Similarities of lifestyles and the occupations of women. In *Gender and stratification*, R. Crompton & M. Mann (eds). Cambridge: Polity Press.

Preston, S. 1984. Children and the elderly: divergent paths for America's dependents. *Demography* **21** (4), 435–57.

Raffe, D. 1984. *The effects of industrial change on school leaver employment in Scotland: a quasi-shift-share analysis*. Working Paper, Centre for Educational Sociology, University of Edinburgh.

Raffe, D. 1986. Change and continuity in the youth labour market: a critical review of structural explanations of youth unemployment. In *The experience of unemployment*, S. Allen et al. (eds). London: Macmillan.

Raffe, D. 1987. Youth unemployment in the United Kingdom 1979–1984. In *Education, unemployment and labour markets*, P. Brown & D. N. Ashton (eds). London: Falmer Press.

Raffe, D. & R. Courtenay 1988. 16 to 18 on both sides of the border. In *Education and the youth labour market: schooling and scheming*, D. Raffe (ed.). London: Falmer Press.

Rainwater, L., M. Rein, J. Schwartz 1986. *Income packaging in the Welfare State. A comparative study of family income*. Oxford: Clarendon Press.

Rees, T. L. P. Atkinson (eds) 1982. *Youth unemployment and state intervention*. London: Routledge & Kegan Paul.

Riley, M. W. 1988. On the significance of age in sociology. In *Social change and the life course (vol. 3) Social structures and human lives*, M. W. Riley with B. J. Huber and B. B. Hess (eds). London: Sage.

Roberts, E. 1986. Women's strategies 1890–1940. See Lewis (1986).

Roberts, K. 1968. The entry into employment: an approach towards a general theory. *Sociological Review* **16** (1), 165–84.

Roberts, K., S. Dench, D. Richardson 1986. Youth labour markets in the 1980s. *Employment Gazette*, July.

Roberts, K., S. Dench, D. Richardson 1987. Youth rates of pay and employment. See Brown & Ashton (1987).

Rubery, J. 1978. Structured labour markets, worker organisation and low pay. *Cambridge Journal of Economics* **2**, 17–36.

Rubery, J. 1988. Employers and the labour market. In *Employment in Britain*, D. Gallie (ed.). Oxford: Basil Blackwell.

Rubery, J., R. Tarling, F. Wilkinson 1984. Labour market segmentation theory: an alternative framework for the analysis of the employment system. Department of Applied Economics, Cambridge. Paper presented at the BSA Conference, Bradford.

Runciman, W. G. 1990. How many classes are there in contemporary British society? *Sociology* **24**, 377–96.

Ryder, N. B. 1965. The cohort as a concept in the study of social change. *American Sociological Review* **30**, 843–61.

Sanderson, W. C. 1976. On two schools of the economics of fertility. *Population and Development Review* **2**, 469–77.

Sawdon, A., J. Pelican, S. Tucker 1981. *Study of the transition from school to working life.* London: Youthaid.

Shaw, C. 1989. Recent trends in family size and family building. *Population Trends* **58**, 19–22.

Shaw, C. 1990. Fertility assumptions for 1989–based population projections for England and Wales. *Population Trends* **61**, 17–23.

Siltanen, J. 1986. Domestic responsibilities and the structuring of employment. In *Gender and stratification*, R. Crompton & M. Mann (eds). Cambridge: Polity Press.

Stafford, A. 1981. Learning not to labour. *Capital and Class* **15**, 55–77.

Stanworth, M. 1984. Women and class analysis: a reply to John Goldthorpe. *Sociology* **18** (2), 159–70.

Stewart, A. & R. M. Blackburn 1975. The stability of structural inequality. *Sociological Review* **23**, 481–508.

Stewart, A., R. M. Blackburn, K. Prandy 1985. Gender and earnings: the failure of market explanations. In *New approaches to economic life*, R. Roberts, R. Finnegan & D. Gallie (eds). Manchester: Manchester University Press.

Stewart, A., K. Prandy, R. M. Blackburn 1980. *Social stratification and occupations.* London: Macmillan.

Stewart, M. B. and C. A. Greenhalgh 1984. Work history patterns and occupational attainment of women. *The Economic Journal* **94** (375), 493–519.

Taylor Gooby, P. 1985. *Public opinion, ideology and state welfare.* London: Routledge & Kegan Paul.

Thompson, J. 1980. The age at which childbearing starts – a longitudinal study. *Population Trends* **21**, 10–13.

Thomson, D. 1989. The Welfare State and generation conflict: winners and losers. In *Workers versus pensioners: intergenerational conflict in an ageing world*, P. Johnson et al. (eds). Manchester: Manchester University Press.

Tilly, L. A. & J. W. Scott 1978. *Women, work and family.* New York/London: Holt, Rinehart & Winston.

Turchi, B. A. 1975. Microeconomic theories of fertility: a critique. *Social Forces* **54** (1), 107–25.

Turner, B. 1988. *Status.* Milton Keynes, England: Open University Press.

Turner, B. 1989. Ageing, politics and sociological theory. *British Journal of Sociology* **40** (4), 588–606.

United Nations, Economic Commission for Europe 1985. *Economic role of women in the ECE Region. Developments 1975–1985.* New York: United Nations.

Walby, S. 1986. *Patriarchy at work. Patriarchal and capitalist relations in employment.* Cambridge: Polity Press.

Walby, S. 1992. *Theorizing patriarchy.* Oxford: Basil Blackwell.

Wall, R. & B. Penhale 1989. Relationships within households in 1981. *Population Trends* **55**, 22–6.

Wallace, C. 1987a. *For richer, for poorer. Growing up in and out of work.* London: Tavistock.

Wallace, C. 1987b. From generation to generation: the effects of employment and unemployment upon the domestic life cycle of young adults. See Brown & Ashton (1987).

Wallace, C. 1987c. Between the family and the state: young people in transition. In *The social world of the young unemployed*, M. White (ed.). Policy Studies Institute, Discussion Paper 19.

Wells, W. 1983. *The relative pay and employment of young people*. Department of Employment, Research Paper No. 42.

Werner, B. 1985. Fertility trends in different social classes: 1970 to 1983. *Population Trends* **41**, 5–13.

West, M. and P. Newton 1983. *The transition from school to work*. London: Croom Helm.

Wilkinson, F. (ed.) 1981. *The dynamics of labour market segmentation*. London: Academic Press.

Williamson, H. 1985. Struggling beyond youth. *Youth in Society*, January, 11–12.

Willis, P. 1977. *Learning to labour*. Farnborough: Saxon House.

Willis, P. 1984. Youth unemployment: thinking the unthinkable. *Youth and Policy* **2** (4), 17–24, 33–6.

Willis, P. 1985. *The social condition of young people in Wolverhampton 1984*. Wolverhampton Borough Council.

Winch, G. M. 1986. The labour process and labour market in construction. *International Journal of Sociology and Social Policy* **6** (2), 103–16.

Wright, R. E. 1989. The Easterlin Hypothesis and European fertility rates. *Population and Development Review* **15** (1), 107–22.

Index